To
Alan
with very best
wishes.

[signature]
March 2008

Skytrucker

Incidents, accidents and romantic attachments gathered over forty years in Aviation

Allen Murray

Writers Club Press
San Jose New York Lincoln Shanghai

Skytrucker
Incidents, accidents and romantic attachments gathered over forty years in Aviation

All Rights Reserved © 2002 by Allen Murray

No part of this book may be reproduced or transmitted in any form or by any means, graphic, electronic, or mechanical, including photocopying, recording, taping, or by any information storage retrieval system, without the permission in writing from the publisher.

Writers Club Press
an imprint of iUniverse, Inc.

For information address:
iUniverse, Inc.
5220 S. 16th St., Suite 200
Lincoln, NE 68512
www.iuniverse.com

The characters in this book are figments of the author's imagination and do not represent real people.

ISBN: 0-595-24729-6

Printed in the United States of America

Contents

CHAPTER 1	The Beginning	1
CHAPTER 2	The Real Air Force	9
CHAPTER 3	A Civilian	21
CHAPTER 4	Rotterdam	33
CHAPTER 5	Parachutists	43
CHAPTER 6	Holiday Airline	53
CHAPTER 7	Nightstop	65
CHAPTER 8	The Tristar	75
CHAPTER 9	Tomatoes	85
CHAPTER 10	The Roar of the Crowd	97
CHAPTER 11	Collapse	109
CHAPTER 12	Malawi	119
CHAPTER 13	After the Otter	137
CHAPTER 14	Cropduster	143
CHAPTER 15	Oostende	155
CHAPTER 16	Trial Lesson	173
CHAPTER 17	Aerobatics	183
CHAPTER 18	First Solo	195
CHAPTER 19	The Circus	213

Chapter 20	The Dove	221
Chapter 21	Skytrucker	239
Chapter 22	Lagos	247
Chapter 23	Eleven Minutes	261
Chapter 24	British Air Ferries	271
Chapter 25	The Ferry Pilot	283
Epilogue		297

1

The Beginning

Deep in the heart of rural England, in the shadow of the Chiltern Hills there was a military establishment that purports to be a school of technical training. A school it most certainly was and it bore a startling resemblance to the popular concept of the English public schools apart from the fact that the scholars were given the title of Aircraft Apprentice and that the graduates were aircraft engineers of a very high calibre.

I had determined that I wanted to be an aircraft engineer, a career choice influenced to a large extent by the fact that I had been building and flying model aircraft since the age of eleven and was totally absorbed by all things aeronautical. The glossy brochures provided to me by the RAF Recruiting Office promised a plethora of all of the better things in life, and showed appealing pictures of young men dressed in smart blue uniforms surrounded by adoring beautiful girls. The prospects of travel to exotic places were also emphasised as was the opportunity to participate in all manner of sporting activities. I was totally entranced and to my great joy, eventually received a letter informing me that I had been successful in the entrance examination and selection procedures and was to report to the School in September of that year.

On arrival at the local railway station, my fellow travellers and I were herded onto an Air Force coach and driven the three miles or so to our destination. On arrival, we were marshalled into a large room where our names were checked off against a list. We were instructed to sit down, to keep quiet and to listen very carefully. A series of totally confusing instructions followed, delivered at high speed by a man wearing an impressive moustache, an impossible number of medal ribbons and a permanent frown. Over the course of the next two days, we were medically and dentally examined, swore an oath of allegiance, had our hair cut and were given uniforms, cutlery, blankets, cleaning materials and the myriad other items deemed to be essential to military existence.

From the outset we were very quickly made to appreciate that we were one of the lowest forms of life and that we were obliged to conduct ourselves in a manner befitting our lowly status. During the first six weeks, we were instructed in the gentle arts of marching and parade ground drill, of the effective cleaning and polishing of our barrack room floor, the correct method of displaying all of our kit for inspection by a fearsome corporal and interminable cross country runs. Despite the almost constant demands made on us, many of my companions found the time to be desperately homesick. I have to admit that I too experienced a feeling of total despair from time to time. During this first period, we were introduced to the well-established ethic that distinguished the more senior Aircraft Apprentices as a kind of deity to be obeyed without question. Disobedience or insolence to such minor gods resulted in swift and dreadful retribution and occasionally physical violence. It was not, therefore a particularly pleasant period.

Eventually, however, the constant cleaning, polishing and drilling subsided somewhat and we were at last receiving instruction in the basics of aeronautical engineering. Along with my fellows, I sawed and filed interminable pieces of steel to produce various test pieces that had to fit together to a high standard of accuracy. We were instructed in the basic principles of piston engines and we stripped a Gypsy Major engine down to almost the last nut and bolt and reassembled it as hundreds, maybe thousands of similar classes had done before us. A wonderful Chief Technician with a real gift for instruction introduced us to the mysteries of a fourteen-cylinder radial engine called the Hercules.

We learned about propellers The operating principles of the jet engine were patiently explained to us. We became familiar with aircraft systems, fire extinguishing devices and documentation. We tried our hand at welding and soldering. In fact, the whole workings of the RAF and its equipment seemed to be included in our curriculum. In addition, we spent three afternoons per week in classrooms improving our grasp of Mechanics, Physics, Mathematics and Current Affairs. The workload was, it seemed, awesome. Even the weekends were planned for us. Saturday mornings were taken up with a parade and an inspection by the Wing Commander, a portly gentleman who always appeared to be slightly confused. On Sunday mornings we were marched to the chapel for Church Parade presided over by the base Chaplain. The only time that we were able to truly call our own was Saturday afternoon and Sunday afternoon. On those days a few of us who were all guitar players of varying degrees of competence would get together and destroy some of the popular songs of the day.

As the first year came to an end, we were a great deal more comfortable with our existence. Since we had joined, two more intakes of uncomfortable, unhappy teenagers had become our juniors. We were no longer at the bottom of the heap and most of us began to actually enjoy the regime. We had all found ways to beat the system and indulge in the small pleasures that made life bearable. We were now very familiar with the hundreds of stories about the place. Some of these stories were based on fact and certainly many of the tales of the paranormal were given more credibility by the rather speckled history of the original buildings. The fine building that had been transformed into the Officers' mess had been the home of an incredibly wealthy and quite famous figure in the earlier part of the century. This person was well known to be a practitioner of black magic and indeed some of the more permanent artefacts of his craft still remain there to this day. In a small outbuilding there is a pentacle laid out in the mosaic of the floor, for instance. Stories of dark happenings abounded and we would frighten ourselves silly by telling ghost stories after lights out. Many of the stories concerned a very strange area of land known to us all as the Pimple. Anyone may visit that area right now and you will discover that what I am about to say is absolutely true.

As previously mentioned, the School lies amongst the Chiltern Hills and is in fact located right at the base of one particularly steep and imposing hill. We all hated that hill because it was the course for our many cross country runs. The runners always avoided the area right at the very top, however for no other reason than that the ground at the very top was totally devoid of any form of vegetation. Not only was vegetable life absent but even birds and insects seemed to avoid the area too. The Pimple was just an area of bare earth right at the very top of the hill. It was said that a team of scientists had visited there and taken soil samples and found nothing untoward. Small trees and shrubs planted there by unbelievers simply died. The area was truly sterile and no sound reason for the sterility could be identified. In the folk lore of the base, this barrenness was obviously linked to the hundreds of ghost stories and much was made of anecdotal visits to the Pimple by Apprentices who were either never seen again or who returned completely mad. It was, therefore, a point of honour that at least one member of each entry would make a solo trip armed with a powerful torch with which he would signal from the Pimple at the stroke of midnight. To be most effective the visit should take place on Halloween or some other suitably notable date. Sitting in the comfort of a well-lit room, surrounded by familiar things, it is easy to scoff at the terrors of such a trip. In the dead of night, however as I left the buildings area and glanced over my shoulder as I left the bright lights behind me I was certainly not at ease.

As I entered the wooded area and started to climb the hill, I soundly cursed the luck that had selected me to be the one to represent my entry at eleven thirty on that Halloween night. I climbed doggedly onwards, aware of the indisputable fact that behind each tree was someone or something just waiting to pounce. The build up to the Trip had involved an hour of recollection of all of the ghost stories and it was not surprising that I was becoming very uncomfortable indeed. To turn back was unthinkable. To go on was by now quite terrifying. Every tree seemed to assume a sinister shape and I was quite convinced that the well-trodden path was leading me in quite the wrong direction. The rocky outcrop close to the path did not appear familiar and I must therefore be on the wrong track.

Still I climbed, startled by every scurrying movement of small animals in the undergrowth. I was totally unprepared for the tawny owl that took off from a tree right beside me. I was by now quite prepared to accord some degree of credibility to the existence of werewolves and had to forcibly restrain myself from breaking into a run. I risked a quick glance behind me and was dismayed to see that the brightly-lit buildings were now totally obscured by the trees. The moon very obligingly appeared from behind the clouds but the comfort gained from the pale light was more than outweighed by the weird shadows cast on the track.

I briefly shone the torch on my watch. Eleven forty. If I was heading in the right direction, I should be at the Pimple in fifteen minutes. I bravely ignored the evil entity cunningly disguised as a tree and forced myself forward and upwards. The climb was at least getting harder so I must be heading in approximately the right direction. There had been several tales of people from the school wandering around in these woods until daybreak and at least two of those had totally disappeared from the face of the earth As I climbed fearfully upwards, it was very hard to dismiss those stories as figments of someone's imagination. It was very easy to see how someone could panic and get completely lost. All I had to do, I realised, was to keep the moon in the correct position and I would be fine. At that point, the moon retreated sullenly behind its dark cloud.

I looked again at my watch. Eleven forty-five. Very soon now I must break out of the trees and onto the bare earth of the Pimple. From that point I would be able to at least see the lights of the buildings far below. Something large and heavy crashed through the undergrowth a foot in front of me and in the light of the torch I saw the shrubs bend as it moved to a position from where it would be able to attack me. I climbed steadily onwards. The moon emerged again for a brief look and I realised that I had veered off to the left. The path had merged into the undergrowth and I had no option other than to navigate by instinct. Without warning, the ground in front of me cleared and I was scrabbling upwards on the bare earth of the Pimple. The moon resumed its station behind the clouds again and the night sounds faded into a complete and deafening silence. There was not even the sound of a breeze to dent the silence. No night flying insect broke the quiet with beating of wings. From far below I heard the derisive call of the owl as it swooped upon some tiny mammal.

It had become extremely cold. The chill in the air bit through my two sweaters and penetrated right to the bone. It was unrealistically cold and even damp. There was a faintly musty smell in the air that I attempted to dispel by lighting a cigarette. At last, the very top of the hill was within my reach. I looked at my watch. Eleven fifty-five. I sat on the ground and tried to calm down. The earth beneath me felt like ice so I stood up again The cold was overwhelming and I assured myself that it was always this cold in November. I got the distinct feeling that somebody or something was watching me. I swung round shining the torch but the light detected no other presence.

At eleven fifty-eight I identified my own barrack block and carefully aimed the torch. As arranged, I flashed six long flashes then six short flashes then another six long flashes. I saw the lights in my block go on then off again. They had seen my signal. Honour had been satisfied. I started down the hill. Immediately on re-entering the trees, all of the demons that had been content to merely observe my progress on the way up now went on the offensive. Huge animals crashed around on every side of me. Demonic trees reached out to grab me and lashed at me with wicked branches as I hurried past them. Tangled bushes reached out over the track to trip me and something large and evil was right behind me. My hurrying pace inevitably broke into a fast trot then into a run as I crashed through trees and bushes to reach the safety of the bottom of the hill. With countless demons close on my heels, I ran flat out, mindless of the branches ripping at me and scratching my face. Sharp twigs snagged my clothes and tore at my hands as I pushed them aside. At last I emerged from the trees and saw the welcome sight of the first of the barrack blocks. I stopped and leaned against the wall to get my breath back.

When I had recovered my composure, I walked back to my own room where my companions waited for me.

"Why did you stay there for so long?" my friend Derek asked me. "We saw your first signal and replied."

"What do you mean?" I asked.

"You signalled again about five minutes later," he said.

"I signalled again?" I asked.

"We thought you hadn't seen our reply so we switched the lights on again. Did you not see our first signal?"

Something inside me stopped me from telling them that I had stayed on the Pimple for only just long enough to signal once. As I realised that I had apparently not been alone up there, I started to shake violently, sure that there had been no other human being on the hill that night. I am not sure to this day whether my friends were trying to scare me or whether there had indeed been a second signal from the Pimple. I am absolutely certain, however that the midnight trip to the most eerie place in the whole county was the most un-nerving episode that I have ever experienced.

It would be comforting to conclude that either my friends were trying to frighten me or even that there had been another Apprentice up there on a similar mission and that we had somehow missed each other. I shall never know but somehow I feel that the second signal did take place and that it just might not have been the work of a human hand.

As I said, I shall never know.

2

The Real Air Force

The ceremonials which marked our successful completion of three years hard training were somewhat overshadowed by the excitement of learning where the Air Force had decided that we put our training to good use. I was delighted to learn that my first choice of posting had been granted. The base at Leuchars located between Edinburgh and Dundee was only some two hours from my family home in Aberdeenshire and I would be able to spend weekends with my parents.

Brimming with a totally misplaced confidence I drove my newly acquired but rather elderly Ford Consul up to the guardroom at the camp and presented myself to the bored RAF Policeman on duty. He looked me up and down with a rather sour expression of distaste and checked a typewritten list.

"You're to report to 29 Squadron," he announced. "Their hangar is the one in the middle over there." He pointed to three hangars close to the taxiway. "Report to Warrant Officer Gillies." His duty completed, he turned and disappeared inside the gloom of his guardroom. I thanked the empty space where he had stood and drove carefully to the indicated building.

Warrant officer Gillies was not easy to locate, but after conducting a few enquiries, I tracked him down in the senior NCO's crew room.

"Fresh out of training?"

"Yes sir."

"And ready to give us the benefit of your skills I suppose?" He grinned at me. "Welcome aboard, son. We'll put you on the line for a start. You'll pick up a bit of experience from the lads out there. The line carries out all the pre-flights, turn-rounds and after-flights on the aircraft. That means menial stuff like re-fuelling and polishing canopies but it's a very important part of the squadron operation. Later on, we'll get you working in the hangar once you've got a bit of experience." I had gathered in a very short time that, despite my intensive training, my value to the squadron was considered to be minimal. Suitably kitted out in overalls and dragging my newly issued toolbox behind me, I duly presented myself to the SNCO in charge of the flight line.

"Fresh out of training?" Obviously a standard greeting.

"Yes Chief."

The Chief Technician indicated a man sprawling in an armchair smoking something that smelt disgusting.

"That apparition over there is called Coulter. He probably has a first name but everybody calls him Bumble. Go with Bumble, stick to him like glue. Do exactly what he tells you despite the fact that he is only an LAC (Leading Aircraftman) and you are a JT (Junior Technician). You and he will be doing turnround servicing on the next pair of aircraft to land."

The squadron operated Gloster Javelin aircraft. The manufacturer had optimistically designed the Javelin as an all weather fighter. Powered by two Sapphire engines and carrying a crew of two, the big delta-winged aircraft had a rather poor performance and suffered quite badly from a high degree of unserviceability. It was, however, the first operational aircraft on which I was to be allowed to exercise my engineering skills. In my eyes, it was awesome. The Javelin carried Firestreak missiles and was, at that time, the front line fighter in the RAF's inventory. Bumble took me out to the flight line and we walked round one of the parked aircraft.

"There are refuelling points under each wing," he said. "The bowsers have two hoses and we keep putting fuel in until it stops automatically." He went on to explain the fitting of fresh cartridges in the starter breeches, how to check the engine oils and if necessary, how to top them up. I was struggling to absorb this new information and learning to avoid the profusion of aerials and protuberances that festooned the airplane when a roar from overhead announced the arrival of two Javelins in the circuit.

"They're ours," Bumble announced. We watched as the two aircraft broke left over the end of the runway and entered the pattern for landing. Several minutes later, they taxied towards us.

"I'll marshall the first one in and you can take the next."

The procedures were not exactly mind bending and involved merely indicating to the pilot the exact spot where the nosewheel was to come to rest. This feat was accomplished by standing in front of the aircraft and making an exaggerated beckoning motion with both arms. When the nosewheel was correctly positioned, the marshaller crossed his arms above his head to indicate 'stop'. The boarding ladder would then be attached to the aircraft and the groundcrew climbed up to make the ejector seats safe and to assist the crew to disembark. I followed Bumble around the aircraft and watched as he expertly carried out the procedures, which he had previously shown me.

Within a few days, I was considered competent to carry out this work without supervision and fairly soon afterwards, I was re-allocated to work in the hangar on maintenance duties. Life on the squadron was very relaxed with scant regard for the unbending discipline, which had been usual during training. Our living accommodation favoured comfort rather than a strict military regime. Meals were more than adequate both in quality and quantity. The bar in the NAAFI was reasonably priced and a very popular watering hole after work. Never one to spurn the attractions of female company, I found the presence of members of the WRAF extremely pleasant. Leuchars is a very short drive from the university town of St Andrews. Also world famous for its golf courses, St Andrews boasted a large number of pretty girls and was therefore doubly attractive to us.

As the months passed and I became comfortable with both the work and the local geography, I forged a relationship with a young lady of statuesque proportions named April. As the liaison progressed, there was little doubt in either of our minds that given an appropriate time and location, nature would take its course. April appeared to be impatient for this course to be taken and late one night as we were driving along the coast road, her impatience took control. I pulled off the road into the entrance to a cornfield and we climbed into the back seat of the car. Regrettably, April's height exceeded the width of the back seat. Perhaps a previous similar experience allowed her to solve this particular logistical problem. She wound down the windows and allowed the surplus length of her legs to protrude outside. Totally oblivious to passing traffic, the mission was accomplished with a great degree of enthusiasm. We were still in a state of undress and enjoying a post coital cigarette when the police car pulled up behind us. A large policeman strolled towards the car with the beam of his torch pointing sympathetically at the ground.

"Good evening sir."

"Evening…" I mumbled, frantically trying to restore both my dignity and trousers.

The copper addressed the dark interior of the car.

"Are you aware that you're on private property sir?" I mumbled something about being sorry and that I would move the car immediately. "Och, there's no need to get too excited. We got a call from somebody at the Camp and we had to investigate."

"Somebody at the Camp? Leuchars?"

"Aye, they were going past in a car, about five of them and they saw your car in the field."

"The bastards!"

"Aye, sir, probably. Ye have to choose your friends carefully. Now then sir, I would be obliged if you would move your car." He grinned and turned to go. "Goodnight sir, Goodnight April." He walked back to his car.

"How did he know who you were?" I wondered. "It's pitch black in here."

"No idea."

I drove April home and slowly and thoughtfully returned to camp. The following morning at work, I wondered aloud just which one of you bastards set the cops on me. Gales of raucous laughter greeted the question.

"Ask Tony. He was driving back from Anstruther with some of his mates and he saw your car with a pair of feet sticking out of the back window," said Bumble. The Chief Tech's interest appeared to be aroused at this.

"Feet through the window? You must have been with April!" He laughed. "A very enthusiastic lady, our April. She's well known for doing that!"

"So that would be why the copper knew who was in the car even without his torch!" Another chorus of ribald mirth.

Second only to sex, the favourite topic of conversation on the squadron was motorised transport. I took part in and witnessed many quite heated discussions on the comparative merits of Ford versus Vauxhall, Triumph versus Douglas and so on. Most people vigorously defended their own choice of vehicle or motorcycle and many were more than prepared to put their assertions of excellence to the test. At that time, in the learned columns of the magazine Motor Sport there was a great deal of approval for the Volkswagen 'Beetle'. This vehicle, it was claimed was so well manufactured that it might be considered watertight. Several pictures had in fact been published showing modified Beetles actually floating comfortably. It will come as no surprise that the sole Beetle owner on the squadron continually flaunted the magazine and its opinions to any party prepared to listen. Inevitably, we decided to make him either prove the point or shut up.

The very wide Firth of Tay separates Leuchars from Dundee. There was at that time, one way only of crossing the river apart from the railway and that was the ferry known locally as the 'Fifey'. The Fifey carried around ten cars, which were driven on board via a slipway. The slipway was a fairly gentle concrete slope that extended some way into the water in order to make provision for the tidal variations of the river. It was to this very slipway that we persuaded Trevor, the Beetle owner, to bring his precious car. He was apparently willing to put his faith in the Volkswagen to the test. A length of hose was fitted to each of the exhaust pipes and taped to the roof to allow the engine to continue to run if the normal outlet became submerged.

I suspect that if there had been only a few spectators present, Trev would have backed down. It seemed, however, that the majority of the squadron had turned up to witness the spectacle. Trevor drove the Beetle to the top of the slipway and opened the window just in case he had to make his escape. To the accompaniment of loud cheering, he slowly started his descent towards the oily, dirty water of the river. With something less than ten feet to go, he changed his mind about risking his car and applied the brakes. As previously mentioned, the River Tay is tidal at that point and the slipway was covered with a fine mixture of moss, oil and weed making any attempt at braking totally ineffective. With all four wheels locked, Trevor and his beloved Beetle slid gracefully down the ramp into the water. To our great surprise, the little car did not disappear below the surface. Instead, a jubilant shout from the driving seat announced to the audience that his confidence in Teutonic Engineering was completely vindicated. Assisted by the two hoses, the air-cooled engine continued to run. Everything, it seemed was going exactly to plan. Until, that is, Trev decided to return to dry land. We had brought a long wire cable with us that had been secured to the rear of the car. We took up the slack on the cable and started to haul the car and rejoicing owner back to the shore. We noticed that the car seemed to be riding lower in the water than before.

"Hurry it up guys," came a plaintive cry from the river. "The water is getting in." We redoubled our efforts but alas, the water level was now almost at the window. There was absolutely no doubt whatsoever that the car was sinking. We continued to heave manfully on the line but even with the combined efforts of ten or eleven people, the Beetle continued a downward journey until the wheels settled on the concrete some four feet below the surface. A very dejected Trev struggled through the window and waded to the bank chest deep in water to resounding applause.

"Well, it floated for a while anyway," he said defiantly. "Can we get it out of the water?"

One of the bystanders had a tow hitch on his car and managed to drag the waterlogged car from its watery resting-place. To our great surprise, after a few days of drying out the Beetle ran as well as ever. Three days after Trevor had got his car back on the road, the squadron was detached to Germany. It was October 16 1962.

The date will most probably strike a chord with only a small handful of people. It was, however probably the most profoundly dangerous period in recent history. The Cold War between the Soviet Union and the Western powers was at its height. The Soviet technology was far behind that of the USA and the Soviet Premier had decided to locate some medium range missiles in Cuba. Subsequent to the failed attempt by the Americans to invade Cuba and overthrow good old uncle Fidel, the Soviet plan found favour with Cuba. It was assumed that in the event of the situation turning totally pear-shaped, the major attacks on the West would arrive via East Germany. Along with the other squadrons of fighters and nuclear capable bombers, we would protect the skies and keep them clear of the bad guys and their nasty bombs. It was, understandably, a somewhat hasty departure. We had less than forty-eight hours to prepare as many aircraft as we could, prepare masses of ground equipment and tooling for shipment and somehow find time for the odd social glass or two. We had no idea at that time of the reason for our expedited departure from Britain. President John Kennedy announced some days later that reconnaissance photographs had revealed the presence of some very naughty missile sites in Cuba. He told the world in no uncertain terms that the US Government would regard any missile launched from Cuba as an attack on America by the Soviet Union. He demanded that all Soviet projectiles be removed from Cuban soil without delay.

We were alarmed to see that the sides of our hangar were now being shored up with hundreds of tons of earth, pushed right up to the walls by bulldozers. All of our aircraft were fully armed with four Firestreaks. We had two aircraft sitting in the Quick Reaction sheds at the end of the runway with the crews strapped in and ready to go within thirty seconds of receipt of the message to scramble. Two further aircraft were ready to go within five minutes and the remaining seven serviceable aircraft could be airborne within thirty minutes. It was a very worrying situation and to some extent at least, prevented our full and unqualified enjoyment of the German beer and food.

Some five days subsequent to Kennedy's ultimatum, Nikita Khrushchev, the Soviet Premier offered to withdraw his missiles from Cuba on the understanding that the Americans would promise to play nicely and not invade Cuba again. Before this agreement could be formalised, however, a high altitude surveillance aircraft—a U2 piloted by Gary Powers was shot down over Cuba. A few more days of a very high state of alert followed until the whole affair calmed down. The US promised not to invade Cuba and Mr Khrushchev took his rockets back to Russia. We stayed in Germany for another two weeks in case the situation got nasty again. Personally, I don't think any Russian or East German troops would have dared to make a move with our Javelins pointing at them. Even if we couldn't get them to fly, they would have made terrific roadblocks.

When the squadron did finally return to Leuchars, I was lucky enough to persuade the boss to let me travel back in one of the aircraft. It was during the course of that flight that I realised that more than anything else in the world, I wanted to be a pilot. I already had quite a lot of experience in gliders but this was totally awesome. By modern standards, the Javelin is about as exciting as a weekend in Belgium and about as lively as a dead sheep but in the sixties, it was a front line fighter and quite advanced both in specification and weaponry. I had never been up so high or travelled so fast. I had never seen the curve of the Earth or the deep dark blue of the sky at seven miles up. We made a high speed descent into Leuchars from thirty thousand feet pointing more or less straight downwards with the engines at idle and the dive brakes extended. To describe that descent as exhilarating would be a gross understatement.

Two days later, I was standing in the CO's office.

"Why do you want to apply for aircrew?" he inquired.

"I want to fly, sir."

"Why didn't you apply for aircrew instead of engineering then?"

"I didn't realise how much I wanted to fly until we came back from Germany."

"It's not all like that you know," he said. He launched into a long and very involved speech about constant medicals, proficiency training, technical considerations and all the other difficulties suffered by military pilots. Some little time later, I emerged from his office clutching my application form with his signature endorsing the request to be considered for aircrew selection. Having taken the first step, I resolved to take every opportunity to fly not only in our own squadron aircraft but also in the two-seat trainer version of the Hawker Hunter operated by 43 Squadron, our next-door neighbours. By the time the selection process had got around to actually interviewing me, I had amassed almost twenty hours as a passenger in fighter aircraft, plus a good deal of glider time. On the debit side, however, my conduct sheet indicated several departures from the required RAF standards of good order and discipline.

The majority of these defaults related to escapades involving the traditional squadron practice of decorating the crew room with various trophies such as road signs, hotel ashtrays, ladies undergarments and so on. Our crew room was also the main holiday resort for garden gnomes. It was considered a point of honour that whenever we spotted one of these little people in a garden, we would liberate it and transport it back to the camp. We would then send a postcard to the deprived owner, usually worded "Having a great time. Wish you were here. Love, Gnome." Some weeks later, we would surreptitiously return the gnome to his home sporting a painted suntan. Regrettably, the vast majority of gnome owners totally failed to see the funny side and tended to visit the base and complain bitterly to whomever was prepared to listen. I also suffered a very thorough and effective character assassination by the local Inspector of Police who had accidentally discovered my somewhat intimate relationship with his daughter when he returned from a dinner engagement with other civic dignitaries somewhat earlier than anticipated. It was therefore with a generous measure of surprise that I eventually learned that my application had found a degree of favour with the selection board and that I was to present myself for initial training as aircrew.

Flying training for non commissioned aircrew was carried out in Chipmunk aircraft in which the student sat in the front seat with the instructor in the rear. Chipmunks are fairly docile little airplanes and tremendous fun to fly. Every second of the twelve-week course was a totally joyous experience and because of my experience in gliders, I was able to grasp the basics quite quickly and flew solo embarrassingly early. At the conclusion of the course, we were awarded our wings brevet and given the rank of Sergeant (Acting, Unpaid) whilst we waited for the Air Force to send us for advanced training on whichever aircraft type we were considered capable of flying. In the interim period, we were required to return to work in our former trades.

The Sergeants' Mess on most Royal Air Force stations is almost Holy ground. Conversation in the reading room is conducted in hushed tones. The President of the Mess Committee (PMC) is regarded with the same awe accorded to the Archbishop of Canterbury. The high point of the week is the Saturday evening bingo sessions, referred to by the Services name of Housey-Housey. Traditionally, the supper served at those sessions would be curry specially created to be sufficiently spicy to excite crusty old Flight Sergeants whose taste buds had been destroyed by years of exposure to Far Eastern cooking. I was very fortunate in that another member of the course accompanied me to my new posting at RAF Kinloss, in the North of Scotland. Bernie and I were almost the same age, and both of us had been groundcrew prior to our elevation to the peerage. It was said that we were at that time the youngest Sergeants in the Air Force. Looking back on our conduct then, I have to confess to a little shame at the way we paid scant respect to the traditions of the Mess. For example, we would sit at diagonally opposite corners of the reading room and conduct pointless conversations in stage whispers. This practice was guaranteed to raise the blood pressure of the other occupants. They would glare at us over the pages of the Daily Express and mutter dark incantations including lightly veiled references to our probable parentage.

Despite the suspicions of some, Bernie and I were not actually responsible for the spate of bicycle thefts that had the local constabulary baffled. RAF Kinloss is situated on the estuary of the River Findhorn. From the shore, a long jetty reaches out to the deep water. This jetty had, at some time in the past, been used to off-load freight from cargo ships but had fallen into disuse some years earlier. Two of the members of 120 Squadron, much given to unseemly behaviour used to visit the Red Lion (known locally as the Beastie) and after several pints of McEwans Export would avail themselves of any unsecured bicycle outside the pub. They would then ride the three miles back to camp and race each other along the length of the jetty. The concept of stopping when they reached the end seemed to be much too difficult to grasp. Needless to say, no bicycle was ever found although the quantity of bikes in the water must have almost constituted a shipping hazard.

After some six months at Kinloss, I received a letter informing me that I was to receive further training and upon completion, I was to report to a Transport Command base in Wiltshire to take up a crew position on Britannia aircraft. Bernie received a posting to a base in the Middle East and although we corresponded for a while, I never saw him again. That is the unfortunate way of things in service life. During the following twelve years, I heard snippets of information about some of those with whom I had struck up strong bonds of friendship. One such item of information caused me great sadness. I learned that Bernie had been taking part in a night exercise in Denmark when the aircraft that he was flying had been involved in a mid-air collision with a German Air Force Starfighter. Tragically, both aircraft and crews were lost.

3

A Civilian

As I drove through the main gate of the base for the very last time, a feeling of euphoria swept over me. After countless years of wearing uniform, saluting, annual inspections and all the other formalities that constitute service life, I was a civilian again. I was totally untroubled by the fact that I was effectively unemployed. After all, I reasoned, with many thousands of flying hours behind me, how could I possibly fail to secure a well-paid job with an airline? It could only be a matter of time until one of the major operators realised the value of an ex service pilot with valuable jet experience. In the meantime, I resolved to enjoy my newfound freedom. I had my Air Force gratuity safely in the bank and was under no pressure to start earning immediately.

The Military policeman at the gate stared dully at me as I waved cheerfully at him. The headache, earned by the copious intake of alcoholic beverages on the previous evening, failed to detract from my sense of well being. At my party last night, had I not shaken the Base Commander by the hand and called him by his first name? He was, I concluded quite a reasonable and likeable chap and had even bought me a drink as he wished me success in the big wide world.

The episode involving removing the Mess piano from the lounge, carrying it down two flights of stairs and setting it on the servery of the dining room would undoubtedly be attributed to high spirits. My undignified descent from that lofty perch during an enthusiastic rendering of the Warsaw Concerto had banged my elbow. By tradition, most of the departure social formalities involved splashing beer about so the first aid that I received for my bruises consisted of a thorough dousing with several pints of bitter.

I felt that the addition of several bottles of washing up liquid to the small ornamental fountain in the foyer would probably invoke some adverse comment. I hoped that the senior WRAF officer would eventually forgive us for removing several letters from her name on the notice board, changing her surname from Spiller to Piles. Generally, it had been a very successful party and one that I was sure would be the subject of conversation in the future.

Before finally leaving the Air Force, I had taken advantage of the pre-release opportunity to prepare for civilian life and had added a civilian Flying Instructor rating and an Air Transport Pilot's Licence to my qualifications. When I decided where to settle, I would seek out a local flying club and offer my services until the airlines came knocking on my door. Driving through the town of Jedburgh I realised that I was hungry and located a small café. I collected a music magazine from the paper shop next door and ordered an enormous breakfast. The advertisement in the 'Musicians Wanted' columns caught my eye and I noticed a requirement for a keyboard player to join a semi professional band in the South of England. I phoned the number and received an invitation to come along for an audition.

The drive from Scotland to Southend on Sea took a good deal longer than I had calculated, and finding the location of the club where the band was rehearsing was not easy. I arrived well after the appointed time, tired and hungry. As I entered the room, I heard to my great joy that they were rehearsing a number made popular by one of my favourite bands. On the stage there was an unoccupied Hammond organ. I introduced myself to the leader who invited me to sit in for a while to get the feel of the band. It had been some time since I had worked with a band, especially a fairly large band but my familiarity with the music that they were playing made it a simple matter to play a fairly convincing part. When the rehearsal was over, Bob, the leader waved towards a table.

"You like Blood, Sweat and Tears then?" he said. "You seemed to fit in very well." He looked across the table to the bass player. "What did you think, Ben?"

"No problems that I could see," said Ben.

"Would you like to give it a shot at least for this weekend and we'll take it from there?"

I replied that such an arrangement would suit me very well but, being unfamiliar with the area, I would appreciate assistance in finding accommodation until I was able to locate a more permanent abode. An immediate offer of the guestroom in Bob's home settled the matter and I became a temporary member of the band.

Over the weekend, I learned that the Hammond belonged to a previous band member who had decided to call it a day. Hammond organs are not the most portable of instruments and he had decided to leave it at the club hoping to sell it to his replacement. I resolved to buy the instrument as I had always wanted a Hammond and Bob agreed to conduct negotiations on my behalf. I also struggled to become familiar with the material. Because the band worked in a popular club, they played cover versions of most of the current top twenty material most of which was vaguely familiar to me.

On the Sunday night, after the last of the audience had departed, Bob told me that the job was mine. We shook hands and I became a full member of the Alvin Jones Sound earning considerably less than I had been in the Air Force, but earning, nevertheless. I concluded that matters were being satisfactorily resolved and started looking for a place to rent. During the following two days, I drove around the town, viewing several seedy apartments in equally seedy back streets. At last, I discovered what appeared to be an ideal flat on the ground floor of an old Victorian house. I haggled a little over the rent that seemed to be a little on the high side and finally came to an agreement. I took possession of the keys and moved in immediately. Moving in involved transferring three suitcases from the car to the flat and took all of ten minutes.

"Now for the airport," I said to the elderly gas cooker. "Let's see what the local flying clubs can offer." Gas cookers, not generally given to good conversation, ignored me.

Southend Airport was, at that time, a fairly small municipal airport, supporting mainly the cross Channel traffic. Two airlines based there served the needs of passengers wishing to travel to France, Belgium and the Channel Islands. One of those airlines, British Air Ferries, operated Carvair aircraft, a version of the Douglas DC4, converted to carry six cars and a handful of passengers. A more ugly airplane would be hard to imagine. Gone were the sleek lines of its ancestors. The forward end of the aircraft had been replaced by a huge bulbous structure opening at the front to allow cars to be driven into the interior from a hydraulic ramp. In deference to the ungainly appearance of the machine, all of the airplanes bore names painted on the side, such as 'Fat Albert', Big Annie' and so on.

The other airline, British Midland Airways, flew the Vickers Viscount, altogether a more aesthetically pleasing aircraft. BMA provided a service for passengers bound for the Channel Islands and, although widely different in standards of passenger acceptance, both companies seemed to enjoy a good relationship with each other. I made a careful note of the addresses of both companies and resolved to approach both to offer my services.

There were two flying clubs on the airfield. I found a phone in the Terminal Building and discovered that one of the clubs was actually short of an assistant flying instructor. Two hours later, I had secured the second job of my civilian life. Again, the remuneration was not exciting, but it was more than adequate coupled with my musical earnings. More to the point, I was doing two jobs that I loved. Life seemed extremely rosy. I had, however, reckoned without Charlie.

The owner of the club was, in every respect, a self-made individual. Charlie had made a great deal of money in ways frowned upon by the Inspector of Taxes and had established the flying club to spend the money before the aforesaid Tax Inspector managed to get his greedy hands on it. He was overweight and given to outbursts of profanity. Money, he reasoned, could buy anything, including the company of any unsuspecting female who happened to cross his path. He drove a huge and extravagant red Plymouth convertible that probably used more fuel than the five aircraft with which he had established the flying club.

The Chief Flying Instructor and I were discussing the flying schedule for the coming week over a cup of coffee.

"So tell me about Charlie," I said.

"Charlie can be very dangerous," Ted responded. "I don't know who taught him to fly, but he pays very little attention to the finer points. One day for certain we will be picking up the pieces from the runway after one of his famous landings. "He paused and looked contemplatively into his cup. "He is basically a good guy though and on certain days can even be generous. Sometimes he conveniently forgets to pay bills, but then I suppose we all do that."

"His flying leaves a bit to be desired then?" I asked.

"We can't really stop him. He owns the club. I can only remind him that I'm supposed to be in charge here and responsible for the standards."

The outer door opened to admit a person in her late twenties. Ted got out of his chair.

"Hello Sally, this is Allen, our new instructor."

"Hi," she said. "Sally-Anne Bone, nice to meet you."

"Sally is also an instructor, building up her hours towards a commercial licence," said Ted. "Allen is ex Air Force." She frowned.

"I wanted to join the RAF but all they would offer me were ground jobs. What did you fly?"

I related the aircraft that I had flown and the frown grew deeper. "A jet jockey! Bit of a comedown flying these things isn't it?" She pointed to the neat row of training aircraft lined up outside.

"I have only been out for a week," I told her. "I have applications going in to the airlines as well."

"Have you met Charlie yet?" she asked.

"No not yet but I'm looking forward to it."

Sally-Anne chuckled. "Not many people take to Charlie at first sight. He can be a bit abrupt. She went over to the desk to look at the flying programme. "My first lesson is at nine," she said. "He's just about ready for solo. Do you want to check him out, Ted?"

I should point out that only a full flying instructor is authorised to send a budding aviator into the sky totally alone for the first time. Ted agreed to accompany the student leaving Sally and me to share the rest of the lessons for that morning. My first session as an instructor was to be with a fairly advanced student pilot about to learn how to handle engine failures. As I had little knowledge of the local area, I asked Sally if there was a preferred area for such exercises. She pointed to an area on the map.

"Usually round about here," she said. "Not many houses and a lot of fairly large fields."

My student arrived and we introduced ourselves. After explaining the purpose of the lesson, I sent him out to pre-flight the aircraft and followed him a few minutes later.

"Everything okay?" I asked.

"Yep, fine. Shall I start up?"

He started the engine and taxied competently towards the runway. I was content to merely sit there and watch as he completed the final checks and lined up for take-off. He called the tower on the radio.

"Southend, Lima Whiskey is ready for take-off."

"Lima Whiskey, Southend, cleared for take-off, not above one thousand feet, right turn after take-off."

"Lima Whiskey, roger." He pushed the throttle forward and we gathered speed. As we climbed, I told him that we would be practising engine failure procedures as briefed and asked him if he had any concerns.

"No," he replied, "I think I can remember most of it."

"We shall see!" I grinned inwardly. How many times in the past had I encountered a total loss of memory about a pre-flight briefing! Once airborne, it is quite common to forget the finer details of a mission brief.

We duly arrived over the area pointed out by Sally. I told my student to make a turn to the right. As the wing went down, I satisfied myself that there was no other aircraft near us and that we were in a safe area for the exercise. He levelled the wings. I reached over to my left and closed the throttle.

"You have an engine failure!" I said. "What are you going to do?"

"Trim the plane for best glide, turn downwind and look for a good field," he said. I had to admit that he carried out the primary actions with considerable efficiency and I waited to see which field he would select as being suitable. I reminded him to attempt to ascertain the cause of the engine failure. He checked the magneto switches and the fuel state. He switched fuel tanks and looked at me with an unspoken question on his face.

"Assume that everything is fine but the engine is still dead," I told him. "Make the radio call."

"Not for real, though?" he said.

"No, not for real, just say the words."

"Mayday, mayday, mayday, Golf Alpha Whiskey Lima Whiskey, one thousand feet over the reservoir, engine failure and making a forced landing. Over."

"You need to repeat that," I told him. "That wasn't quite right but it will do for the moment."

"I think that field down there would be fine," he announced. It was a fair choice. A grass field, certainly long enough and nothing in the way of obstructions on the approach.

"Okay," I said. "What are you going to do now?"

"Select a final turning point and aim to be there at five hundred feet."

We continued down. Everything was going quite well and according to the book. A good field had been selected, he had the airplane under control and looked as if he had every chance of making a successful forced landing. It is customary on these practices for the supposedly inert engine to be 'warmed up'. This is done by restoring the power for a moment to make sure that the engine resumes its function when the instructor has decided that the exercise is over and that a practice forced landing is not converted into the real thing.

"I'll just warm the engine for a second," I told him. I opened the throttle. The propeller continued to turn idly in front of us. There was no reaction whatsoever.

"Oh shit! This one *could* be for real," I exclaimed. "I have control." I swiftly checked all the engine controls, the magnetos, the fuel pump and the priming pump. I examined all the engine instruments to see if there was any clue as to the engine's malfunction. There was plenty of fuel but the propeller continued to idle disdainfully before us. I made a real mayday call on the radio and thankfully received an immediate response. We were almost abeam the turning point and I decided that there was no option left open. My first instructional flight was going to end in a forced landing. We checked and re-checked the safety harnesses and I started a gentle turn towards the field.

"Just before we land," I said, "I shall unlock the door. When we land, I will bring the aircraft to a stop and we will get out as quickly as possible. Make sure your headset is disconnected."

We continued towards our projected landing spot. I made a very quick further check of all the engine controls again. We were at around three hundred feet and I was cautiously lowering the flaps when it suddenly hit me. *The fuel tanks! We had switched fuel tanks!*

"Switch tanks again!" I shouted. "Quickly!"

He reached down and turned the tank selector to 'BOTH'. Two hundred feet. I should certainly not be fooling with the engine at this height. The rules state that at this height, all of my energies should be directed towards a safe landing. I pumped the throttle again. The engine coughed slightly. One hundred feet. I pumped the throttle again. We were now very low. The engine coughed again then roared into life. I retracted the flaps and held the nose down to build up the airspeed. This was an act of almost criminal insanity. If the engine's recovery should be short lived, we would miss the carefully selected field and be committed to land wherever we happened to run out of height. The engine thankfully continued to howl at maximum power and the airspeed climbed steadily. We thundered over the field at fifty feet and I gratefully started to climb back up to a safe height.

At two hundred feet I keyed my microphone.

"Southend, mayday Whiskey Lima," I said, "I am cancelling the distress call at this time. We have got the power back but we are returning to base immediately."

"Mayday Whiskey Lima, Southend. Your message received. Distress call is cancelled. Southend standing by."

I turned to my companion. "Right," I said. "Spot the two deliberate mistakes!"

"Umm, we should have landed even if the engine *did* pick up?"

"Yes, definitely. And the other?" He looked at me and shook his head.

"We changed tanks without checking that the tank we changed to was actually feeding the engine. Always make sure that you don't switch to an empty tank by letting the engine run for a few minutes on the new tank. My guess is that there is only a dribble of fuel getting from the right tank." I looked at the fuel gauges and my suspicions were confirmed. The right tank was still indicating full whilst the left tank was showing about three-quarters. Obviously the right tank was simply not feeding.

Our journey back to the airfield was uneventful and my student carried out a very passable landing.

"If anyone should ask you," I said as we taxied towards the club, "we got the power back at eight hundred feet. Okay?"

He grinned at me. "Of course! It was nearer nine hundred feet I thought."

"Don't *ever* try that! That could have been a real disaster. You picked an excellent field and all the other things were fine. You could have made a very safe landing there and we could have flown it out without any bother. Just put it down to my ego."

Ted, recently landed from his lesson was there to meet me as we climbed out.

"Not a bad entrance really," he smirked. "How did you get the power back?"

"Switched tanks to 'BOTH'," I told him. "With a bit of reluctance it caught again."

"We got a call from Air Traffic, said you were going to put it down in a field near the reservoir."

"We had a good field selected and it would have been a safe landing." I pointed to my student. "He did well."

Ted grinned at me. "Air Traffic said your mayday was very faint and you didn't say your height." He looked at me quizzically. "How low did you *actually* get before you got the power back?"

"Oh around eight hundred feet, give or take a few inches."

"I once aborted a forced landing from about fifty feet. I wouldn't want to hear of any of my instructors doing that." He stared at me. I was sure that I was wriggling uncomfortably but he seemed not to notice. "Anyway, if you're ready, you have to fill in the reports and the other paperwork. The CAA (Civil Aviation Authority) will be quite happy with a recovery from eight hundred feet."

"That's what I will be reporting." Ted nodded with satisfaction and disappeared into the clubhouse.

My report told of a power failure during a forced landing practice, and that selecting both fuel tanks had restored the power. The power, I related, had been fully restored at eight hundred feet and a successful recovery made to a safe height and the aircraft returned to base. The engineering report stated that some debris had been found in the fuel line, which had partially blocked the flow of fuel from the tank. The aircraft logbook showed that the airplane had apparently flown for rather a long time without consuming very much fuel. I mentioned this interesting fact to Ted. He looked briefly at the log and pointed to the column indicating the name of the previous pilot.

"C. Smollett," he said. "Charlie to you and me. He sometimes takes the aircraft over to his farm. He has a landing strip there, and my guess is that he's filled the thing up with four star from a can."

"Hence the dirt in the fuel line."

"Exactly. Thank your lucky stars he must have only filled one side."

That is precisely what I did.

4

Rotterdam

My new life as a civilian suited me very well. I was able to live quite comfortably from my earnings from flying instruction and music. The band worked every weekend and additionally on Wednesday nights and I had struck up a friendship with a very petite barmaid who worked at the club.

"Jackie has her eye on you," Bob told me with a grin. "You could get lucky there!"

"I'll have you know that I am a happily divorced man." I was not, in reality, actually divorced but my marriage had deteriorated over the years in the Air Force and just prior to my final posting, my wife had announced that she and my children would not be accompanying me to my new base. It had been a very civilised parting of the ways and I saw my two daughters and my son on a fairly regular basis.

After we had played our final set on one Wednesday night, I asked Jackie if she would care to come for a drink with me.

"I'd love to," she said, "but I have to get home. My dog needs to go for his walk and there's no-one else at home just now." She looked up at me. "You can come back to my house if you like. I'm sure there is some beer around somewhere."

"Sounds good to me," I replied. "Is there usually someone else there?"

"I share with a friend but she's on holiday at the moment, so I have the place to myself." She looked at me again. "I'm not usually this forward but you are nice to talk to."

I drove Jackie to her flat and waited outside until she came down being pulled along by a very excited Basset Hound.

"This is Wordsworth," she said. "He's very friendly but a bit mad." I stooped down and patted the elongated animal.

"Hello Wordsworth," I said.

"I'll just take him into the park for a minute. You coming too?" We walked on the wet grass with the dog snuffling in every direction and tripping us with his lead. At last he performed the expected function and we headed back. Once inside the flat, Jackie set about towelling the dog dry and suggested that I look in the fridge for some beer.

"What are you going to drink?" I enquired.

"I'll just have coffee for the moment, I think. I don't really drink much."

I found the beer and made some coffee for Jackie. We sat together on the couch making idle conversation with Wordsworth surveying us solemnly from across the room.

"He's keeping an eye on you," I laughed. "In case you get up to anything."

"He can mind his own damn business!" she said. She put her cup on the table, reached out and put her arms around my neck. "I know this isn't very ladylike, but it's been a very long time." Her mouth was warm and soft and I felt her body arch as she pressed against me. I slid my hand inside her shirt and felt the smooth skin of her back as she unbuttoned my shirt and threw it on the floor. My exploring fingers traced a path round to her firm breast. She pulled my hand away.

"We can't," she said. "Not here. Not with him watching." She stood up. "Come to bed with me?" She laughed. "Unless you really have to go home!"

I followed Jackie to her bedroom and in the semi darkness, we undressed each other then fell onto the bed and made love until the early hours of the morning, passionately at first, then tenderly as the first urgency turned to sensuality. I fell asleep with Jackie in my arms as the grey light of the new day crept into the room.

At somewhere around seven, I was awakened by a cold nose investigating the small of my back. I was also aware of a great weight across my legs. A Basset Hound is a very solid animal and Wordsworth was quite a substantial Basset Hound. His amiable demeanour dispelled any lingering doubts that I may have had regarding his views on my relationship with his mistress. Jackie stirred and opened her eyes.

"Hello," she murmured sleepily. "Did you sleep okay?"

"Yes, darling, but I have to get going. I'm flying at nine-thirty."

"Want some coffee?" She pushed ineffectively at the dog. "Wordsworth! Get off!"

"I don't really have time, sweetheart. I should get back to the flat and get ready for today"

"I'm absolutely shattered," said Jackie. "You are a very naughty man and I want us to do that again soon."

"Me too Jackie, you are wonderful."

"If you really have to go, I'm going back to sleep. Can you see yourself out?"

"Sure!" I bent over to kiss her. "I'll phone you later."

"Mmmm..."

She was asleep again before I had dressed. I left the room silently, under the steady gaze of the dog.

I arrived at the club to find Charlie's outrageous car parked in front of the building. He was in deep conversation with Sally as I walked in and there was a good deal of head shaking taking place. Sally turned to me.

"Will you tell him the requirements for a commercial charter? He won't listen to me."

"Mainly a properly certified airplane and a properly qualified pilot," I said.

"And I do not have a Commercial Licence, Charlie," said Sally. Charlie turned to me.

"*You* have a Commercial don't you?"

"Yes, I do. What aircraft are you thinking about and what sort of charter?"

"British Air Ferries have an aircraft on the ground in Rotterdam with a burst tyre and they want us to fly a spare mainwheel out to it right away. I can get the big Cessna from across the airfield."

"That is an old heap!" scoffed Sally.

"It might look a bit tatty but it's in pretty good shape and it's legal for the job," said Charlie. I considered briefly then said,

"How much?" Charlie flinched. Parting with money, I had discovered was not a topic that Charlie found pleasant.

"You work for me anyway. Why should I pay you extra?"

"You pay me for instructing, not as a charter pilot."

"You're a bloody crook. Fifty?"

"So are you. Seventy-five."

"Sixty?"

"Make it sixty-five and I'll do it."

"Right then. I'll take you over to collect the aeroplane then you taxi it over to BAF to pick up the wheel."

We hurtled across the airfield in Charlie's car with screeching of tyres and arrived at the hangar where the aircraft was stored. A Cessna 206 is a much larger version of the four seat touring aircraft. It has a bigger and more powerful engine with a three bladed variable pitch propeller and usually six seats. The main attraction for our purposes was the fact that the aircraft has a very wide freight door on the right hand side of the fuselage. Sally had not been unkind when she made the scathing reference to the condition of the machine. The paintwork could certainly not be described as pristine. There were several dents in the wing leading edge and quite a few patch repairs had been carried out in other areas.

Charlie got the keys and the tech log and I started the engine. Whilst it was warming up, I read the log and discovered that despite the shoddy appearance, the airplane appeared to have completed many trips without a hitch. The engine appeared to be sound and most of the vacuum driven instruments seemed to work. I shut the engine down.

"Okay Charlie, it seems pretty good. I'll get it over to BAF and file the flight plan. Cash when I get back, right?" He looked hurt.

"Of course," he said. "I'll be here." He drove off in a cloud of tyre smoke. Charlie never went anywhere quietly.

I taxied the airplane to the BAF hangar and watched as a forklift truck lifted the pallet with the wheel up to the freight door. Two BAF engineers pushed and struggled the load into the aircraft and lashed it down. According to the engineers the weight of the wheel was well under the load capacity of the Cessna. As the safe working load marked on the fork truck was less than the maximum payload of the airplane I felt reasonably confident in their judgement.

Before undertaking a foreign trip, there are of course certain formalities to be undertaken quite apart from the sensible things like checking the weather. It was necessary to clear Customs of course and to file a flight plan. I also took the opportunity of acquiring some duty free goods from the bonded store. I carried out a very careful pre flight inspection of the airplane and checked the refuelling figures. All seemed to be in order. I climbed in and started the engine.

"Southend, good morning, BAF3340 request taxi clearance for Rotterdam"

The tower cleared me to the end of the active runway and gave me the altimeter setting figures for the sea crossing. Southend to Rotterdam is a long way in a single engined aircraft over water. I checked that the lifejacket was accessible and hoped that it wouldn't be necessary to use it.

"BAF3340, Southend, clear for take-off, not above two thousand feet initially. Report leaving the zone."

"Southend, BAF3340, rolling," I replied. The aircraft responded to the power and we lifted off the runway into a clear sky. The eastern part of the Thames Estuary slipped below us as we climbed and the northern part of Kent with its huge grain silos was just visible in the haze. Soon, we were cruising at two thousand feet over the North Sea. The Cessna had no autopilot but the air was smooth and there was little turbulence to disturb our passage. Below me I could see the wake of the Scandinavian Seaways ferry ploughing through the sea, bound for the Hook of Holland.

I recalled the previous occasion when I had flown over this stretch of water. That flight had been carried out at thirty-five thousand feet and at over five hundred miles per hour. On that previous flight, I had been searching for another of the squadron aircraft in an exercise known as a practice interception. Far above the weather, all we were concerned with was finding our target and locking our attack radar on him. Once that radar had acquired a target, the interception was deemed to be successful and the role of each aircraft would be reversed so that the hunter would become the quarry

The grey sea passed slowly beneath me. I checked my watch and fiddled with the radio navigational instruments. By taking bearings from two radio beacons, I was able to pinpoint my position. Looking on the chart, I concluded that I was pretty much where I was supposed to be. There was a check point coming up fairly soon and I calculated an estimated time of arrival. The radio emitted a constant stream of chatter as the many aircraft crossing the North Sea reported their positions and requested permission to climb or to descend.

I waited for a break in the chatter then reported my own position. I received clearance to make the initial approach to Rotterdam by a somewhat circuitous route and before being allowed to descend, I had to climb to four thousand feet to keep us clear of other inbound traffic. With some difficulty I broke into the chatter again and reported to the Rotterdam controller that flight BAF3340 was a light aircraft carrying spares for the stranded British Air Ferries aircraft presently on the ground in Rotterdam. The mood of the controller changed immediately.

"BAF3340, Rotterdam, confirm please that you are carrying a wheel for this aircraft?"

"Rotterdam, BAF3340, yes that is affirmative"

"BAF3340, Rotterdam, we clear you inbound to Rotterdam direct. Ignore previous approach instructions. Can you accept radar vectoring to the airfield?"

"Rotterdam, BAF3340 that is also affirmative. Do you wish me to expedite the approach?"

"BAF3340 we wish to get the BAF Carvair repaired and away from Rotterdam as soon as possible. Please expedite your approach as much as possible."

I am fairly confident that several aircraft were repositioned to allow me to make a priority landing on the huge runway. Certainly the authorities in Rotterdam bustled around and arranged a crew to off-load the wheel. Seemingly, the continued presence of the wounded Carvair was causing more than a little embarrassment to the busy airport as it was occupying a stand very close to the passenger terminal. Rotterdam's airport fathers tended to discourage ungainly old propeller driven aircraft in favour of KLM's new shiny jets.

My task had been accomplished and I was once again cleared to depart for a flight across the miles of grey sea. On the way back, despite her age and dishevelled appearance, the airplane behaved impeccably and indeed was very pleasant to fly. A large single engined machine like this could earn a good amount of money, I thought. Perhaps it could be used for pleasure flights in the summer and carrying small items of freight. The possibilities appeared endless and I idly wondered how much an aircraft like this would cost.

By the time I got back to Southend, the weather had closed in and I had to request a radar approach. The 206 proved to be a very stable airplane in difficult weather conditions. I decided to make some very discreet enquiries to see it was for sale. After landing and clearing Customs, I went in search of Charlie to claim my just reward. Predictably, he was unavailable and had gone away until Saturday. In a foul mood, I taxied the Cessna back to her owner.

"Just as a matter of interest," I asked the owner, "how much would an aircraft like this sell for?"

"Why? You thinking about making me an offer?"

"Just interested really, it flies well."

"Carries a lot of weight too," he told me. "I don't really use it enough to justify keeping it. I used it for flying parachutists until last year. It's ideal for that because of the wide door."

"So you might be interested in selling?" I asked.

"I'll work out a price and let you know. You work for Charlie Smollett, right?"

I agreed that Charlie was my employer and that I could be reached at the club. He drove me back to the Terminal Building where I consoled myself with a cup of coffee and thought about becoming the actual owner of an airplane. Quite apart from the actual cost of the airframe, there was insurance and maintenance to consider. I supposed that I could probably make a decent aircraft pay for itself. Other people did after all. An airplane of that size could be used for almost anything. I considered seasonal pleasure flying. With five passenger seats available, a useful amount of revenue seemed possible. Perhaps I would be able to hire myself to the airlines to ferry spares and crews around. Clive had mentioned parachuting work and I decided to investigate that aspect too. By the time I had finished my coffee, I was in such a positive frame of mind that I was almost ready to phone Clive and make an offer. I did use the phone but it was to call Jackie.

"Hello, Jackie," I said. "It's Allen. Would you like to eat out tonight?"

"Oh, hi! No sorry I can't tonight. My friend is coming back tonight and I really want to be here."

I was disappointed but kept a stiff upper lip in the best traditions of an officer and a gentleman.

"Oh well then, I shall have to dine alone. I wanted to tell you that I am going to buy an airplane." When I listened to myself actually saying that, it sounded so good that I wanted to say it again. Jackie did not appear to be terribly impressed.

"That's nice," she said. "Sorry about tonight but I really should be here when Wendy gets back."

"Don't worry darling, I'm sure there will be other times." I began to realise how it felt to be on the receiving end of a one night stand type of relationship. I was definitely getting the brush-off and felt rather indignant. How could she turn down the company of the *owner of an aircraft*! I ambled back to the club and ascertaining that there were no further lessons scheduled for the day, settled down to write up my logbook.

The phone rang. Ted called me from the office.

"It's for you. Clive wants to talk to you." I picked the receiver up.

"Hello?"

"Are you still interested in the old girl?"

"Yes I think so, have you worked out a figure?" Clive had, and mentioned an amount somewhat higher than I had expected but still within reach.

"Let me think about that, Clive. I'll get back to you later."

"Look, if you think it's too high, lets have a beer and talk about it. Maybe I can lease it back from you sometimes. I can still get work for it." That was an option which I hadn't considered.

"Are you free tonight?" I enquired.

"Meet you in the Flarepath around seven," he said. The Flarepath was the airport social club and was the watering hole favoured by all of the pilots, hostesses and airport staff. It was justifiably famous for being the venue for very discreet affairs and covert meetings. Next to the trade magazine, Flight International, it was probably also the best airline job market in the area.

I was halfway down my second drink when Clive came in. I bought him a drink and we sat at a corner table. Several drinks later and not without a good deal of haggling, I had agreed to purchase the 206. Clive would put the wheels in motion the next day and I would demolish my bank balance to pay for it. In the meantime, until the formalities were completed, I would have full use of the aircraft and assume responsibility for all the numerous extras such as hangarage and maintenance.

The following morning, I drove straight over to Clive's hangar and collected the keys to *my* aircraft. Like a child with a new toy, I played with it for the best part of two hours. I started the engine, played with the radios, fiddled with the cigar lighter, sat in each one of the six seats and finally polished the instrument panel until the vinyl shone. Now all that remained was to put the machine to work.

5

Parachutists

I have always been puzzled by the fact that a cross section of the community, although giving every indication of complete sanity in their everyday lives, suddenly abandon logic and are conveyed into the sky for the express purpose of jumping out in mid-air. The thought of departing from a perfectly serviceable aircraft in mid flight in order to descend attached to a canopy by lengths of string seems pure folly.

At a small airfield in Kent there was a thriving parachute school catering to the needs of those brave and foolhardy souls and one morning just as Summer was finally struggling to make an appearance I received a phone call from Clive.

"Got a job for the Cessna," he said.

"Oh great," I responded. "What sort of job?"

"Headcorn Parachute School just called me to ask if the aircraft was available tomorrow. Are you free?"

"Yes I can be available but I've never flown parachutists before."

Clive suggested coffee in the Terminal building when, he said, he would give me all the briefing necessary for the safe departure of the terminally insane.

The secret apparently lies in first of all locating the correct drop area. Having arrived over the correct spot and at the required height, one of the parachutists would throw a long paper streamer from the aircraft to assess the wind speed and direction. He would watch the progress of the streamer until it reached the ground. Based on the results of this experiment, the lead parachutist, known as the Jumpmaster, would then direct the pilot to fly the aircraft to a position from where the jumpers would naturally drift towards the target.

At this point, the pilot is required to fly the aircraft as slowly as possible and in a sideways direction in order to reduce the airflow over the door. This involves flying in a very unnatural way with the controls almost crossed. The behaviour of the airplane is unpleasant. It is very noisy and usually quite turbulent as the machine protests against proceeding through the sky in a sideslip. At the appropriate point, the jumpers disappear through the door and make their own way to the ground. After all those who wished to go ashore have gone ashore, it is usual for the aircraft to perform a wide circle around the jumpers, presumably in case any of them have changed their minds and wish to rejoin the flight.

Clive suggested that we take the Cessna up and practice the required manoeuvres. In order to make the exercise more realistic, we removed the large freight door from the aircraft. Much to my surprise, there was little to complain about regarding draught or even excessive noise as we lifted off the runway. We climbed to three thousand feet over the reservoir and I reduced the speed to about five knots above the stall.

"You'll have to fly slower than that," Clive told me. "They expect somewhere around fifty miles per hour. Put the flaps down about thirty degrees and slow down until the stall warner starts to beep." I did as directed and raised the nose a little more until the airplane started to buffet as the stall approached.

"That's about right," said Clive. "Now you have to make the thing fly a little sideways." I applied right rudder and stopped the natural turn by turning the control wheel to the left. The buffeting increased as the unnatural attitude of the aircraft brought us even closer to the stall. A small power increase was required to prevent the development of a spin but apart from that the airplane seemed quite happy to fly in this crab-like fashion. Clive grinned across at me.

"That will do nicely," he remarked. "When the jumpmaster is happy with the position and speed, he will clear the jumpers to go. The jumpmaster will be the last one out and he should tap you on the shoulder to let you know that he will be leaving you. After that, you'll be on your own and you can get back to flying like a real airplane again."

We headed back to the airfield and I offered the controls to Clive who brought us safely back to earth with an ease borne of long familiarity with the Cessna. We parked outside Clive's hangar and set about removing the passenger seats and stacking them against the wall.

"You happy with all of that?" he asked.

"Yes I think so. When do I have to be at Headcorn?"

"Somewhere around nine thirty. The first drop is usually at about ten. The jumpers are usually first timers and nervous as hell." I followed him into his office. "Have you flown from Headcorn before?" I shook my head. "There are nearly always some sheep grazing on the airfield. You usually have to do a low pass over the runway to clear them away before landing." I mentally filed this information away for future reference. After chatting for a little while, I made my way back to the Club.

Ted met me at the door.

"Can you take these people up for a pleasure flight?" he said, indicating a middle aged couple and a spotty teenager. "I have to stay on the ground because there are students flying and Sally is already instructing."

"Sure," I said. "No problem." I walked over to the family. "Hello, I'm Allen. Where would you like to go?"

"We live near Maldon," the man told me. "Can you take us over our house?"

"That's only about five minutes flying from here," I said. "Yes we can easily do that. The normal pleasure flight is about twenty minutes so we can stay a little while over Maldon if you like."

The spotty teenager and his father climbed into the back of a Cherokee and their mother nervously took her seat in the front. I gave them the usual safety briefing and made sure that all their seat belts were properly fastened.

"Do we not have parachutes?" she asked nervously. I concluded that today was my day for being involved with parachutes. "What happens if the engine stops?"

"In the extremely unlikely event of the engine stopping, we just glide until we find a field and land there," I said. "A lot of people actually operate this sort of aircraft from a field. We don't really even need a runway." She did not appear to be very convinced and wriggled uncomfortably in her seat.

The pleasure flight was, as pleasure flights go, uneventful. Predictably, the nervousness decreased as mum saw familiar surroundings from a completely new aspect. The three of them pointed out landmarks to each other and chattered excitedly as I flew them in a wide circle over their home. As we approached the airfield again, the Tower asked me to hold in our present position.

"Southend, Whiskey Alpha roger," I replied. "What's the problem?"

"Whiskey Alpha, Southend, we...ah...we have a student in difficulty at this time and we are keeping traffic clear of the runway until she lands." I acknowledged the message and listened attentively to the radio. The man in the back tapped me on the shoulder.

"What's going on?" he asked. "Why are we circling here?"

"It's only a bit of heavy traffic," I told him. "We have to wait here for a while before we can land." The radio came to life again.

"Charlie Lima, Southend, do you read?" Almost immediately, a female voice replied.

"Yes, Charlie Lima can hear you. I can see a big lake over to the right. I think it's the reservoir but I'm not sure."

"Charlie Lima, Southend, we have you identified on radar approximately eight miles from the airfield. Make your heading one three five degrees and climb to two thousand feet. Tell me when you can see the airfield. It will be at your twelve o' clock position and you should see it very soon."

"Charlie Lima, okay, I'm climbing now to two thousand feet. I still can't see the runway."

"Charlie Lima, Southend, please say your fuel state. How much fuel do you have?" There was quite a long pause.

"Both tanks are reading about half full," came the reply.

"Southend Tower, roger." The controller's voice was reassuring. "Just keep going the way you are. You're doing fine." There was another period of silence during which I almost held my breath, then suddenly,

"I can see it! I can see the airfield! It's right in front of me."

"Well done Charlie Lima, maintain your present heading and descend now to one thousand feet to join downwind right hand for runway two four."

We continued to circle. The man tapped me on the shoulder again.

"Robert feels sick. Are we going to land soon?"

"Yes," I said, "we should be down in about five minutes or so." I keyed my microphone. "Southend, Whiskey Alpha, can you get us in before Charlie Lima? I have an unwell passenger after all that circling."

"Whiskey Alpha, Southend, roger you are cleared to finals number one on runway two four. Report on final approach." I thanked the controller and turned round to tell my passengers the good tidings just in time to witness Robert's lunch landing on the floor of the aircraft.

Because of the sad fact that airsickness is contagious, I carried out what the books call an 'expedited approach and landing' As we rolled out after touchdown I opened the door to allow fresh air into the aircraft. The controller kindly cleared us to fast taxi back to the club by the shortest route, but even then the atmosphere in the cabin was far from pleasant. My passengers climbed out of the Cherokee and headed for the office, probably full of complaints about my flying. I watched as the student, now completely recovered from her ordeal, executed a copybook landing.

"That recovery was thanks to some previous good instructing," I thought. Basic principles, if properly taught can save your life many

times over. I walked back towards the Club in time to see my passengers getting into their car.

"That was great," the woman said to me. "Pity about Robert being sick. I told him about the stuff he was eating." She shrugged her shoulders. "Teenagers! Anyway, thanks for the flight, it was fun." They drove away. I made a fast phone call to the airport cleaning company and gave them the rather unpleasant job of cleaning the Cherokee.

The following morning dawned fair. By eight o' clock, the sun was shining and little white cumulus clouds were dotted over the sky. I drove over to the airport and unlocked the Cessna. As I planned to fly her down to Headcorn and remove the freight door there, I borrowed a pair of pliers from one of Clive's engineers to pull out the lock pins. The big engine pulled us into the sky and I turned south towards Kent. Headcorn was not the easiest airfield to find. It was a small grass field conveniently located amongst hundreds of other almost identical grass fields. Only the single hangar with "Headcorn" painted on the roof gave the game away. I identified the runway and prepared to make the required low fly past to move the sheep. The animals scattered as I roared overhead and pulled round tightly for a fighter approach and landing.

As soon as the engine had stopped, I turned round to see that two people were already removing the freight door. Patently, they had seen this airplane before. Six more people moving with discomfort in their awkward parachute harnesses were walking towards the aircraft. This was obviously the first wave of jumpers. One of them climbed up inside.

"Hi!" he held out his hand. "I'm Harry. I'm the jumpmaster today for this lot. Have you done much para flying?"

"Not a great deal," I admitted, "Clive gave me a pretty good briefing and we did some air work too."

"Should be no problem then, Clive tells me you're ex Air Force." I nodded. "We like about fifty knots or thereabouts for the jump. We'll fly over the target area, which is this field and throw out a streamer then we'll come around in a big circle. I'll give you course corrections until we get exactly over the jump point. I will be the last one out and just before I go I will give you the signal by tapping you on the shoulder." He paused to let all of that sink in. "Any questions?"

"No," I said. "What height do you want?"

"Three thousand for this jump. They have all jumped before and they're going to free-fall the first thousand." He turned to the other five lunatics. "Right guys, lets get airborne."

As I taxied into position for take-off one of the men leaned over.

"If you have an engine failure below three hundred feet, we'll stay with you. Above that, you're on your own!" As he obviously meant what he had said, my estimation of their sanity dropped yet another couple of points. As we thundered down the grass runway I glanced back into the cabin and noticed that Harry was sitting casually in the doorway and not even holding on. The other five were sitting on the floor of the airplane apparently unconcerned about the magnitude of the insanity which they were about to perpetrate.

At last, we reached our assigned height and I put the aircraft into the slow sideways mode while Harry did his paper streamer thing. Eventually he was satisfied and told me to start the approach to the jump point.

"Left,…left more,…Hold that, steady…steady…GO! GO! GO !" I was aware of a change of trim as the jumpers dived out in quick succession. Harry hurriedly came forward and tapped me on the shoulder as promised.

"Okay," he said. "They're all gone, I'm the last to go." Without warning, he reached in front of me, pulled the mixture control to fuel cut-off. He snatched the key out of the switch, laughed out loud then ran back and jumped out of the airplane.

As Harry and my key plummeted out of sight I quickly reviewed my position. I was at three thousand feet above an airfield. Without the key I had absolutely no means of re-starting the engine. Even I had to admit that a forced landing was extremely likely. With my level of experience I had damn well better not screw this up. On the credit side, I had more than enough height to play with and the best landing area in Kent was right below me.

The eventual landing was not the best nor the smoothest that I have ever made, but it was, at least bloodless. I sat there in my aircraft on the runway at Headcorn, unable to even move. Harry and the jumpers sauntered over to me.

"Having a bit of bother? Broken down?" He laughed and handed me the ignition key. Suddenly I too saw the funny side and roared with laughter.

I flew seven more jump teams that day but kept a very close eye on my possessions just in case Harry had any more little tricks up the sleeve of his flying suit. As they put the door back on the aircraft for the trip home, one of them said to me,

"Harry pulls that trick almost every week on some poor unsuspecting pilot. I should have thought that Clive would have warned you. He always carried a spare key, just in case!" Clearly I had to have a friendly whisper in Clive's ear at the earliest opportunity!

Despite working with the band three nights every week plus one afternoon for the strict-tempo dancers, the limited amount of income from all of my activities, both musical and aeronautical was rapidly becoming insufficient to support my preferred lifestyle. To my great disappointment, my relationship with Jackie had been unilaterally terminated. She confessed with some degree of embarrassment that she actually preferred the company of other girls. I decided that it was high time that I once again took control over my life. It cost me a small fortune in postage, but I think I applied to almost every aircraft operator of any significance on the British register.

For several days, the postman brought me, along with the usual crop of bills, a bundle of letters regretting that they were not in a position to offer encouragement at that time. When the letter bearing the logo of a very well known holiday airline fell on the doormat, I was confidently anticipating dropping it into the bin. This letter however suggested that I might care to present myself for a meeting with their chief pilot at their Luton base. I should bring with me my logbook, licences and service record They were the letter said, actively recruiting for the forthcoming holiday season.

On the appointed day, I flew up to Luton in the Cessna and found the Chief Pilot's office. Some two hours later, I had received a firm job offer as a First Officer with the Company, providing that I was successful in passing the technical and flying courses, which would be provided by the Company. I would also be required to sign a bond tying me to the Company for a period of two years. The lifestyle of any aircrew member is one of constant study and examinations. The subsequent weeks found me studying the technical aspects of the BAC1–11, learning company procedures, enduring countless hours of simulator rides and then, when that was all over, many hours of non-passenger flights conducted under the eagle eye of the training captain. After what seemed to be a lifetime, the training and assessment was over for the time being. I was ready to join the workers again.

6

Holiday Airline

Five thirty in the morning. The rain hammered on the window of the bedroom and leaked in through the gap at the bottom, forming puddles on the windowsill. Being early March, it was still dark as I struggled out of bed and commenced the ritual of coffee, washing, shaving and dressing. As I gradually recovered consciousness and dressed in the still new uniform the anticipation of the forthcoming day dispersed the gloom of the morning. Today was to be my first day as a fully qualified line pilot on a trip to the sun drenched Algarve.

The process of becoming so qualified was a somewhat tortuous one. From having been an Air Force pilot on a fairly large four engined transport aircraft, an appropriate civil licence was necessary in order to operate civilian aircraft. Although the basics of flying skills were already firmly in place, I had to assimilate the masses of technical information applicable to the BAC1–11 aircraft that was at that time the typical holiday airline ship. Having studied and struggled with fairly unfamiliar concepts, I then had to have the extent of that knowledge examined and assessed by an examining board that finally agreed that the appropriate endorsement might be added to my Air Transport Pilot's Licence. My employers, who had subsidised the period of study and the not inconsiderable expense involved, were now in a position to use my newfound expertise in the right hand seat of the type. Subsequent to the actual aircraft qualification, known as a Type Rating, new pilots had to undergo a succession of trips on a particular route before being entrusted with the duties of First Officer. The title of the latter varies with the position of the user. If one is a Captain, the person in the right hand seat is usually referred to as 'co-pilot'. If the co-pilot refers to his own position, the term 'First Officer' is used. The level of experience of a co-pilot may also be assessed by the form of timepiece worn. Very junior people will usually affect a very large, heavy and complex wristwatch with facilities for telling the time in several time zones, a split second stopwatch and other chronological functions. Senior Captains, on the other hand will probably wear a comic-strip watch or even no watch at all, claiming to rely on others if they wish to know the time.

That grey March day was to be my first day of productive work with the airline and I determined that I would discharge my duties to the complete satisfaction of my Captain and my employers. In such a positive frame of mind, I drove the fifteen miles to the airport and arrived ridiculously early for check-in. Hoping to create a favourable impression, I requested the technical log for the aircraft and studied every detail of the previous few trips to see what defects, if any, had impeded the course of operations. Finding nothing of any note, I accepted a cup of coffee from a sympathetic dispatcher behind the Operations desk and settled in an armchair to await the arrival of my revered leader. Some thirty minutes later, the door opened and Captain Des Walsh entered. He greeted the two dispatchers with an easy familiarity, addressing them by first names. He was handed the tech log at which he glanced briefly then signed his name with a flourish at the bottom of the page.

"Did they finally get the cabin pressurisation fixed then?" he enquired.

"Yes, they did engine runs last night and found a sticking outflow valve which they changed. It's fine now."

To my abject horror, I realised that I had not even noticed the defect nor the rectification work. The great man turned to me. "You with us today? Glad to have you along. Name's Walsh, Des Walsh. We'll have a coffee whilst you do the fuel calculations and flight plan then we'll go out and count the wings just in case the technicians have missed something."

I busied myself at a desk working out diversion airfields, flight plans, fuel quantities, weights and the thousand and one other little calculations that are necessary prior to launching an airliner into the sky. We always assumed that every seat would be filled and that every passenger weighed exactly the Civil Aviation Authority approved amount, and that each passenger would carry precisely the regulation amount of baggage. On this calculation, and knowing the distance to be travelled, we were able to calculate the amount of fuel that we would need to take on, allowing for possible diversions and delays. Most flight crews elect to add a few gallons just to be on the safe side. Fuel, of course has a weight and excess fuel carried adds to the cost of the flight. This calculation, along with the other paperwork keeps the co-pilot in a flurry of activity whilst the captain lounges about in the ops room, greeting other captains and joking with the cabin crew. Captains very rarely conduct direct communications with First Officers other than their own. Remarks made to such people are kept to a minimum. Even then, eye contact is studiously avoided, the gaze of the senior man being focussed at a point just above the menial's right eye.

At last, the work was done and I handed the result of my deliberations to Des who glanced at it then handed it back to me.

"You happy with all of that?" I nodded. "You have a lot of air time I notice. Most of it military?"

"About four thousand hours turbo-props and around six hundred jets. Yes mostly military."

"Well, at least you probably won't get air sick then. Let's go and look at the beast."

He led his crew out to the ten seater crew bus that was parked outside. In the Air Force, the AC (aircraft commander) boards the bus first, followed by other crew members in order of rank. Des, however stood aside to allow our cabin crew, five pretty girls, attired in uniforms designed by a leading fashion house to board the bus. He then gestured me on board and swung his bag into the bus.

"Morning, Tony," he said to the driver.

"Hi Des, where you off to today?"

"Don't know," he said. "Ask him." He indicated me. "They never tell me a damn thing."

We drove out to where the aircraft was parked, surrounded by the umbilical cords of the fuelling process and trailing ground power lines. A catering truck was just pulling away and the cleaning supervisor greeted us as we climbed aboard.

"Morning, Captain. She's all spick and span, ready to go."

"Thanks, Janice." Yet another first name. "Don't suppose we'll come back in the same condition though." Janice shrugged.

"It's what we get paid for."

The five girls busied themselves with stowing the things that cabin crew stow and making the final preparations for boarding as Des and I strolled round the aircraft. As we came round to our starting point at the foot of the stairs he asked me

"Happy enough with it?"

"Looks fine to me."

"Right then, let's saddle up."

We climbed up the stairs and entered the flight deck. The check list of things that have to be done is carried out as a 'check and response' procedure. Des picked up the manual and with a sigh, started reading out the various items that had to be variously, set, checked, observed and counted.

"Nose gear indicator?" he enquired.

"Green," I replied.

"External lights?"

"Off."

"Pressurisation amplifier?"

"Flight and no red light."

"Axe and lifejackets?"

"Stowed."

The door to the flight deck opened and Sandy, the chief stewardess poked her head in.

"We're all ready back there for boarding," she said.

Des picked up the hand microphone.

"Hello Sarah, wheel them out."

I looked out of my side window and soon a crocodile of happy holidaymakers emerged from the terminal building and, led by one of the ground staff, headed for the aircraft. It is a strange fact that even very intelligent people who are being loaded onto an aircraft seem to be totally incapable of identifying a nominated seat even if the number of the seat is indicated on the boarding pass and on a placard on the seat itself. They will therefore mill around aimlessly, trying to force overlarge carry-on bags into an overhead locker, usually several seats removed from where they ought to be sitting. When they eventually locate the correct seat and the family arguments about who gets the window seat have subsided, they inevitably practice reclining the seats, lowering the tables and examining the honey bags (the cabin crew name for the polite little paper sacks stowed in the seat back). They do this despite instructions to the contrary issued by the cabin crew. The confusion is always sorted out eventually and the cabin resumes some semblance of order.

The list went on and on. In fact the pre take-off checks ran to about ten pages of the manual. At long last, we came to the bit where the passengers stop being bored and start getting excited about the imminence of flight.

"Air crossfeed?"

"Closed."

"Ignition?"

"High and low."

"Start master then please."

The number one engine was started up and the tug attached to the nose wheel pushed us back from the gate to a position where we would be able to start number two engine and taxi forward. As we taxied towards the runway, the cabin crew would have been delivering the required pre-flight briefing to the passengers about the various safety features most of who totally ignore this most essential demonstration.

The journey to the end of the runway was unremarkable punctuated for me by more of the apparently endless co-pilot duties such as copying the airways clearance and reading it back to the tower. This ensured that there could be absolutely no doubt as to where we were going and how we were going to get there. When we turned for take off I was exhibiting the sort of quiet confidence that I hoped would impress the Captain.

"Brakes?" he asked.

"Checked, pressure sufficient."

"Flight instruments?"

"Checked, my altimeter set to QNH."

"Mine also. Thrust reversers?"

"Checked."

Sandy entered the flight deck and confirmed that the cabin was prepared for take-off. Finally we were finally ready to go. The appropriate exchanges on the radio were made and Des increased the power to the take off setting. The aircraft shook with the anticipation of the headlong rush down the asphalt and the leap into the air. He released the brakes and I started the stop watch.

"Acceleration normal, airspeed building," I called. We sped along the runway and then, when the speed reached the point where we were committed to take off.

"Vee one." I called.

"Your throttles," said Des. I closed my hand over the two power levers.

"My throttles."

'Vee' speeds are the critical speeds on an aircraft. Vee two is climb speed and Vee three is usually called 'Rotate' in civil aviation and is the speed at which the aircraft is flown off the runway.

"Rotate!" I called. Des eased back on the control column and we were airborne.

I took my hand off the power levers and hovered near the landing gear selector.

"Gear up!" said Des. I moved the bulky gear selector lever and the landing gear retracted smoothly into the wheel wells. A BAC 1–11 climbs well and we were very soon enveloped by the dark grey murk of the low clouds. We turned on course for our first waypoint, the radio navigation beacon at Biggin Hill. Still climbing, Des reached above his head and turned off the no smoking sign.

"Here's your big moment, then. Do a passenger announcement," he said with a grin.

I picked up the handset.

"Ladies and Gentlemen, this is the First Officer. On behalf of the crew, I'd like to welcome you on board this morning. The Captain has now turned off the no smoking sign so those of you who wish to smoke may do so. Please remain seated, however until the seat belts sign has been turned off. You may be interested to know that the weather in Seville is forecast to be very pleasant today with a high of 24 degrees. Thank you for flying with us today and we wish you a pleasant flight."

Des looked across at me with a puzzled grin.

"You can expect a riot any time now. Most of these people want to go to Faro."

Somewhat ashamed, I realised that I had inadvertently read the weather for our diversion airport instead of our destination. Not one passenger had even noticed. The remainder of the flight proceeded without incident and it was soon time to start down. The descent is one of the busiest phases of a flight and we both worked quite hard in a well-prepared routine to prepare the aircraft for the landing at Faro. We swept over the sewage works at the end of the runway and Des very gently settled the aircraft onto the runway.

"Reverse thrust, please," he called. I engaged reverse thrust and increased the power until the speed had decreased to the speed at which the nosewheel steering could be engaged.

"Very nice landing, boss," I remarked. "Hope I can do as well."

"We'll see on the way back. You'll be in the driving seat. I shall look forward to being flown by a former protector of the skies."

The cabin crew were making the usual exhortations to the passengers to remain seated whilst we taxied to the terminal in the early morning sunshine. As usual, the instructions were almost universally ignored and I could visualise the flurry of activity as they attempted to retrieve hand baggage from the overhead compartments.

We were scheduled to remain on the ground at Faro for forty-five minutes. We used the time to file the return flight plan and have a cup of the particularly noxious liquid masquerading as coffee, served in the terminal building.

Again, we trooped out to the aircraft and carried out the pre departure checks. This time, acting as Aircraft Commander, I called out the checks and Des carried them out. Somewhat self consciously, I called the terminal crew and asked them to board our passengers. Once again, the ritual of confusion took place and was sorted out with the same enviable efficiency by Sandy and her team. The subsequent take off and climb to our cruise altitude was achieved with no drama and we settled down to enjoy the view as we sailed serenely over the Spanish mainland. I had selected the autopilot and my function as Aircraft Commander was that of monitoring the performance of that very complex piece of machinery that was maintaining our airspeed, heading and altitude far more accurately than the most proficient human pilot.

The flight proceeded to the accompaniment of the sort of occurrences that I would later come to expect from these holiday charter flights. Drunk male passengers made clumsy attempts to grope the stewardesses, countless children ran up and down the aisles, inevitably, somebody was airsick, we had several passenger visits to the flight deck and so on. I was enjoying the experience of flying the 1–11 and congratulating myself at having made such an easy transition from service life to a civilian position. I started doing some mental arithmetic to try to compute when I might reasonably expect to achieve a command with the Company. I was fairly confident that Des was satisfied with the manner in which I had discharged the duties of co-pilot. I was relaxed and feeling quite at home on the flight deck of the 1–11 when there was a very loud bang and the window in front of Des became completely opaque.

"Windshield Failure! "Des cried in upper case letters. He looked across at me, waiting. To my great astonishment, I instantly remembered the primary emergency drill for this occurrence.

"Cabin pressure selector to 8000 feet. Emergency descent power please."

Des trimmed the cabin pressure selector to reduce the pressure in the aircraft and pulled back on the power levers. I disengaged the autopilot and pushed the nose down to reduce our altitude. When we were established in our descent, I requested the full depressurisation check list. With all the items on that procedure taken care of and nothing further to do until we had descended to 8000 feet, I asked Des to make the passenger PA announcement.

"Ladies and gentlemen," he began, "This is Captain Walsh. I expect you have noticed that we are reducing our height. You may feel some discomfort in your ears but I can assure you that there is no cause for concern. We are descending to a lower level for precautionary reasons. We will keep you advised of any further developments. In the meantime please return to your seats and make sure that your seat belts are securely fastened. Thank you for flying with us today."

When we reached 8000 feet, the height at which the cabin pressurisation could be turned off, we reduced our speed to the 210 mph required by the flight manual and reviewed the situation. According to the flight manual, there was no danger to the airplane if the speed did not exceed the stated maximum of 210 mph. We decided, therefore to continue to our primary destination rather than saddle the Company with an expensive diversion. A jet aircraft consumes a great deal more fuel at low altitudes than it does at its normal cruise height so Des made some calculations and pronounced that we would still have sufficient fuel to reach Luton with the required reserves. A BAC1–11 becomes a noisy lumbering beast at low speeds and at low altitude but eventually we crossed the English coast and obtained the required modified clearances to proceed to our destination.

"Now we shall see what sort of landings you air force people can do," said Des. "I can't see a damn thing except through the side window."

I looked across at him and shrugged. "It's not too late to change seats you know!" I offered.

"You stay where you are. I have every confidence in your abilities. Just tell me what you want and your wish shall be my command."

"OK then, Descent check list please."

"Seat belt notice?"

"On, in fact, still on."

"Pressurisation?"

"Set."

"Reference speed?"

"Set."

We continued our progress to Luton and eventually commenced our final approach to the airport. As the 'pilot flying' the responsibility for the crew landing briefing was mine and I rather self-consciously instructed Des as to what actions I expected him to take in the event of a missed approach (which seemed quite probable) or other departure from the norm. As we got close to the airfield, I decided to cancel the autopilot and hand fly the final approach. The approach is usually flown using the Instrument Landing System (ILS). The ILS indicator on the flight deck shows the pilot whether the aircraft is on the correct glide slope and whether it is following the runway centre line allowing a correct approach even in very bad visibility. As I would be the only one able to actually see the runway, I requested Des to fly the ILS approach until I had visual contact with the runway. At that point I would take control and put us on the ground.

"Final Checks please," I requested.

"Altimeters?"

"Set QFE."
"Flaps?"
"Set."
"Landing Gear?"
"Checked down, 6 green lights, no red lights."

Des flew the approach with scarcely a deviation although there was quite a lot of turbulence then at about a mile out I positively confirmed that I had the runway in sight through the haze.

"I have visual contact." I called
"Confirm contact?"
"Visual contact confirmed."
"You have control."
"I have control," I replied putting my hands on the yoke.

Des made the final radio calls and we were cleared to land. With one eye on the ILS indicator and the other on the rapidly approaching runway, I continued the approach. We swept over the threshold and Des reduced the power as I felt for the ground. Much to my surprise, the wheels settled on the tarmac with barely a squeak. I released a breath that felt as if it was five days old.

Des looked at me and grinned. "Very nice. The passengers will be impressed."

"Thanks," I said. "Reverse thrust please."

As we taxied to the terminal, I was aware that none of the trusting souls traveling behind us had been given any indication that there had been a problem with their airplane. Our abrupt departure from the heights and our subsequent snail-like progress had not been explained to them. To all but a knowledgeable few, it had been a normal flight except that the pilot seemed to have gone low, probably to enable them to view the countryside over which they were flying. I could almost hear them saying what nice chaps we were.

Although there had never been any real prospect of danger, I was glad that we were once again safely on the ground. At the de-briefing over a cup of coffee, Des was kind enough to comment on the way that I had handled the problem.

"As long as the wings hold on and the engines keep running, a 1–11 will take a hell of a lot of punishment and still keep flying!" he remarked. "So how was your first day? It's not normally as boring as that. You'll get used to it. Next time we'll try an engine failure on take-off. That'll make you sweat a bit!"

I got up from the chair and picked up my bag.

"See you tomorrow, Des," I said.

"Yeah, see you Al."

Somehow, I knew that I had passed a test and gained some measure of acceptance. Although the test had been simple and set for me by pure circumstance, it was a very satisfactory feeling.

7

Nightstop

Flying along in the cruise at thirty-three thousand feet, at a speed of some five hundred plus miles per hour is a very comfortable way to make a living. I was idly considering this fact on the flight down to the Balearic Islands. The flight deck was a comfortable environment and Des Walsh was an excellent companion and a first class skipper. We had just finished our in-flight meals (one at a time, of course and different meals) when Des remarked that he was bored. Not *ordinary* bored, but *bloody* bored. The airplane was perfectly happy flying on autopilot and apart from monitoring our progress and making radio calls, we had very little to do. Des twiddled one of our navigation radios and managed to find a Portuguese radio station that we listened to for a while.

"Not exactly lively," said Des as the sound of a string quartet issued from the cockpit speaker. I nodded my agreement.

"What do you think of the new girl in the back?" I asked.

"Not your type, Al. Anyway, it's captain's privilege to get first refusal."

"You'll be too busy doing the paperwork for the return," I said. "It's your sector on the way back."

"I might just delegate that." He was rudely interrupted by the radio.

"Autair334, this is Bordeaux Information." Des pressed his transmit button.

"Bordeaux, Autair334, go ahead."

"Autair334, descend to flight level three one zero for traffic separation." I immediately reached up and reset the autopilot for the new level.

"Roger that. Descend to three one zero. Autair 334," said Des.

"Three one zero set," I told him.

"Thank you. Going down." Losing the required two thousand feet took only two minutes and Des called the controller when we were established at the lower height.

"That came very close to waking me up," he said. I pretended to be asleep. Just as we were about to resume our discussion of the new face in the crew, the door opened and she came in.

"Anyone care for a drink?" she asked.

"Jack Daniels on ice for me," Des said.

"I'll just have coffee please, Gemma, I'm driving." She looked nonplussed. I grinned.

"They *warned* me about you two," she said. "You both have a reputation for winding the hostesses up!" She smiled. She had a very beautiful smile. "You'll both have coffee and like it."

"You have a very beautiful smile," Des remarked.

"Hey! I just nearly said that."

"But I actually *said* it," Des said. "I'll take you up on the drink offer when we get back to Luton." The radio came to life again.

"Autair334, Bordeaux, Descend immediately to flight level two niner zero. Please expedite. We have unidentified traffic at your eleven o' clock, range nine miles and flight level three one zero"

"Bordeaux, three three four, descending to two nine zero." He turned to Gemma. "Get in the jump seat quick as you can."

"Cabin signs please," I said to Des. He reached up and switched the seatbelt and no smoking signs on as I disconnected the autopilot and pushed the nose down into a high-speed descent. Des pushed his transmit switch again.

"Bordeaux, three three four, I am looking but I have negative contact with the other traffic."

"Roger three three four, the traffic is now at your eleven o'clock, range five miles. We think it is military but he is not responding to our transmissions." Des turned to me.

"That thing is bloody *moving*!" I looked anxiously through the windshield.

"Why can't we see him," I said. "We should turn right to get clear."

"It's your call. I would recommend that we stay on this heading. He will miss us provided he stays on heading too." Gemma was looking anxious as we levelled out at our new height.

"The passengers will be a bit worried about that dive," she said. "Can I get back to the cabin yet?" She looked out of the left-hand window. "Hey! I see it!" She pointed excitedly. I looked where she was pointing and sure enough, about a thousand feet above us, a USAF Phantom flashed across from left to right. Des wiped imaginary sweat from his forehead.

"Well, he has definitely seen us now," he said. "I'll tell Air Traffic." I listened as Des advised the French Air Traffic Controller that we now had contact with the conflicting traffic. The response he received was, however, a little surprising.

"Autair334, be advised that the Phantom was aware of you all the time. We receive the message from his carrier that he mistakes you for an English Air Force tanker and he tracks you since one hundred miles." Des and I rolled our eyes in unison. We heard a new voice on the radio.

"Bordeaux, this is Airforce51, may we talk through to Autair?" The controller gave his assent.

"Autair, this is Airforce51, Hey you guys I'm real sorry if I scared y'all back there. That airplane looks real like a VC-10 tanker from far away, y'know with the rear engines and the high tail an' all."

"Fifty-one, this is Autair, You had us just a teeny little bit worried there, old boy. We couldn't hear you on the radio and we didn't know exactly where you were. If you're not too low on fuel you might care to fly alongside us for a minute. Give our passengers a look at you. Don't get too close in, though."

"Roger that, Autair, I won't come closer than 'bout a mile. That okay?"

"Fifty-one from Autair, one mile will be absolutely topping thank you. Des was doing his British Airways Captain impersonation.

The Phantom slowly appeared on our left, flying nose high to match our speed. The American pilot waved, the sunshine glinting off his visor. Des picked up the cabin interphone.

"Ladies and Gentlemen, this is the captain. If you look out of the windows on the left-hand side of the aircraft you will notice that we are currently in the company of an American Air Force fighter aircraft. The reason for this is that he is just a little bit lost and we are showing him the way back to his aircraft carrier. I'm sure that he would appreciate a little wave from you folks."

I felt the aircraft lurch a little as all the passengers congregated on the left side of the aisle. The helmeted hero in the Phantom waggled his wings twice then pulled up hard and broke to the left, giving us a view of the underside of his aircraft. We saw the twin flames leap from the jetpipes as he lit up the afterburners. Within a few seconds, the Phantom was just a dot in the sky.

"I wonder why he wasn't talking to Air Traffic," Des remarked. "Kind of worrying when jets start leaping about in your airspace."

"You're only mad because it woke you up!" I said. "Would you request a return to our original flight level please?"

Gemma got up from the jump seat and went back to look after her passengers, Des settled back in his seat and I resumed my duties as 'handling pilot'. For the benefit of those who are unaware of the sharing of the workload on the flight deck of a transport airplane, two pilots carry out the flying. Both pilots are fully qualified to fly the aircraft but the captain, who occupies the left-hand seat is totally in command. The actual business of flying the aircraft is shared between the two pilots one of whom is designated the 'handling pilot' and the other the 'non-handling pilot'. The handling pilot makes all the decisions, gives the instructions and actually flies the airplane. The non-handling pilot operates the radios and carries out the myriad other duties necessary for the safe conduct of the flight, such as operating the flaps, speed brakes and landing gear as requested. I trust that wasn't too boring.

Eventually, it was time to start our descent into Palma. Everything appeared to be going well and we were well into the approach procedure when the cabin interphone rang. Des listened for a few seconds then said,

"Explain to him that if he does not follow instructions, we will hand him over to the police as soon as we land." He paused, listening. "Well tell him again. Make bloody sure that he understands."

"What's the matter?" I asked.

"We have a passenger who is pissed out of his mind and refusing to get back in his seat." He ran his hands through his hair "How did he get into that state without the cabin crew noticing, I wonder?" He listened again to the interphone. "No, not a chance, we're both busy up here, you'll have to manage as best you can. Use as much force as you need to and get a couple of other passengers to help. We'll abort the approach until it's sorted." He looked across at me. "You comfortable with that?"

"Fine with me. Advise Palma that we will proceed to the holding pattern direct from here and advise them when we're ready to give it another shot."

We trundled round the oval holding pattern three times and I was just about to enter the pattern for the fourth time when Gemma put her head through the door.

"We've restrained him. He's struggling and swearing a lot but I put a big guy on the seat beside him and he's keeping him in order."

"Thanks Gemma," Des said. "Ask the passenger who helped you to have a word with me before he gets off."

We started down again and this time we actually made it onto the runway. As we taxied towards the terminal, Des remarked that if the trip back was as eventful as the trip down, he might well use his prerogative as aircraft commander to make me fly back to England. I steered us carefully onto the stop mark and applied the brakes. The usual procession of refuellers, baggage trolleys and catering vehicles surrounded the aircraft and the passengers filtered out of the doors and down the steps to the waiting buses. Gemma appeared at the flight deck door accompanied by an enormous man, his bulk filling the narrow doorway.

"This is Mr Brownlow who helped us with the disruptive passenger. This is Captain Walsh," she said.

"Thank you very much indeed for your help," Des said. "I will be making a formal report to the Company as soon as we get back and I feel sure that they will contact you." The big man looked embarrassed and replied,

"Aw, it was nothin'. The young lady just asked me if I could persuade the guy to sit down and strap in so I just told him to sit down and behave otherwise I would give him a fuckin' spankin.'" He blushed furiously and said "Oops, sorry miss!"

"Well it certainly seemed to have the desired effect, Mr Brownlow. Thanks again for your help." He held out his hand. Mr B shook the proffered hand and headed off towards the stairs and his two weeks in the sun.

Our problems, however, were not over. We had taken on the required amount of fuel, the catering had been loaded and the aircraft interior cleaned and the returning passengers boarded. Everything seemed to be going according to plan until Des attempted the start on our number two engine. The engine reached the speed required for light up and immediately there was a loud bang and the whole aircraft shook.

"Shut-down!" Des called. I closed the high-pressure valve and watched the engine indicators intently. "We have no fire warning."

"Sounded like a compressor stall to me," I ventured.

"Whatever it is, we're shutting down. Still no fire warning but tell the girls we will be off-loading the passengers." He picked up the public address handset. "Ladies and gentlemen, this is Captain Walsh. I regret to advise you that we have had a problem with one of our engines as you probably noticed. This means that I will not be taking this aircraft for the time being, so as soon as we can get the coaches back here I will be asking you to return to the departure lounge. Please make sure that you take all your carry-on baggage and personal belongings with you. Once again, we regret the disruption to your plans but every effort will be made to enable you to be on your way as soon as possible." He looked at me and grinned. "And thank you for trying to fly with us this afternoon."

"Des, that was cruel!" I said. "Maybe we get to stay down here until they fix the engine."

"We'll be here tonight at least," Des remarked. "Both of us will be out of hours at ten tonight."

"So it's a shower, a few drinks, dinner and out on the town then?"

"Mmmm, could be. Don't forget, Gemma is mine."

We closed down the rest of the aircraft and wrote up the problems in the technical log to give to the engineers. Des briefly discussed the situation with the ramp agent who responded by waving his arms around quite a lot. I told the cabin crew that we would be staying overnight in Palma and that the agent would be organising a hotel for us. We should meet up in the bar before dinner, I suggested. The Agent came running over and announced that he had, with great difficulty, managed to acquire some accommodation for us in town and that the bus, driven by his cousin would take us there as soon as we were ready to leave. We should be aware, he told us, that it was only because of his influence and his standing in the community that such benefits could be offered to us at such short notice. We nodded vigorously, carefully omitting to remind him that the Company had an arrangement with that very hotel guaranteeing accommodation for stranded aircrews.

The agent strutted off with an air of immense importance and we climbed onto the coach.

We met in the hotel bar about an hour later to discuss plans for our unexpected evening out. Des and I would have been quite happy to stay in the hotel and eat in the restaurant, but the three girls who had joined us wanted to go out. With little difficulty, we found a taxi. A ten-minute drive took us to a restaurant decorated in typical Spanish fashion, with tables outside and soft lighting from oil lamps on each table. We chose from the excellent menu and everyone except Liz and I ordered paella. As I am wildly allergic to seafood, I decided on steak. Liz thought steak was a good choice.

"*Poco hecho por favor*," I told the waiter.

"*Gracias, senor*" he said and turned to Liz. "And how do you prefer your steak, ma'am?"

"Rare too, please," Liz replied. "You speak excellent English."

"That's probably because I *am* English," he said. "I originally came from Birmingham." He gestured towards the bar where the bartender was juggling with a cocktail shaker and a martini bottle. "My partner and I opened this place two years ago." I assumed that the word 'partner' inferred more than just a business arrangement.

During the meal and the subsequent drinks, it was fairly obvious that Des was making significant progress in his bid for Gemma. I realised with something of a shock that he had not been joking on the trip down. "*Good ol' Des!*" I thought somewhat drunkenly. We had all been consuming vast quantities of red wine and none of us could possibly have been described as sober.

"Bloody good job we're not frying tomollow" I said to no one in particular.

"Hey! You said frying!" said Des.

"That too, Des. I think it's about time we moved on. They're trying to close up."

"I think we should go back to the hotel," said Wendy. "I'm knackered."

Des whispered in Gemma's ear. She pulled away from him and said loudly,

"Yes, okay, but I'm not going to sleep with you. Just a drink and no more."

"I might not even ask you!" Des retorted. Gemma giggled.

I suddenly realised that as Des and I were sharing a twin room, my presence was obviously going to be surplus to requirements. I mentioned this to Liz. She gave me a little smile and whispered to Wendy. Wendy laughed then nodded.

"If you promise to behave, you can spend the night in our room. I wouldn't trust you with just one of us, but two of us should be able to control you!"

And that, Chief Pilot, Sir is exactly why I finished up spending the night between two of our stewardesses. And no Sir, I have absolutely no idea where our clothes had disappeared to.

8

The Tristar

The whole Company was buzzing with excitement. Even the rather staid lady who did something unidentifiable in the Accounts department was heard to be singing. The Managing Director walked with a spring in his step. The reason for the feeling of well being that had arrived at Luton was that, subsequent to a prolonged period of hard negotiation, the Company was shortly to take delivery of not one, but two Lockheed L-1011 wide bodied aircraft. We were to be the European launch customer for the aircraft and our joy was augmented by the knowledge that we had even beaten British Airways to the punch. BA was indignant that we had usurped their inalienable right to be first with all things new and wonderful. We missed not one opportunity to brag about our achievement whenever we came across a BA crew at a night stop.

The entire airport observed the arrival of the first Tristar. Painted in bright yellow, the huge aircraft slid gracefully down the approach and the delivery crew put her down smoothly with a little puff of smoke from the mainwheels. The three engines bellowed as the reverse thrust was applied. Eventually, she came to a stop outside the hangars and was immediately surrounded by almost everybody who could find a reason to be on the apron. I found myself standing beside one of our senior captains and together we walked towards the great beast.

"There is little doubt," he pronounced, "that a thing like that is just too fuckin' big to fly."

"It's smaller than a 747," I ventured and was rewarded with a scornful glance that clearly labelled me as a bloody know-it-all and an ex-air force know-it-all at that. I attempted to make immediate reparation. "I suppose that it'll only be senior people like you who will get to fly it."

"They will probably ship in a whole bunch of type rated guys for that," he snorted. "Probably bloody yanks who talk in inches of mercury instead of millibars as God intended." I should mention that the British (who are, as everyone knows, the only *proper* pilots) set their altimeters in millibars whilst our American cousins use inches of mercury as a pressure measurement. "And another thing," he continued, "the seniority system will now be completely pointless."

The so-called seniority system represented the ladder on which we all were climbing. Substantially, a crewmember who had been with the Company for many years enjoyed several privileges denied to more junior folks. Pilots with high seniority, which meant a low employee number, got first crack at the rostering options and therefore the cream of the trips. They were allowed to pick and choose the lucky individuals who were to form their crew. I could well appreciate his concern. Obviously, this magnificent new aircraft would be used on our most prestigious routes such as the Canary Islands. Hitherto, the Canary Island sectors were the almost exclusive domain of the senior crews and it seemed probable that the new guys would snatch this prize from under their noses.

As my own position on the ladder was almost at ground level, I felt little in the way of threat and idly considered whether I might usefully express an interest in becoming a Tristar person.

"Don't even consider it," he said, having read my thoughts. "You could get a command on the 1–11 years before you would even get a right hand seat on that contraption. I've heard that you are making a fairly passable attempt at flying the 1–11. Des appears to be happy with your progress and there's a lot of life left in the aeroplane. That…*thing*…is totally inappropriate for our operation."

Inappropriate or not, our passengers adored the aircraft. With a total seating capacity of three hundred and fifty-five souls plus three flight deck crew and fourteen cabin crew, the mighty aircraft flew back and forth from the Canary Islands, Cyprus and Italy making huge amounts of money for the Company. Additionally, when the second Tristar arrived, it made frequent trips to the West Indies and Florida, which was just emerging as a holiday attraction within reach of the package holiday public.

There had to be a down side, of course. It happened on a Friday afternoon. Tristar number two was across in Barbados and number one was in the Canaries when a substantial bird disappeared down the air intake of an engine during landing. The aircraft was, of course, unable to make the return trip, leaving three hundred plus travellers unable to return to the plethora of unopened mail and unwatered plants. Simple mathematics showed that our BAC1–11s, with a capacity of one hundred and fifteen passengers would struggle to retrieve the situation. Our operations staff deduced that it would take precisely three point two one BAC 1–11 trips to recover the stranded passengers and crew. The main problem, however, was that we had only one uncommitted aircraft available.

Eventually, two further aircraft were chartered from Monarch and the procession returned to England in somewhat less stylish surroundings that those in which they had departed. The episode had cost the Company a great deal of money and the appeal of the aircraft diminished somewhat.

Around this time, I had decided that commuting from Southend to Luton was not only tiresome but also expensive. My rosters usually involved three duty days and one standby day so I decided to become a part time lodger close to the airport. A long distance truck driver and his French lady friend owned the house I finally settled on. She was a somewhat voluptuous lady in her early thirties who spoke little English but was an undoubted expert in sign language. I spoke very little French and our conversations, therefore were conducted usually in raised voices and extensive use of body language. The only other occupants of the house were two Jack Russell terriers named Effing and Blinding. As both animals were given to high speed chases around the house, and their command of both the English and French languages was somewhat limited, it was customary for Annette—my landlady—to converse with them in a series of high pitched screams accompanied by a great deal of French arm-waving. The result was an awesome cacophony of noise as the two dogs added their excited yelping to the melting pot.

I gradually became aware that Annette suffered quite badly from loneliness when Paul was away from home. Her loneliness manifested itself in a manner devoid of any vestige of subtlety. I returned to the house one evening to find her dressed in an almost transparent negligee. She had a glass of wine in her hand and an almost empty bottle by her side.

"Hello!" she bellowed at me. Both dogs bounded towards me yapping excitedly. I adopted a defensive stance ready to fend off the assault of the animals. I love dogs but I was getting just a little bit weary of trying to remove white hairs from my uniform trousers. "I have, in the…the…*merde!*" She waved her arm in the general direction of the kitchen, "some casserole of the rabbit. You will eat, yes?" The concept of eating bunnies did not appeal to me so I indicated by sign language that I had already had dinner on the flight. "Then you will drink with me?"

"Okay Annette, yes a glass of wine would be nice." She set sail for the sideboard and returned with a wineglass. I sipped appreciatively at the dark red liquid. "That is very nice," I said. "Is it French?"

"But of course," she said. I slumped into an armchair and both dogs launched themselves onto my lap and started licking my face. "Effing! Blinding! *Couche tois*! You will become so many white hairs upon the trouser." I had to agree about the white hairs upon the trouser. Jack Russells as a breed tend to shed enough hair to stuff a mattress but they are very selective and only shed the white hairs on dark material and my uniform was rapidly assuming a somewhat piebald appearance. Annette was seized by what appeared to be a good idea. "You must off with the trouser and I shall pick from it the hairs of the dog," she said, punctuating the sentence with meaningful waves of her wineglass. She stood up and swayed gently. "Come. I show you."

I protested that the idea was flawed and that, at any minute, Paul might return home and then what would he think? Paul was in Folkestone she replied. She pronounced it 'Follkestonee."

"Come," she repeated. "We have the good times." She started towards the staircase then as an afterthought, she returned for another bottle of wine. I am invariably weak in the presence of powerful women and I meekly allowed myself to be led upstairs and into Annette's bedroom. Once there, however, the wine took effect and she collapsed onto the bed and fell into a deep sleep. As I crept out of the room, Effing (or maybe it was Blinding) bit me goodnight. I felt that my honour had been preserved and that I had done nothing of which I should be ashamed. I went to my room and quickly undressed and fell into bed.

Somewhere in the early hours of the morning, I woke with a start to find Annette, apparently fully recovered, climbing into bed beside me. Someone once said, if something is inevitable, then just make the best of it. Someone else apparently said that the French are very accomplished lovers. The point about wise sayings is that you can either accept them or leave them alone. Annette, although statuesque, was well proportioned and certainly proved to be an amazingly accomplished and tireless lover. As the darkness gave way to dawn, she apparently decided that our frolics were over. Announcing that I was a 'very bad man' and that she was going to go to bed, she sailed out of the room.

The next day was my standby day and I could very easily have stayed in bed or just lazed around the house, but the occurrences of the previous night had made me somewhat uneasy. I decided to go over to the airport and investigate the Tristar, which was in the hangar receiving some tender loving care from Engineering. To be more accurate, only the front two-thirds of the mighty beast was actually *in* the hangar. Because of the height of the tail fin, the aircraft was too tall for the building and a moveable extension had been constructed to enclose the tail end.

I got permission from the senior engineer and climbed the steps to reach the flight deck. For someone used to the BAC1–11 and even smaller military aircraft, the sheer size of the 1011 was awesome. The flight deck was spacious and well arranged, but the passenger cabin seemed to go on forever. I was just concluding that I might very easily get used to becoming Tristar crew when Des appeared in the doorway.

"Somebody else who can't stay away from the place," he remarked.

"It's a bloody impressive piece of aircraft," I said. "Don't you fancy driving it?"

"It had crossed my mind, but I thought the better of it. What about you? You thinking about crossing over?" I confessed that I was considering applying for a fleet transfer.

"I think it would be a bad move at this stage," he said. "It's still early days and who knows what could happen." Several airlines had grown too rapidly both in fleet numbers and aircraft size. When the travelling public failed to fly in the expected numbers, the problem became one of over capacity (too many empty seats) and the financial troubles started. Des continued,

"If the crunch comes, the first people to go will probably be the Tristar crews. If I were you, I would stick with the 1–11 for a while." He paused briefly. "Personally, I will be surprised if you don't get some promotion quite soon." I raised my eyebrows. He grinned at me. "Don't quote me though!"

We climbed out of the aircraft and wandered around the company seeking some pleasant diversionary activity. Eventually we found ourselves outside the cabin training building; a structure made to exactly duplicate the middle section of a BAC1–11 fuselage. In this place, new trainee hostesses were taught evacuation procedures and the correct way to do the Flight Safety ballet (the safety demonstration using arms, legs, oxygen masks and life vests) There was nearly always an urgent requirement for members of the public to act as passengers for the trainee hosties to evacuate and we decided to offer ourselves for the ritual.

Sandy, who had been the senior on my first trip had in the meantime been promoted to a training position and was in charge of that day's proceedings. She ushered us into a pair of seats and gave us stern 'Don't try anything silly' looks. We watched as the new girls pointed out the emergency exits and demonstrated the correct method of donning a life vest. When it came to the part where the simulated emergency evacuation took place we were almost the first out and decided to award the remaining 'passengers' points for the style in which they left the 'aircraft.' As usual, there was a contingent of secretaries and typists from various companies joining in the fun so predictably there was a fairly attractive display of underwear in evidence as they came down the slide.

"Almost worth calling an evacuation for," Des remarked. He looked at his watch. "That's my standby over. I'm heading off home. See you on Tuesday."

Tuesday was bright and fair. I was feeling decidedly happy as I parked my car in the company space allocated to flight crew. As I retrieved my bag from the car, one of the girls pulled into the adjacent space.

"Morning Dawn," I called.

"Hi Al," she said. "Is Des with us today? I have a present for him."

"Yes he is," I replied. "What's the occasion?"

"It's his birthday. Didn't you know?" She pulled a package from her car. "He's going to love this!"

"I had better go through the terminal and get a card," I said. "See you inside." Although Luton was, in those days, a small regional airport, it did boast a fairly good airport shop and I managed to find an absolutely insulting card. As I walked through the terminal, I was aware that several pairs of eyes were following my progress. I concluded that it must be the uniform as there was a fascination shown by the travelling public for the people who sit up front. All things considered, I was in a very happy frame of mind as I met Des in operations.

"Happy birthday, you old bugger!" I greeted him. I handed him the card with an exaggerated flourish.

"When did you learn to do joined up writing?" he asked me. "The girls have given me a present but I'm not allowed to open it until we're in the air. Do you know what it is?"

"Sorry, I don't have a clue," I said. "Probably something obscene. As it's your birthday, shall I check the fuel and do the externals?"

"No," he said. "But you can do the fuel and externals if you like." Des grinned at me.

"We should synchronise our watches. At my mark it will be exactly sixteen seconds to four and a half minutes to 08.41. Mark at twelve seconds ago." I made pretence of setting my watch and strolled outside. Larry, one of the engineers was just finishing off the refuelling process. He handed me the clipboard with the fuel figures.

"Everything okay, Larry?" I asked.

"Looks pretty good to me," he said, "but then I'm only an engineer, what would I know!" I walked under the wing and looked at the brakes.

"It's a wheel," Larry said. "And the black rubber things are tyres."

The rest of the crew arrived at the aircraft and the job of readying the airplane for the trip continued. With ten minutes to spare, I called the dispatcher and announced that we were ready for boarding. As usual we were full, and the excited holidaymakers squabbled noisily as they milled around in the cabin. Eventually Dawn came through the door and announced that the folks all appeared to be sitting down and were strapped in and that we might reasonably assume that the cabin was prepared for departure.

Without incident or delay, we started the engines and taxied out to the runway. Des turned the aircraft onto the runway as I got our take-off clearance and we started our take-off roll.

"We'll go with full power, please Al. Sod the noise abatement. Let's wake the locals up." Des pushed both throttles up to the stops and I put my hand behind his.

"Your throttles," he said. "Cross check."

"My throttles." A very short time later "One hundred knots." Moments later we hurtled into the air.

"Gear up," Des called

"Gear in transit," I replied, then, "Gear up and no lights."

"Flaps twenty please." I retracted the flaps to twenty degrees. In a very short time we were levelling off at five thousand feet. The climb out from Luton was achieved in several stages. Des reached to the central overhead panel and switched off the no-smoking lights.

"That's two of the three out of the way." I looked at him quizzically. "Gear up, Flaps up, and the third is Coffee up. Where is the captain's coffee? Who does a guy have to shag to get a cup of coffee around here?" I pressed the call button and a little while later one of the girls came in bearing two cups of the required brew.

"You can open your present when you're ready. Oh and can you take a couple of flight deck visits?" she inquired. "Two folks have asked already."

"Yes okay," Des replied. "Give us about ten minutes until we're out of the TMA" (London Terminal Movement Area) he started ripping the paper from his present. When he saw the contents he burst out laughing. "My God," he cried, "Where on earth did they find this?" He held up a World War Two flying helmet, complete with goggles. "That is just brilliant." Des took his headset off, put the helmet on and pulled the goggles down. "Curse you, Red Baron," he snarled through clenched teeth. "Get Dawn to send one of the visitors through."

I shall never forget the look of total disbelief on the faces of the two visitors as they entered the cockpit to find me sitting back, relaxed and communicative. The captain with his seat all the way forward, helmet on, goggles down was hunched over the control column and scanning the empty sky for any sign of bandits. I suspect that they were very relieved when we finally touched down smoothly in Spain.

9

Tomatoes

As sunrises go, on a scale of one to ten, it scored a miserable three. The heavy stratus sullenly parted just enough to allow a pale yellow sun to illuminate only the far corner of the airfield. It was unseasonably cold for June, with a hint of the rain that had been forecast and certainly was not far away. Des Walsh looked up from the paperback novel that he was reading. He looked out of the window at the flurry of activity around our aircraft. The engineers had the cowlings off the number two engine and were peering inside.

"Not bad so far," he commented. "Another three hours delay and we will be out of hours for the trip back." He grinned comfortably "That would mean a very inconvenient night stop in Italy. My wife is not convinced that you are well behaved at such times and thinks that you might lead me astray." I snorted, displaying what I hoped was an air of righteous indignation.

"I couldn't even hope to keep up with you, Des. Especially in Italy. Spanish is my language, not Italian." He shook his head in mock sadness.

"Did they not teach you anything in the Air Force?" he said. "The language of love is universal."

The phone rang on the operations desk. The fair haired and rather effeminate young man behind the desk picked it up. He listened for a few seconds before replacing the receiver.

"Captain Walsh," he called, "your aircraft will be ready in twenty minutes or thereabouts." Des rose from his chair and stretched.

"Right then, we'll go and start the ball rolling. Can you give the girls a shout please William?"

"Of course, Captain. Anything you ask, Captain. I exist only to serve." Des grinned at him.

"And don't you forget it young man," Des said sternly. William minced towards the door.

"Although why they don't stay in here with you boys is a total mystery to me," he said over his shoulder.

I consulted my watch.

"If we get in the air within the next thirty minutes we will be fine for the return trip," I said. Des picked up his bag and headed for the door.

"We could save a bit of time by starting the number two and doing the slam checks before the passengers board," I suggested. Slam checks are carried out to ensure that the engine accelerates from idle to maximum RPM within the specified time. To carry out this check, the operator, usually an engineer rapidly advances the power lever and times the spool-up with a stopwatch whilst carefully watching to ensure that any temperature limitations are not exceeded. The defect that was in the final stages of rectification had manifested itself on the previous flight, the crew having complained that the offending engine had consistently displayed very high temperatures during any increase in power.

We strolled out towards the aircraft. Des looked up at the sky and shook his head.

"Don't like the look of the weather," he sighed.

"Not scared of a bit of cloud are you?"

"My tomatoes need more sun. They're never going to ripen in this." I had forgotten that gardening was a passion with Des. His home life revolved around his vegetable plot, his flowerbeds and his manicured lawn. On his sideboard there were several testaments to his expertise in the field. Trophies and photographs asserting his success at various flower shows bore witness to his many years of contact with the soil. On the three occasions on which I had visited the Walsh family I had been tremendously impressed by the man's undoubted expertise in horticultural matters and by his wife's excellence in culinary matters. They also owned the most monstrously overweight black Labrador that I had ever seen. Their two children, a boy of sixteen and a pretty seventeen-year-old girl displayed an almost total lack of interest in their father's profession. Mary Walsh was a devoted wife and mother who fussed over her family although she had enjoyed a successful career as a Legal Secretary prior to their marriage.

The engineers greeted us as we arrived at the aircraft steps. I left Des to talk to them whilst I carried out the pre-flight external checks. When I arrived back at the stairs, Des was still deeply involved in what appeared to be a serious discussion with one of the engineers.

"Everything okay?" I asked

"Mmmm," he mumbled. "You go on up, I'll be there in a minute."

I got the distinct impression that all was not well. I hoped that Des wasn't going to accept the aircraft with a defect. Such a practice was known as making a "commercial decision". Most aircraft commanders would not even consider accepting an aircraft with even a moderately serious defect. An engine problem of any description definitely fell into the moderately serious category and I felt quite sure that Des would not take a risk unless he was quite sure that the odds were very heavily stacked in our favour. As he took his seat, however, and started the check list, I could tell that he had something on his mind.

"You sure everything is okay?"

"Well, since you ask, no it's not. Lets get this show on the road then I'll tell you."

"Now you really got me worried," I said. "Is this thing going to fall out of the sky?" He looked at me and raised one eyebrow quizzically.

"Not unless you know something that I don't."

"So we carry on with the departure?"

"We carry on with the departure."

"And the airplane won't fall down and break?"

"It won't fall down and break."

Later, as we climbed out over London, I discovered the reason behind the concerns that Des was experiencing.

"Gordon told me that I have probably been overfeeding my tomatoes," he grumbled. "Apparently you should only feed them every other day."

"And that was all that was on your mind?" He looked horrified.

"All?" He retorted. "What do you mean 'all'?"

"I thought Gordon was chatting to you about the aircraft."

"You have a lot to learn about Gordon. He never talks about work."

We progressed comfortably for the next three hours or so. Cruising high above the weather, we chatted idly about this and that although Des kept returning to the subject of his confounded tomatoes. At last, I ventured to ask him why he was so hung up on the subject. With just a shade of embarrassment, he confessed that he had been having a difference of opinion with one of his neighbours and had unwisely agreed that the only logical means of deciding who was the better gardener was to enter the flower show. Since then, he had been lavishing undue amounts of care and attention on his charges. The tomatoes, being ungrateful creatures, were being totally unresponsive to his ministrations. With the great day only three weeks away, he felt that they were not really showing the anticipated world-class development. Indeed, Des was a worried man.

The Rome controller interrupted our learned discussion to advise us that the destination weather had deteriorated. Ciampino, he said, was experiencing wet, squally weather with a quite nasty wind almost across the runway gusting to twenty knots. The BAC One-eleven was supposed to demonstrate adequate controllability in crosswinds up to thirty knots but even at twenty, the aircraft was going to take very careful handling. The fact that the runway would also be wet added another factor. The aircraft was known to be rather prone to aquaplaning and several instances of One-elevens failing to come to a stop before the end of the runway had been reported. We studied the performance tables and reached a decision.

"We'll give it a shot," he announced. "If we are in good shape by decision height, we'll go in. If it looks wrong, then we'll go around and divert. It certainly looks acceptable according to the book."

"The unknown factor is the amount of water lying on the runway," I said. Italian controllers are not noted for their ability to communicate with pilots of any nationality other than their own. If there was a lot of water on the runway, our landing distance could even double. Des, as the Captain and handling pilot was responsible for the landing briefing.

"As soon as possible after touchdown I shall get the nosewheel down and keep straight with rudder. I will call for reverse thrust early and we'll start braking soon after. If we should start to weathercock into the wind, I will cancel the reverse immediately." He looked across the cockpit at me. "Okay?"

"Yep. All copied."

"I suppose I had better tell the people in the back that the landing might be a bit on the hard side." He picked up the public address handset.

"Ladies and gentlemen, this is Captain Walsh We have now commenced our descent into Rome and I regret to tell you that the weather is rather unpleasant with rain and a fairly strong wind. Consequently, we will be putting the aircraft on the ground fairly firmly. This is a precaution to ensure your safety and is not a reflection on the ability of the First Officer who will be carrying out the actual landing. Will you now please give your attention to the cabin staff for your arrival briefing. Thank you." I glared at him.

"You are doing the bloody landing, not me."

"Yes, but Captains, being superior beings, cannot be associated with anything other than a silky-smooth arrival on the ground."

"That will cost you a large vodka. I will crease myself laughing if you make a balls-up of it."

As we got closer to the airport and established ourselves on the ILS (Instrument Landing System, for those who have not been paying attention) the turbulence increased to a rather uncomfortable level. We were being thrown around from side to side with quite significant height deviations. Des was flying the approach manually and making constant corrections to keep us honest. The runway appeared through the rain. It certainly looked very wet. I pushed the transmit button.

"Rome, Autair 337, do you have any reports on the runway surface?" I asked.

"Autair 337, Rome, we have a recent departure by Alitalia within the last ten minutes with no problems," the controller responded.

"No standing water?"

"Negative, 337. The runway is just fine." Des remarked that the Italian controller probably didn't understand what standing water meant. I shrugged and went back to concentrating on the approach.

"We'll find out soon enough," Des said.

We continued our descent towards the runway. Des was flying the aircraft with one wing slightly low to stop us being blown sideways by the crosswind. Despite that, he was almost constantly putting in small amounts of rudder to stop the natural tendency of the airplane to weathercock into the wind. It was certainly not the most comfortable approach that I had ever experienced and I wondered how the passengers were faring.

"Twenty-six flap please." I selected the flap setting.

"Twenty-six degrees selected."

"Gear down."

"Gear is down. All green lights."

We reached Decision Height, also known as Minimum Descent Altitude, or MDA for short.

"That's MDA," I called

"MDA, roger. We're continuing the approach. Flaps forty-five please."

"Flaps forty-five. Looking good Des."

We swept over the runway threshold and Des levelled the wings and chopped the power back. The aircraft hit the runway hard but without a bounce. He lowered the nosewheel.

"Reverse please," he called. I selected thrust reverse and increased the power. Almost immediately, the aircraft began to swing into the wind.

"Cancel reverse!" He slammed in opposite rudder to try to stop the drift. Gradually, the nose came round and pointed straight down the runway. I felt the brakes come on but almost immediately realised that we were not slowing down appreciably.

"Bugger it. We're aquaplaning." He looked concerned. "Try reverse again. More power on the upwind engine." This was not a standard procedure. Differential reverse thrust can be very unpredictable. I cautiously increased the power.

"It's working," I said. The airspeed indicator was unwinding. Looking at the runway DTG (distance to go) markers flashing past, it was going to be pretty tight. Our speed was still over one hundred.

"More reverse. Increase the power. I don't think we're going to stop." I increased the power again. We were definitely slowing down. Just over ninety knots. I kept the power on. Des glanced at me.

"Good lad. I think we're going to get away with it."

The airspeed indicator hovered just above seventy. The aircraft shuddered.

"Okay, that's it, Des said. "Cancel reverse. We've stopped sliding. The brakes are working again." Sixty knots. "Nosewheel steering engaged."

Although we had landed safely and without damage, we had used up all but seven hundred feet of the runway. As we taxied towards the gate, I told Des that in my opinion, that was a pretty crummy landing. He grinned across at me.

"Yes it was a bit hairy wasn't it."

"I think I owe you a drink when we get back."

"I agree totally."

My chance to buy him a drink came sooner than expected. As we were off loading the holidaymakers, a Boeing 737 experienced the same runway conditions on landing, despite the warning that we had given to Air Traffic about water on the runway. The crew of the 737 clearly did not have pilots of the calibre of Des Walsh. The Boeing drifted off the side of the runway with both engines in full reverse. The mainwheel contacted the grass and immediately sank, spinning the aircraft around until it was almost at ninety degrees to the runway. As the crash crews raced across the airfield, we saw the doors open and the evacuation slides pop out. Although there was no injury on board, it was obvious that recovery was going to be a protracted affair. There was absolutely no chance that the runway would be open again in time for us to return to England. Des used the phone in the weather briefing room to call the Company and relay the bad news Although the probable delay would be only a few hours, it meant that we would be out of duty time and another crew would be required to return the aircraft to England.

"What's the betting that they will bring the spare aircraft into Fiumicino?" I suggested, referring to the other Rome airport.

"Odds on, I would say. I wonder if they'll leave us here to take ours back."

"That would mean that we'd be stuck here until tomorrow."

"Oh dear," I sighed. "That's terrible. When will we know?"

"I'll give them a couple of hours then I'll call them again. In the meantime, see if the Hilton has any rooms. You can have one on your own and I will share with the girls."

"I suppose this is the old 'Captain's prerogative' again." He gave me an innocent look as I headed for the phone. In an act of total defiance, I booked rooms for all of us. If Des wanted to make alternative arrangements, that was none of my business.

In order to further enhance our sense of membership of a crew and not just existing as individual beings, we all had dinner together in the luxurious surroundings of the hotel dining room. The three girls, immediately on discovering that we were spending the night in Rome, had rushed out to the sort of shops where a girl could buy the sort of clothes that would guarantee the turning of heads in downtown Littlehampton, or wherever it was that flight attendants lived. They were wearing the results of their shopping expedition, much to the appreciation of our waiter who spent a totally disproportionate amount of time standing slightly behind them whilst pouring wine and generally fussing around.

I had managed to find reasonably uncrumpled clothes in the emergency bag which I always carried. Des had visited the hotel shop where he had acquired an extremely lurid shirt. I enquired as to whether he was wearing it for a bet and was rewarded with a disdainful glance. Diana, our Number One flight attendant put her hand on his arm.

"Pay no attention, Des. It is a perfectly *nice* shirt." She smiled serenely. The other two giggled appreciatively. Des glared.

"Is this what I am reduced to?" he said. "To provide entertainment for the Cabin Crew? To be trotted out when the conversation flags?" He rolled his eyes towards the ceiling. "Bring on the Dancing Walsh in fancy dress?"

"Never mind, Des," I said comfortingly. "At least if you spill spaghetti on it, no one will notice. You could even show it to your tomatoes. That would brighten up their day." The mention of his botanical friends seemed to cause Des some distress. To add insult to injury, the waiter materialised at the table bearing a tray of salad, the centrepiece of which was a truly enormous tomato, artistically carved into the shape of an exotic flower. "Now, if you could persuade your miserable little specimens to grow like *that*," I continued with a smirk. I was rewarded with a cold and disdainful glance.

"Is this some kind of private joke?" Diane inquired. "Come on Des, you should have no secrets from your crew."

"I agree," said Jenny. "Otherwise we'll only talk about you." I decided to reveal all.

"Des has unwisely entered into a contest with a neighbour in the ancient Olympic sport of tomato growing. As he is not well versed in the more advanced aspects of the care and training of the fruit, he is rather afraid of losing the race." The girls looked somewhat nonplussed at this snippet of information as if their deeply respected Captain had suddenly developed a case of terminal senility.

"You mean you actually *grow* things to eat?" asked Mandy, a somewhat serious girl. "In a garden? How fascinating."

"My mum does that," Jenny remarked. "But she never lets her tomatoes ripen. She cuts them off when they are still green and makes chutney."

"Chutney?" Des asked thoughtfully. "Now there's an idea." I had to confess that I did not find the subject of chutney worthy of much thought but I was obviously missing something. The conversation turned to other matters such as the unorthodox arrival of the Boeing 737.

"The runway surface was really nasty," I pronounced. "Des did very well to keep us on the tarmac."

"Using somewhat unorthodox braking techniques!" Des laughed as he drained his glass of the hotel's house red. "I would have been really worried if I had been in the back and someone else had done that." He rattled his empty glass on the table and looked meaningfully at me. "The carafe is empty. Get us another, there's a good chap. I have to make a phone call." He headed off in the general direction of the lobby.

When he returned to the table, he was smiling broadly, as if a tremendous weight had been suddenly lifted from his shoulders.

"You seem very happy all of a sudden," Mandy remarked. "It must have been a good phone call."

"Yep, it certainly was. That little remark Jenny made started me thinking."

"Not more about tomatoes I hope?" I groaned loudly and rested my head in my hands in despair.

"A solution, dear boy. A perfect solution." He leaned back smugly. "Mary is going to persuade my neighbour's wife to steal all his tomatoes and make chutney with them. I sadly had to allow Mary to do the same, but at least it gets us both out of the daft bet." I felt that a round of applause was called for but when I started clapping, I was met by blank stares.

"Well, at least now that that is settled, maybe we can get back to being flying people again."

Des grinned at me.

"Party?" he suggested, pointing to the crew of the Boeing who were standing disconsolately at the bar. I looked around. We were, after all, being flown back to England as passengers. It seemed like a very good idea.

"Party," I agreed.

10

The Roar of the Crowd

The game of Association Football has always been shrouded in mystery as far as I am concerned. I confess that I am not even sure which end of the bat is supposed to be used to strike the ball and the rules of the game are as incomprehensible to me as nuclear physics. I am, however, prepared to concede that I form part of a very small minority of the population of this green and pleasant land. It should therefore have come as little or no surprise when I was told that we would be flying a full load of loyal supporters of a London football club to Holland.

Because of the regrettable association between football supporters and alcohol, our sales team, having done a superb job in selling our services, specified that nothing stronger than fruit juice would be allowed on board the aircraft. Needless to say, this condition drew strong disapproval from the customer despite similar restrictions being imposed by the other transport companies in competition for the contract. The restriction was extended to allow the operating crew to examine more closely than usual items of hand baggage which might conceal booze, and additionally, to refuse boarding to any prospective traveller displaying an unsteady gait or showing signs of having recently been on the sauce.

As Des Walsh had fallen foul of a particularly virulent species of the 'flu bug, I was considered to be a 'floating' crew member and not assigned to any particular Captain. On the day before the charter to Holland, the short straw was pushed firmly in my direction. The more experienced crews avoided these charters like the plague on the grounds that there was invariably some form of disturbance during the flight. My lack of seniority proved a great hindrance when it came to the avoidance of flights that other crews shunned. Had Des been on the register of those classified as fighting fit, I have no doubt that as a team we would have been able to wriggle free. Alone, I stood no chance and was assigned to the tender mercies of another commander, as yet, unidentified.

Reasoning that I was by now sufficiently experienced on the aircraft to be able to acquit myself with a reasonable degree of proficiency, I was not particularly concerned to discover that my Captain was to be Angus Gordon, the Fleet Training Captain. Angus, or Gus as he preferred to be known stood an impressive six foot three inches tall and was a product of an aristocratic Scottish family. He was almost universally considered to stand for no nonsense from either passengers or crews, and most pilots who had flown with him could testify to his devastating oratory when some trifling rule had been infringed. Rumour had it that Gus possessed an amazing collection of malt whiskies which he had been known to share on occasions.

We all met, as was customary, in the Operations office. When all the flight planning was completed Gus summoned the cabin crew.

"I am not going to pretend that this will be a normal trip," he intoned. "There will be a high level of excitement on the outbound sector and either intense grief or overpowering elation on the return In either case, we will have to keep a very close eye on the passengers to prevent any sort of situation from developing." By 'we' he of course meant the cabin staff. We would be carrying five flight attendants on the trip, one more than was customary, meaning that one of the girls would be occupying the jump seat for take-off and landing.

In the terminal building, the check-in procedures for the flight were proceeding fairly normally. The passengers were enduring the extra security checks with some impatience but without too much verbal protest as their hand baggage was systematically searched by airport security staff. Predictably, several containers decorated the counter as a result of confiscation. The range of containers gave some insight into the ingenuity of dedicated drinkers. Amongst the bottles and hip flasks were such items as a vacuum flask, several soft drink bottles and even a re-sealed Coca Cola can.

At the appointed time, we walked the short distance out to the aircraft and busied ourselves with the pre departure checks. For once, the aircraft was perfect. Every defect on the Tech Log had been cleared and every system worked faultlessly. Gus remarked as we prepared to board the passengers that a special effort must have been made.

"Probably because there is a high ranking pilot in command," I replied.

Gus made a Scottish noise, which I assumed to be an indication of scorn.

"If they made this sort of effort all the time it would be nice," he replied. "Can we get the self loading freight on board yet?" He was, of course referring to our passengers to whom we usually referred as 'Self loading freight,' 'Sheep,' 'Breathing ballast' and several other less complimentary names. I called the dispatcher on the company radio frequency and told them to start loading up,

To be honest, although we had expected otherwise, this collection of football fans did not appear to be very different from our usual passengers. They made the same fuss about finding the correct seats and stuffing bags into the overheads as normal people did. The only real difference apparent to me was the total lack of young children and that the majority of them were male. Gus finally made a microscopic adjustment to his seat position and wiped a tiny smear from the side window.

"Right," he said. "I'm ready."

"All set here."

Fiona came through the door and announced that we were three passengers short. One had not turned up at all and two more had been denied boarding because they had partaken well but not wisely at the airport bar. Needless to say they were not best pleased and had vented their wrath on the young lady at the departure gate. Commendably, she had stuck to her guns and had not even needed to call Gus to make a final decision. So, with two empty passenger seats and a third occupied by Fiona we set off towards the runway.

"It's pretty safe to assume that there is at least one unauthorised bottle on board." Gus looked across at me, patently expecting agreement. "We might have to consider keeping the seat belts sign on."

In an unusual display of co-operation, Luton cleared us for immediate line-up and take-off. As we climbed steadily into the scattered cloud, the cabin crew started the snack service.

"You have control," Gus said as he picked up the PA handset.

"I have control."

"Good morning, folks, Captain Gordon speaking. We are currently climbing through fifteen thousand feet and we'll be crossing the English coast in ten minutes or so. I regret that there is no bar service today, but our flight time is only forty-five minutes and the liberal Dutch licensing laws will allow you to make up for lost time. I must caution you, however, that any passenger who is considered to be unsafe to travel will be refused boarding for the return flight. After all that, we wish you a pleasant flight and an enjoyable stay in Holland. Thank you."

"That was very well put, Gus."

"Thank you."

"Do you want the aircraft back?"

"No, the autopilot is managing to resist any of your attempts to disrupt our progress." He grinned at me. "Just in case you get too confident though, and to demonstrate my magnanimity, I shall permit you to carry out the approach and landing."

"I shall try my very best not to make you famous."

"That would be greatly appreciated."

The flight proceeded, free from incident or interruption and the coastline of Holland appeared in exactly the correct place. We had started our descent some time previously and Gus had disconnected the autopilot. By good fortune, the weather was fair and the wind light. As we swept over the threshold and felt the gentle rumble as the mainwheels contacted the runway, I was conscious that I had probably carried out the best approach and landing of my life. Gus looked at me suspiciously.

"Of course, all of your landings are like that, I suppose."

"I wish!" I remembered several situations where my contact with the ground could at best be described as an arrival.

We arrived at the terminal and heard the sounds of our passengers studiously ignoring the exhortations to sit down and remain seated until the engines were shut down. Eventually, a single set of stairs arrived at the aircraft and the forward door was opened. The 1–11 has an integral set of stairs for the rear door and passengers disembarking using this door appear from the underside of the rear fuselage. We watched from the flight deck as the travellers boarded the buses sent to collect them, noting with some amusement that the reputation of English football fans had encouraged the Dutch to put two policemen on each bus. Despite the presence of the constabulary, even before the coaches had started to move, Union flags sprouted as if by magic from almost every window. The cavalcade with its singing, cheering occupants and its worried police presence moved majestically towards the terminal building.

"We have the whole day to fritter away." Gus had a gleam in his eyes. "Don't know about you, but I intend to spend some time in the town."

"Don't get yourself arrested, Gus. The police might mistake you for a football hooligan and throw you in the slammer just to be on the safe side." My earnest solicitations were rewarded with a Scottish stare as cold as if it had just spent a night on the top of the Grampians.

"I'll look after the airplane then, shall I?"

"That would be a kindly thing to do," he conceded.

"I might even have time for lunch."

"Perhaps you might." He grinned and climbed out of his seat. "I would invite you to come with me but somehow I don't think that art galleries would appeal to you very much."

"Art galleries?"

"Yes. Boyman's Gallery has some original Van Goughs. We Scots are a cultured race."

"I think I will see if the girls want to have lunch. Might even take the harbour trip."

"See you at six then." He pulled a sweater from his bag and headed for the door. "We'll do the fuel when we come back. Have fun and don't get lost."

"Gus," I called after him. He turned round. "Keep away from the red light district. You don't expect me to believe that stuff about Van Gough do you?"

◆　　◆　　◆

Although Rotterdam is a city with much to commend it to those of a cultural disposition, there is plenty of less highbrow entertainment available to the less culturally inclined. Accompanied by two exceptionally attractive girls, I took a taxi to the city. At the taxi driver's suggestion, we stopped in Delfshaven, one of the historic areas of the city. In excellent English, he told us that this would be an ideal area to eat and he pointed in the direction of one of the many restaurants for which the Delfshaven is noted. My scant command of the Dutch language, gained from a stay in Holland whilst working for Her Majesty only served to confuse the waiter. It is entirely probable that I had ordered deep fried teapot, but we eventually conveyed our requirement for steak, two medium-rare and one very rare with chips and mushrooms. We discovered that the rather optimistic "Just be a few minutes," could be translated as something approaching forty minutes, Dutch restaurant service being somewhat leisurely. From our table, we could see the church of the Pilgrim fathers and an imposing statue of a naval person brandishing what appeared to be a baseball bat. Subsequent enquiries revealed that the statue was that of an admiral, one Piet Heyn whose maritime activities in the seventeenth century had excited the good citizens of Rotterdam to such an extent that they had erected the imposing memorial.

Well fed and happy, we decided to take the boat trip round the harbour. Rotterdam harbour is truly enormous, with vessels of every shape and size jostling for space. The boat crew spent very little time in the actual business of steering the boat. They were glued to the radio, and the amplified voice of an excited Dutch commentator was giving a blow by blow account of the football match. It appeared from their jubilant cries that the English team was not faring too well. I wondered whether the probable result would impact on our trip home

I took the girls up to the top of the Euromast, a structure standing some 185 meters high. The view from the top is nothing short of spectacular but, because of the outward sloping windows, it can be somewhat disconcerting for those without much of a head for heights. Even at the top, there were six local men huddled over a small radio. They too appeared jubilant. We started to become concerned about possible reaction by the thousands of disaffected English fans and I suggested that we head back to the airport before the disenchantment manifested itself in street fights. On board the taxi, the driver was very anxious to tell us about the game. The English, he told us, had been soundly defeated by a totally superior Dutch team. Already, he announced, the citizens of Rotterdam were celebrating in the time honoured way, but there was certain to be trouble in the streets caused, understandably in his opinion, by the bad tempered English fans. He shook his head sadly in a Continental fashion.

"Always, when English teams come to the Netherlands, they drink too much Amstel." He turned around in his seat and explained by means of exaggerated sign language, raising an imaginary glass to his mouth. We narrowly missed a head-on collision with a large truck. Our driver leant on his horn and waved his fist at the other driver.

"There will be fightings in the streets and many people become arrested." He turned around again to ensure that we had grasped his meaning narrowly avoiding a collision with a bicycle. We breathed a sigh of relief when we finally turned into the airport entrance. I paid the man who looked sadly at the tip. With all the dignity that we could muster, we disappeared from his view into the terminal building.

In the small sparsely furnished office belonging to the handling agents, we found Gus giving a learned dissertation of the subject of Scotch whisky. His audience consisted of a lady of indeterminate age, a man in overalls and two attractive girls wearing the fluorescent jackets required for work in the aircraft manoeuvring area. He stopped in mid sentence and peered at us through a dense cloud of cigarette smoke.

"You managed to find your way back then. There's hope for you yet." Gus leaned nonchalantly on a filing cabinet and surveyed his attentive audience. His air of casual indifference was somewhat ruined by the fact that his elbow had knocked over a plastic cup half full of cold coffee and the contents were slowly but surely soaking his shirt. I felt it my duty as a member of his crew to apprise my revered commander of this fact.

"Gus," I started.

"Yes, yes, I know," he said. "Oh *shit*! he dabbed ineffectually at his shirt front with a handful of tissues, thoughtfully handed to him by a yellow jacketed beauty. With some difficulty I stifled a grin and was rewarded by an icy glare.

"Should I get going on the fuel and externals?" I inquired, anxious to make my escape from the office.

"Yes. Do that. I don't suppose for a second that you have the slightest inkling as to how much fuel we might actually *need* to get home."

"I'll work it out then add a bit for navigational errors." I grinned at him. "After all, you are taking us home." Before Gus could work out an appropriate response, I was out of the office and heading for the aircraft.

We did not require the services of the refuelling truck as we had loaded enough for both the outbound and return journeys prior to departure so I took a leisurely stroll around the aircraft. I had always considered the BAC1–11 to be a thing of beauty and even in the rather garish colour scheme favoured by our company, the clean lines of the aircraft were very appealing. The company logo on the forward area of the lower fuselage gleamed in silver against the light blue paintwork and the engine air intakes shone as if an industrious housewife had continually polished them. I completed the inspection of the outside of the aircraft and was about to climb the stairs when my attention was attracted by a vehicle heading for the aircraft. The driver, one of the girls from the office, braked the vehicle to a standstill and climbed out.

"They want you at check-in," she said. "I'll give you a ride over there if you like." I got in the passenger seat and we sped off towards the terminal. On the way, I discovered that there was some disturbance involving three of our passengers and that Gus was unable to attend owing to the condition of his uniform. Once inside the building, it was easy to locate the disturbance. A small interested crowd of spectators watched a large person apparently of Dutch origin, restraining a man who, by his language and vocabulary, was unquestionably English. The Dutchman was seated on his victim's chest and his large hands encircled the throat. Two other English passengers were attempting to liberate their compatriot with little success. The spectacle was enlivened to a great degree by the arrival of three burly Dutch policemen. They attempted to pry the Dutchman from his seat and were rewarded with a torrent of abuse. At last, they succeeded in tearing him from his prey and pinned him up against the check-in desk. At this point, they were set upon by the other two passengers, seemingly intent on revenge on anyone of Dutch origins. I felt it was my duty to intervene. After all, our passengers were not only English but were our responsibility.

"Now look here," I started. That was as far as I got before the Dutchman broke free from his captors and lunged at me. To my horror, the two other passengers joined him in this assault. The policemen attempted to resolve the situation by producing handcuffs and looked around hopefully for someone to arrest. Discretion being the better part of valour, I resolved to put some distance between us. As I was engaged in making good my escape, I found my way blocked by police reinforcements recently arrived to join in the fray. A stentorian shout brought the proceedings to an abrupt halt.

"Stop this nonsense immediately!" Gus, resplendent in a clean white uniform shirt and wearing his jacket appeared as if by magic in the midst of the writhing mass of pugilists. "I will take the aircraft back to England empty if I have to. Unless order is restored immediately, I will refuse to allow any of you to board." I had to marvel at the sheer power of command. Reluctantly, the fighting stopped. "This totally outrageous!" Gus bellowed. "You are British! Remember that. Now line up properly and quietly, do what you are told and we will say no more about this disgraceful behaviour." He turned to walk away then stopped. "I have instructed the check-in staff to ensure that only those people who are in a fit condition to travel are allowed to board my aeroplane. Kindly remember that." I followed meekly as he stalked out of the hall. As we walked out of the building into the afternoon sunshine, he turned to me.

"It was commendable, although somewhat foolhardy to get involved in that sort of affray." Then, in a more kindly voice, "Are you all right? There were three of them piling into you."

"No, I'm fine. They just got a bit out of hand." I looked at his shirt. "Where did you get the clean shirt?"

"I went to the KLM uniform store. They have tons of them. Better than ours."

"But it's white." We wore light blue shirts.

"Very observant. I can see why you decided to take up flying for a living."

We walked to the aircraft in silence. As we reached the top of the ladder, Gus looked at me.

"Take the left seat for the trip home. It's about time you got some exposure to the command chair." This was an incredible act of generosity on Gus's part. The left-hand seat is the exclusive domain of captains and very few of those elevated souls were prepared to allow a mere First Officer to occupy that sacred throne. On the way home, I concluded that this was the measure of the man. Authority stemmed both from his excellence as a commander and from his sheer physical presence. Such men are few in number and I count myself very fortunate to have encountered several.

The return journey was not entirely without incident. As Gus had so accurately predicted, a sizeable amount of alcohol had been smuggled on board. As most of the travelling public will be well aware, airline coffee, when mixed with booze becomes a quite lethal cocktail. Three of the passengers, although in general agreement that they had been robbed and that the referee suffered from acute myopia were engaged in an animated discussion regarding the various competency of the players. The discussion degenerated, as such conversations are wont to do, into a brawl in the aisle which the cabin crew were powerless to stop. Fiona burst through the cockpit door.

"Gus, there are people fighting in the cabin. We can't separate them."

"You have control." Gus got out of his seat and plunged through the flight deck door. Towering over the combatants, he produced his front door key from his pocket.

"This," he said, waving the key in front of the brawlers, "is the key which opens the internal door to the freight hold. As we are at a height of thirty thousand feet, and as the hold is not insulated, the temperature in there is approximately twenty degrees below zero." The fighting subsided. "Unless you return to your seats and undertake to stay there for the duration of this flight, I shall have no hesitation in putting you both in there for the safety of this aeroplane and the rest of the passengers."

"You wouldn't dare."

"Try me."

"Well, he started it."

"Both of you."

"Well, maybe it did get a bit out of hand."

"Are you both going to behave or is it to be the freight hold?"

"We'll sit down."

"See that you do." Having supervised the return to peace, Gus smiled a captain's smile around the cabin and returned to the cockpit.

As we touched down at Luton there was the customary applause from the cabin. We stood in the forward galley as the passengers left the aircraft. The passenger who had taken a swing at me in the terminal held out his hand.

"Sorry about all that back there," he said. "I realised a bit too late that you were on our side."

"No harm done," I said. "Maybe your team will win next time." Immediately I sensed a certain coolness.

When the last of the passengers had left the aircraft and the cleaners had come on board, Gus and I walked over to the office. It was a pleasant evening. The air was filled with the gentle sounds of engineers swearing and engine runs. The sweet perfume of jet fuel was in the air. Steam and smoke poured from the Vauxhall factory on the airfield boundary. All things considered, I thought myself extremely lucky to be able to spend my life engaged in a pursuit that I truly loved. True, there had been several occasions when I would have gratefully exchanged the more than adequate annual salary for the privilege of being safely on the ground but such occasions had mercifully been few and far between. I had now been a First Officer for quite a considerable period of time and surely, I thought, the responsibility of command could not be far removed.

"There's a thought!" I told myself.

11

Collapse

The runway stretched out ahead like a black ribbon. I looked across at my fellow crewmember in the left seat.

"Ready?"

"Ready," he replied. I pushed the two throttles forward and watched the engine speed indicators climb. I released the brakes and we started to move. The captain punched the stopwatch. We started to accelerate more quickly.

"Power checked," he called, then "Cross-check airspeed."

"Power and airspeed cross-checked," I responded. The speed built much faster now as we overcame the inertia. The airspeed indicator moved relentlessly higher.

"One hundred knots."

"One hundred knots confirmed," I replied. The runway was slipping past us, the centreline markings becoming blurred. As handling pilot, I was responsible for any decisions during the flight and I was happy to observe that we were at least staying on the centre of the runway.

"Ten to Vee one," said the Captain. Vee One is the speed at which the aircraft is committed to take-off. If something dramatic happens before that speed is reached, it is considered safe to abandon the take-off. Above Vee One, the probability is that the aircraft would be unable to come to a stop before the end of the runway and would, therefore, run off the end with subsequent damage to aircraft and ego. 'Ten to Vee One' meant ten knots below the critical speed. At our calculated weight of the aircraft, some forty-one tonnes, our Vee One speed was

134 knots. At the rate we were accelerating, the last ten knots would take a very short time indeed. I swiftly scanned the instrument panel for any sign of problems. Finding none, I relaxed slightly. One hundred and thirty knots. Everything running like clockwork.

"Vee One," came the call.

"Vee One, roger. Your throttles."

"My throttles." The captain took over the throttle levers and I put both hands on the yoke. Our lift off speed was calculated at 143 knots. We raced towards the end of the runway. One hundred and forty knots. Then the number one engine started to wind down.

"Engine failure!" I shouted. "Full power please."

"Full power," he said and pushed both throttles forward to the stops. "Five knots to Rotate."

The speed crept towards the rotate speed at which we could safely become airborne.

"Rotate!" he shouted. I pulled the control column smoothly towards me and we lifted into the air. "Target speed is one-five-eight knots." He looked at the vertical speed indicator. "Positive rate of climb."

"Gear up!" I called. The captain moved the landing gear selector upwards and the undercarriage started to retract into the wheel wells.

"Vital actions please," I said.

"Landing gear?"

"All lights out."

"Flaps?"

"Thirteen degrees." We checked all of the seven engine failure vital actions from memory. I remembered another mandatory procedure.

"Two hundred feet. I am going to turn left onto two five five degrees to avoid the water tower."

"Roger," he said. At Luton there was a water tower about two miles from the airfield, which stood about six hundred feet high. There was a standard procedure for engine failure on take-off, which necessitated the left turn as soon as possible. In accordance with the procedures, I continued the climb to 1500 feet and requested the skipper to call the tower.

When the required radio calls had been made, we settled down to the business of flying the aircraft on one engine.

"We agree that number one has quit?" I asked.

"Definitely number one."

"Shut-down vital actions then, please."

He quickly carried out the nine emergency shutdown tasks then turned to me.

"High pressure valve?"

"Identify number one please?" He put his hand on the number one engine high-pressure valve. I also placed my hand on the same valve. "Agreed?"

"Agreed."

"HP valve to closed please."

"HP valve closed." He smartly pulled the lever to the shut-off position. At that precise second, the sky froze. All engine noise ceased abruptly. All the instrument indications stopped. It was almost as if the whole world had suddenly ceased to function. The door opened and a short, balding man entered the flight deck.

"Okay," he said, "That was pretty good. Speed control was a little bit out but within limits. Crew communication was fine and you both identified the correct engine. You will be pleased to know that the situation was contained with no blood."

We got out of our seats.

"It's lunchtime," said the captain. "I'll see you later, Jock."

I followed him from the simulator building out into the bright sunlight.

"That was a good sim ride," he said. "I'll sign your logbook this afternoon, then you're legal again for a few months."

I had spent the whole morning in the simulator under the eagle eye of our training captain. During the four hour session, they had inflicted major hydraulic failures, engine fires, depressurisation, total electrical failure and God knows what else. This 'sim ride' was a regular requirement for all pilots designed to ensure that if any real emergency were to occur in flight then we would be prepared for it. The fact that the training captain had not bawled me out was, I felt, a favourable indication. I decided that the least I could do was reward myself for my performance. Failure on the emergency procedures would have meant that I would be grounded until such time as I was able to satisfy the Company that I could handle any situation that might arise in the air. I was now officially off duty for four days.

I went along the brightly-lit corridor in our main office building, known to us as the 'Gin Palace' until I came to the operations room. The crew roster sheet was pinned up on the wall. Happily, Liz was also off duty. Her home number was carefully written down in my newly acquired Filofax. I dialled the number from the phone on the desk. It was answered on the fourth ring.

"Liz? It's Allen. Are you doing anything special this afternoon?"

"Oh hello," she said brightly. "No I'm not. What do you have in mind?"

"I wondered if you might care to take a little trip," I said. "I think there are some spare seats on tonight's Faro flight."

"That sounds like fun," she said. "When is the return flight?"

"Thursday."

"That's three days," she said. "Can I put up with you for three days?"

"Sure you can," I responded. "I am terrific company."

"I'll throw some stuff in a bag then. Where will you be?"

"I'll nip home and change. Meet you in the bar in the Terminal in about two hours."

"See you soon then. Cheers!"

I left my logbook on the training captain's desk for signature and asked the duty operations officer to allocate two seats for us on the Faro flight. He wanted to know where we would be staying. I told him that we would sort that out when we got there and that he shouldn't worry.

He grinned and scribbled on a scrap of paper, which he pushed towards me.

"It's not exactly five star but it's better than the average Portuguese doss-house and the place is clean. My wife and I stayed there last month."

"Thanks Simon. Appreciate that." He wrote two flight coupons by hand and rubber-stamped them 'Crew travel. Non-revenue.' He passed them over the desk.

"I owe you one," I said.

When Liz turned up at the Airport bar, she looked stunning. I told her so and she fluttered her eyelashes at me. The bartender looked her up and down as he poured our drinks.

"Off on holiday?" he asked.

"Just to Portugal for a couple of days," I replied. He looked sad.

"All right for some," he sighed and went back to polishing glasses. Business was slow that day. At last, our flight was called and we went through to departure. The security man at the barrier recognised us and waved us through the security gate. He expressed the hope that we would have a good time. Our company status meant that we were allowed to board early and we greeted the crew as we entered the aircraft. I stuck my head through the cockpit door and said hello to the flightcrew.

The first officer was fairly new to the company but I had worked with the captain a couple of times.

"Sure you know the way?" I asked him. He threw a crumpled ball of paper at my head and said to his co-pilot,

"If this guy tries to get on the flight deck during the trip, brain him with the fire axe." Always helpful, I pointed to the fire axe in its stowage behind his seat to make sure that he knew where it was. We took our seats next to the exit and waited patiently for the rest of the passengers.

It is only a short flight to Faro and it was pleasant sitting in the back of the airplane with a drink in my hand. Liz spent a while in the galley chatting with the cabin crew, no doubt talking about girl things. It was by no means unusual for company personnel to take advantage of empty seats on these holiday flights and nobody jumped to any conclusions about the intentions of a stewardess and a first officer travelling together. When she came back to her seat, Liz said

"Jenny said she hopes your intentions are not totally honourable."

"Jenny should mind her own business." Liz gave me a little smile.

"Maybe I hope that too." She squeezed my hand and turned to watch the clouds go by. "I might get you all to myself this time," she said apparently addressing the right wingtip. She turned to me and I got the full force of her blue eyes. They were the sort of eyes that a man could happily drown in.

We landed gently at Faro and taxied to the gate. As soon as we had passed through Immigration, I found a phone and called the hotel. The proprietor assured me that she had plenty of room. She was delighted that Mr Simon had been so kind as to recommend her little hotel. The hotel was some distance from the airport, in the town of Portomao, one of the favourite resorts on the Algarve. We begged a lift on the tour coach and about forty minutes later we were dropped off in the town. I had changed some money into Escudos before leaving Luton and we hailed a taxi to take us to the hotel.

The hotel room was bright and airy with a large window from which we had a magnificent view of the Atlantic Ocean. It was already evening, and the lights of the nearby town reflected on the water. I watched an aircraft climb away from the east and wondered idly if it was our aircraft homeward bound. It was good to be away from the daily routine of airline work. I breathed in deeply, savouring the night air. Liz came up behind me and put her arms around me. I turned and held her close. Her hair was soft against my face. I tilted her face towards me and gently kissed her mouth. She pressed against me.

"Mmm, this is wonderful," she murmured. I kissed her again.

"Hungry?"

"Starving. I haven't eaten since breakfast."

Portomao is the absolute centre of the sardine fishing industry. The fish dock is lined with restaurants mainly aimed at tourists but also frequented by locals, always a good sign. I suggested that we might eat there. Liz released me and slipped her shoes on.

"That sounds great. I could eat a horse."

"If they don't have a horse, would you settle for a sardine?"

"One sardine?" Liz asked.

"These are real sardines, sweetheart. About the size of a rainbow trout. Not the little ones you get in cans back home." She looked unconvinced. "You'll see."

The restaurant was busy but we found a table and very soon a waiter was heading purposefully towards us, carrying a large tray on which there were at least ten large fish.

"*These* are sardines," I told Liz "Pick the one you want and they cook it for you." She pointed to one of the fish. The waiter thanked her and offered the tray to me. I selected a sardine and ordered some drinks. A short time later, we were presented with our meal. The sardines are cooked whole over charcoal, not even cleaned and the head is left on. Liz looked doubtful.

"They don't even take the insides out?" I laughed.

"No, but don't worry, all the innards just shrivel up and look like a bit of black string. Just hook it out." I demonstrated the technique. She put a brave face on it and gingerly prodded at the fish. Having disposed of the head and other doubtful items, Liz was soon demolishing the sardine with startling alacrity.

"That was wonderful," she said, leaning back in her chair and surveying the tidy pile of debris on the plate. "I certainly didn't expect sardines to taste like that!"

"What now, then?" I asked. "There's not a great deal of night-life here but there are a couple of bars with live bands."

"You can listen to the local musicians, I'll do the drinking then." I settled the bill and we wandered off in search of entertainment. After trying a few likely looking places we settled on a tourist bar where a four-piece combo was ritually murdering a selection of Beatles songs. We stood it as long as we could then bid farewell to a truly appalling version of 'Can't buy me Love' complete with totally wrong words and headed back to our hotel. It might have been the generous amount of Crystal beer that I had consumed, or it might have been plain fatigue but I had no sooner climbed into bed and folded Liz into my arms than I fell into a deep sleep.

When I woke, the sun was shining brightly and the air was already warm. Our window was wide open and I could hear the sound of the waves crashing onto the sand. Beside me, Liz stirred. I kissed the tip of her nose.

"Good morning gorgeous," I said.

"Coffee," she mumbled. "And aspirin." I had a better idea. I pulled her towards me.

Some time later, we were strolling along the beach, dodging beach balls thrown by obnoxious children. Liz pushed her sunglasses up into her hair and turned to me.

"That was nice this morning. Great way to wake up." I grinned at her.

"And we still have tonight. And tomorrow morning." I thought for a few seconds. "And this afternoon."

"I need to get some stuff to take home I don't often get a chance to wander around resorts." That was one of the problems with being aircrew. We got to know hundreds of airports and very few countries. One airport is pretty much the same as another and all of the international standard hotels seem to have been designed by the same team and the name drawn from a hat. The Singapore Hilton is therefore pretty similar to the Ramada in Rome. The advantages of this arrangement include never having to look too hard to find the bathroom in the middle of the night.

We walked around the busy main streets avoiding the smiling approaches of time-share salesmen. Liz bought several bits and pieces for her seemingly innumerable relatives. We had coffee and local pastries in a kerbside café and I came up with the idea of taking one of the boat trips from the fish quay. The trip was fun. It was a glass bottomed boat and the view of the thousands of brightly coloured fish visible under the boat was fascinating. We pulled into a sheltered cove where the boatman dropped the anchor and started opening bottles of local wine.

"Is here the swimming please," he announced. "Is very safe and water warm." Neither of us had thought to bring swimming clothes but without hesitation, Liz slipped out of her sundress and disappeared over the side of the boat. I quickly followed suit and jumped into the sea after her. The boatman was right. The water was warm and as we swam lazily around, shoals of fish parted to make way for us.

"I suppose our clothes will dry out soon enough," Liz said, her hair clinging to her face.

"I expect so. You might have to take yours off and spread them out on the boat though." She grabbed my hair and pushed me under the water. I put my arms around her and unhooked her bra with a practised flick. I swam as fast as I could but she was a much better swimmer than I and very quickly caught up with me.

"I'll get you for that!" she said grabbing for the waistband of my shorts. I pulled her under the water again and kissed her. We stayed under until we could stay submerged no longer and came to the surface, gasping for air. I wondered how fish ever manage to make love. We climbed back into the boat and stretched out on the deck.

We went for dinner that evening in a restaurant owned by an English expatriate. In order to keep in touch with events at home, he had installed an impressive antenna, which enabled him to receive one or two British television stations. We had just started our main course when the ITV News at Ten came on. Over the introduction to the programme there was a picture of one of our Tristars. The announcer launched into the first news item, which was that our Airline had collapsed, the receivers had been called in and all flights both outbound and home had been suspended. The stranded passengers and crews would be returned to the United Kingdom on board other carriers and wherever possible, alternative holidays would be offered to those who would no longer be able to travel with us.

"Looks like we're out of work, darling," I said.

"How are we going to get home? What are we going to do?" She brushed a tear from her eye.

"We'll be fine," I told her. "We'll get back very soon. They don't like having crews stuck away from base." We finished our meal and went straight back to the hotel. As soon as we were in our room, Liz put her arms around me.

"Take me to bed," she whispered. "I really need you to make this go away."

We made love until the early hours of the morning when we finally fell asleep, her head on my chest.

In the morning, I called the Company to ask what we should do. By chance, there was a Britannia flight departing in the afternoon with one spare passenger seat and the supernumary crew seat unoccupied. When we got back to Luton, we discovered that not only had the company collapsed, but that there was no money available to even take care of salaries. Liz and I realised simultaneously that it was very unlikely that our paths would cross again. We said our goodbyes tearfully in the car park and I held her close for a very long time. She eventually pulled away.

"Try to keep in touch, Al," she said.

"I will," I replied, "You are terrific." She got into her car and started the engine.

"You're not so bad yourself," she smiled. "Take care darling!" She drove off with gravel spitting from her spinning wheels.

12

Malawi

On the collapse of the airline, I was, needless to say, one of the unemployed and I spent a good deal of my time hanging round the terminal building at Southend hoping that a job with another airline would materialise. Naturally enough, British Airways do not, as a rule, sniff round small municipal airports seeking to recruit BAC1–11 first officers so my time was, to a large extent, totally wasted.

One morning, an enormous man of about six foot four with jet black hair and a deep suntan approached the table where I was sitting with a couple of Viscount pilots.

"You guys interested in some real flying?" he asked. His accent was strong, Polish, I thought but with something else there as well. "You boys, all pilots, right?" We all agreed that, yes we're pilots and therefore always interested in "real flying". All pilots are interested in career moves.

"Got some real work for you if you can handle it," he said. "Bloke at the crop spraying place said I'd find you here."

We all wanted to know more and said so. Our potential benefactor who introduced himself as Joe went on to explain that he represented a mining syndicate in darkest Africa who operated two Twin Otters and an Islander to ferry men and materials from their base mining town to the mine which was inaccessible by road. The current pilots were now at the end of their contract and he needed replacements bloody quick.

I pointed out that, alas, my licences only allowed me to fly UK and US registered aircraft otherwise I for one would be very interested indeed. I noticed that my two companions were making got-to-go motions, I thought of Africa, mines and probably dirt strips and King Solomon's Mines. It really sounded good. Pity about the licence cover. My problems were soon resolved. Joe thumped a fist the size of a leg of lamb on the table,

"Hey boy, that no a problem. Got a big rubber stamp," he said, stretching the word "big" to the length of three words, "we stamp that in you logbook and you okay to fly anything in Africa." He paused for breath. "You fly a Twin Otter, boy?"

"I'll fly a London bus if you put wings on it," I claimed. The touching arrogance of the young!

Joe exclaimed that I was just the sort of guy he was looking for and we arranged to meet later in his hotel to go into more detail. My two companions had by now, melted silently away, no doubt to their safe, secure, boring employment. No spirit of adventure, some people.

Later that evening I learned more about my new job with its attractive, tax-free salary and benefits. The company was based in Livingstone, Malawi and the base camp was situated some forty miles to the south. The mine workings were about twenty miles away, across a minor (by African standards) lake, and totally unreachable by road. All the mining engineers and equipment had to be airlifted across the lake and every morning one of the aircraft took six relief engineers and odd bits of freight to the mine and brought another six back to base.

It sounded fine, I told him. The money was certainly fine, almost twice what the holiday airline had been paying. Joe looked pleased and carefully wrote my name, address, passport details and licence numbers in a little notebook.

"Be in touch next coupla days. You get a package with airline tickets and stuff like that through the mail." He picked up the phone. "You want a drink, boy?" Even after long experience in various air forces, I should have known better than to accept. Don't ever drink with a six foot something Polish gentleman. By four in the morning I had given up and had fallen asleep in the hotel lobby to the great consternation of the night porter,

Two days later, a jiffy-bag containing a South African Airways ticket (tourist class) to Nairobi and an Air Malawi ticket from Nairobi to Blantyre dropped through my letterbox. There was also a very poorly typewritten set of instructions detailing flight times and who I was to contact on arrival at Blantyre. Apart from the departure date, which I realised with a shock was only two days away, everything seemed pretty straightforward. I set about doing the mundane things like giving notice to my landlord, collecting all the assorted bits that I supposed I would need like insect repellent, suntan cream, quinine tablets and so on. After wandering around Boots in the forlorn hope of finding medicines aimed at preventing tropical diseases, I just threw a few lightweight clothes in my bag and went to have a final drink with my friends at the airport.

The flight to Nairobi was uneventful and boring. I had been to Kenya before but the wonderful smells and sounds of the Country brought back a mixture of memories, not all of them pleasant. I found the Air Malawi desk and checked in for the flight to Blantyre. Air Malawi used a Viscount for that sector and I wondered how long the trip would take. I seemed to recollect that the distance was something in the order of a thousand miles in a southerly direction. That's a bloody long way in a Viscount. About four hours or so. I had about three hours to kill so I tried to catch up on my survival shopping in the airport shops. Predictably the flight had a technical delay and I had just settled down in the lounge to read when a voice like a portable foghorn exploded in my left ear.

"Bloody hell! *It is* you! What brings *you* to God's country?"

The owner of the voice was, I realised with great joy, Gerry Roe, with whom I had suffered at initial flying training in the Air Force and with whom I had spent many many evenings getting totally destroyed in the mess. Gerry and I had also endured jungle survival courses together and we had run into each other several times during our flying careers. The flying business is not that well populated and people pop up in the most unlikely places. Like Nairobi at seven in the evening.

I explained that I had a new job and that I was, as we spoke, awaiting the convenience of Air Malawi to transport me and my goods and chattels to Blantyre. Gerry looked at me dubiously and announced that he also was awaiting the departure of the Blantyre flight. I suggested that perhaps we might sit together on the flight. Talk about old times and all that sort of thing. With a grin, he said that might be arranged but that his seat was up in the front on the left hand side of the bloody aeroplane, Gerry a Viscount skipper!

"So you did learn to fly something with more than one engine

"Only just. Last tour in the Air Force was on Britannias out of Brizenorton. This is actually a lot of fun. Good laugh."

Putting my book away, I joined Gerry in the operations room where he changed from tee shirt and shorts into his uniform. Four bloody rings! Four! Gerry, the guy who could never got the hang of navigation! Finally the engineers declared the aircraft fit for flight and I went back into the terminal to check in and have my baggage loaded. The other passengers and I walked out to the aircraft in the evening heat. Nairobi is as near as dammit right on the equator and therefore never really gets cold. I settled down in my seat to await departure.

The faintly accented voice of an extremely pretty Malawi stew bade us welcome, on behalf of Captain Roe and his crew, to this night flight to Blantyre. She hoped that we would enjoy the flight and suggested that our wish would be the crew's command. Would we please read the safety leaflet in the seat pocket in front of us and kindly give our attention to her colleagues who would now demonstrate the positions of the various safety features of the aircraft.

Probably after some head scratching, Gerry remembered the start sequence and the engines slowly came to life. In its day, the Viscount was a very fine airplane and in the opinion of a great many people, it still is. Notwithstanding that, they shake rather a lot when the engines are running up on the ground. Not like the posh one-elevens that I used to fly before I got a real job. We taxied out to the end of the runway and held on the brakes until all four Dart engines were howling,

Brakes off and we lurched forward. Thirty seconds later, we're airborne. I don't know of any pilot who, when flying as a passenger does not time the take-off run! As soon as the seat belt lights went out, the pretty stew whose left breast appeared to be named Adelle leant over me and said that Captain Roe would like me to join him on the flight deck.

I went forward and knocked on the flight deck door. The foghorn voice invited whoever was without to come within. Gerry was leaning back in his seat. tie loose and smoking one of those disgusting cheroot things. The sort that smell like burning camel droppings.

"Hi Gerry," I said. "Lost again?" This is a traditional greeting exchanged between aviators when one visits the flight deck of another. Back came the traditional answer.

"Of course! That's why old M'bongo there is flying"

The African first officer looked at me and grinned.

"He's only jealous. I had a grammar school education, got a BSc in engineering and did my flying training at CSE Oxford. My name's Martin Lovell. It's only people who can't pronounce Martin that call me M'bongo,"

Africa is a very dark place at night and as I looked through the flight deck window, only a few lights could be seen on the ground. It was hard to imagine that anybody actually lived down there. We were flying over the mountains of Tanzania and Gerry explained that this route was not by any means available to everyone. The Tanzanians, he claimed, were twitchy about people flying over them and only Malawi aircraft with properly qualified English captains were accepted. I seemed to recall something about Malawi and South Africa being close trading partners, which would obviously upset some of the other African nations.

"Very pretty girl, that Adelle." I remarked to the darkness outside the flight deck. "Mixed race, I guess."

Gerry glanced at me.

"Yeah, her name is short for Adelaide. Her father is, or was an Aussie and her mother is Spanish, I think. She's been through a bit of a rough time just lately, poor girl. Got dumped by one of our engineers and took it pretty badly. Lives somewhere up near Livingstone, I think."

"That's where I'm going." I told him. Small world, even in Africa.

"What's this job you've got yourself? Tell me more. Somebody's not actually going to allow you to command an aeroplane are they?" I told him as much as I knew, which I realised was precious little. I only found out the name of the company when Joe's package arrived. Gerry said that he had heard of the mining company and that, as far as he was aware they were no better and no worse than any other in the area. Mining, he said, was a pretty difficult business in Malawi and people better have a bloody good idea of what they're doing before they commit time and money. He glared at me as if I should have known better.

"Any port in a storm, Gerry. This port seems as safe as any of them right now." Martin turned round.

"They are actually a very well run company," he said. "It's German money and Polish mining know-how. A pretty good combination in my book."

"You only just recently learned to read, M'bongo" said Gerry with a barely concealed grin. I was becoming aware that there was tremendous mutual respect between these two men. From the little I had seen, they worked together extremely well and each seemed to have complete confidence in the other. "Any time we run into problems," Gerry continued, "I get to handle the technical situation and fly the plane while Martin gets out his magic bones and his prayer mat. Back at his village he's some kind of witch doctor."

There was a knock on the door and Adelle entered with coffee.

"Al is going up to your neck of the woods, 'Del," said Martin. "Perhaps you can tell him how to get there. The Caucasian races do have trouble finding their way around."

"When are you leaving Blantyre?" she asked looking into my eyes. She was certainly a beautiful girl. Big eyes, perfect skin and a stunning figure.

"I'm supposed to meet a man from the company tomorrow night in Blantyre and we're flying up to Livingstone in the Islander."

"This is my last shift for four days. Do you suppose I could get a ride up to Livingstone with you?"

Now we were cooking on gas! I said with some conviction that I couldn't see any problem. It would be nice to have her company. Perhaps we can meet after we land and make some arrangements.

"If you're not meeting your company man until later, I can show you round Blantyre if you like."

If I like! Believe me, I like! Adelle left the flight deck. Gerry turned round in his seat.

"You no doubt appreciate that there is a problem in Blantyre with different race mixtures? Can give problems, especially in the current political climate. She's a hell of a nice girl. Don't you get her or yourself into any bad situations. You'll be okay in the main streets but be careful anywhere else."

I'll be careful Gerry. If you gentlemen will excuse me, I'll go back and catch up on some shut-eye."

"Nice meeting you, Al," said Martin. "Maybe we'll catch you on the way back up"

"Yeah, I'll look forward to it. Nice meeting you too. Keep Gerry right for me. He's a good guy but sometimes he gets confused by all the clocks and dials, I always said that one day he would meet a real pilot and here he is with two on the same flight."

"Go back to sleep, Al," Gerry said with a smile. "Adelle will wake you in time for the landing. That'll be a first for you. Come on M'bongo. Fly this bloody thing will you."

I returned to my seat and dozed for the rest of the flight.

The landing was simply perfect. I supposed that Martin had done the landing and said as much to Gerry when we were leaving the aircraft. He snorted and Martin laughed out loud. I arranged to meet Adelle in the coffee bar when she was finished with her paperwork. At Blantyre, the restaurant looks out over the apron and the combination of heat and aircraft engine fumes overcomes all other sensations, Especially the smell of food. Great place to diet, Blantyre. At around one a.m. Adelle walked over to my table.

"Where are you staying tonight?' she asked me,

"I'll wander over to the airport hotel, I think. Where is it?"

"There isn't one yet, they're still building it. Why don't you use the crew hostel right here on the airport? Gerry can fix it for you."

"That would be great. Where is he?"

"You don't need to bother. I've already asked him and he's organising it for you now."

"Adelle, you're brilliant. Thanks."

"No problem," she said. "I'll pick you up in the morning and we can go for a drive."

Things were sounding better all the time. I was beginning to like Africa all over again. Adelle walked with me to the crew hostel and used her pass key to open the outer door.

"Don't go out again or you won't be able to get back in. There's a board in the hallway with keys on. Any key is for a free room, See you around ten thirty"

"Yeah, great. Thanks Adelle."

"That's okay. Goodnight, sleep well."

"Thanks. You too

A pause.

"Goodnight then."

"Goodnight"

On impulse, I leant forward and kissed her on the forehead. She pulled away.

"Sorry, not here. That's what Gerry meant by problems. See you tomorrow about ten thirty."

The room was comfortable with air conditioning but I slept only fitfully. Around five, I must have gone out for the count and I woke with a start at half past nine to find the cleaning of the room was under way. Two ladies, one very large and the other probably her daughter were vigorously mopping the floor. As I was wearing nothing but my wrist watch and had thrown the cover back during the night, this came as something of a shock.

"Mornin' massa." said the larger of the two. "Okay we clean now?"

I mumbled something about taking a shower. They giggled and said that they would come back later.

At half past ten on the dot, as I was sitting on the wall outside, a blue Nissan pulled up.

"You going to sit there all day?"

Adelle looked simply devastating as she got out of the car Knee length skirt, of course and everything else well hidden. That's how it is in Malawi. Women don't wear trousers or short skirts. Men don't have long hair. All very moral and upright. Apparently.

We drove off, heading out of town. As we left the urban sprawl, Adelle told me that the word 'malawi' means a place where the sun reflects on the water like fire. I remarked on the beauty of the scenery and added that I had a better view than she. More to look at, I mean. She turned and looked at me. Once again I was struck by the incredible eyes.

"Adelle, if you look at me like that again, I'm going to have to kiss you. That is if it's okay with you and the government."

"I won't look at you then, Not yet anyway."

We drove on for thirty minutes or so admiring the profusion of bird and animal life for which Malawi is renowned until Adelle pulled over onto the side of the road. She set the parking brake and switched off the engine.

"I'm going to look at you now, I'm sure Dr Banda won't find out and I really want you to kiss me."

I stretched across the car and gently kissed her on the mouth. Her arms went round my neck and she pulled me closer. The second kiss was long and sensuous and, had it not been for the cramped conditions, would have led to some fairly major developments I'm sure.

After a little while, she suggested that we get out of the car and walk around. She looked around her then reached for the back of her skirt and let it fall to the ground revealing a scanty pair of shorts. She undid the lower buttons on her shirt and tied the ends just below her breasts. The effect was stunning.

"I thought the regulations didn't allow that sort of dress. I'm very glad I was wrong. You look wonderful."

"We're in a Natural Park site at the moment. The restrictions are relaxed out here. You can grow your hair long if you like."

"Adelle," I said, 'You're beautiful." Always original. Never stuck for something clever to say.

"I've been hurt too often to be beautiful. Back there in the car, I just wanted you to hold me. I'm not really that forward."

"Never doubted it for a moment."

We walked along a path for a little while until I spotted a tree stump.

"Let's sit down for a while." I suggested.

"You can if you like. Take a closer look."

On inspection, the stump was a seething mass of bugs, every last one just waiting to sink its poisoned fangs into my Caucasian backside.

"Perhaps not then!"

"Why don't we go back to my place in a little while and I'll cook us some pasta." I actually hated pasta but refrained from saying so. "Jane and Martin will be back now. That'll stop your baser instincts getting the better of you. Of us!" she added with a smile.

"Martin the co-pilot?" I asked. She nodded. "Who's Jane?"

"Jane is one of the other girls on the trip down here, She's my flat-mate and she and Martin are very much an item."

I looked sad as she put her skirt back on and re buttoned her shirt,

"Adelle, can I see you in Livingstone? I'd really like to see a lot more of you. I mean I'd like to see you a lot more."

"I'm only there for three days then I have to get back here. I expect you'll be pretty busy at first anyway."

"Can we try anyway?"

"I'd like that." She kissed me again and we set off for the car, All too soon the return trip was over and we spent the afternoon talking with Martin and Jane who told me that they were setting off in a month or so to get married in Barcelona with Gerry as best man.

I was due to meet the man from the company at four in the airport and it was already three fifteen. We picked up our bags, said goodbye to Martin and Jane and drove the mile or so to the terminal,

The Islander was already there on the apron, MMC on the side in large blue letters.

"Stands for Morgan Mining Corporation." I told her She looked out at the aircraft.

"It's a long way to Livingstone. And it's all uphill. Can that thing climb to four and a half thousand feet?"

"Probably," I assured her "anyway they use it on this run all the time."

A tall man with thinning hair and wearing an American Air Force MA1 jacket came over.

"I'm Hogan. You the new Morgan pilot?"

"That's me. Be all right to give this young lady a lift to Livingstone?"

"Sure, man. No problem. Glad to have you along, miss."

We threw our bags into the airplane and climbed in after them. For an Islander, the standard of the interior was very high. Decent seating and a good quality wall covering.

"Afraid it's no smoking but it's only a three hour trip. You'll survive." With that, Hogan hefted himself into the left seat and started the engines. Adelle and I sat side by side for the whole trip and in the gathering dusk, she finally fell asleep with her head resting on my shoulder.

We landed at the company strip at somewhere around seven thirty and we managed to arrange for Adelle to borrow one of the company cars until the next day Although glad that my long journey was finally over, I was genuinely sorry to see the tail lights of the Toyota disappear into the darkness.

"That's Doc Helen's daughter ain't it?" said Hogan. "Thought I recognised her. Pretty girl."

"Who's Doc Helen?"

"She's the doctor around here, Always up here doing medicals and bandaging cut fingers, We get a lot of accidents here."

"Is there a mister Helen?" I asked.

"No, he died about a year ago back in Australia." He pointed to a low building. "That's your home for the duration. Better go and settle in. Plumbing's a bit basic but it should all work.

"Thanks. Do you have a first name?"

"I don't use it. Everybody calls me Hogan,"

I thanked him for the ride and went to examine my new home. As a parting shot, Hogan had said that he would see me at the aircraft at seven am sharp for a checkout on the Twin Otter and don't be bloody late, I decided to go straight to bed. I woke the following morning to the ever-present sounds of Africa. Up there, in the north of Malawi, the climate is quite comfortable, although in the hot season, the temperature gets quite high. I did a full functional check on the shower and decided that it was adequate, if unpredictable. I dressed in a short-sleeved shirt and shorts and wandered over to the flight line to meet Hogan. He arrived in a beaten up Land Rover and gave me a doubtful look.

"Insects will have a bloody field day with that much white skin," he said, 'You'll learn."

He opened the door of the aircraft and climbed in, He showed me all the important features of the aircraft then we got out again to look at the various walk-round items.

"Right. Let's see how you fly. You handled turbo prop engines before?"

"Some. I Have some flying time on C-130 and Bandeirantes."

Hogan grunted and climbed back inside. He quickly ran through the start sequence and when the right engine was running, asked me to start up the other one.

"We're light today, so she'll be off quickly. Lift her off at around seventy knots or so, It's not critical. Thing'll fly at about sixty if you want." I found the aircraft very easy to manage on the ground using the nosewheel steering tiller on the control column. The subsequent take off, although bumpy because of the dirt strip, was quite pleasant. Hogan showed me one or two of the aircraft's behaviour patterns during the climb and I had to agree that, on the whole, the Twin Otter was, as he put it, "a pussycat". When we had reached two thousand feet above ground level we did some steep turns, a simulated engine failure and some stalls. All were very straightforward and we headed back to the strip for some landings. I discovered that once again, DeHavilland had produced a virtually viceless aircraft and even a short-field landing on the dirt strip produced no white knuckles from either of us.

"I got a lot to do today so I'll leave you to get familiar with the aircraft. She's not needed again until this evening's shuttle. You can do it tonight and I'll come with you to show you the mine strip."

The Otter and I spent the morning getting to know each other. I certainly liked her and I got a feeling that she was reasonably happy with me. I told her so and she replied with a contented purr from her two Pratt and Whitney PT6 engines. Together, we tried all sorts of different power and flap settings on take-off and landing, a single engine climb and getting off the ground at terrifyingly low speeds. I found that, unless you are really determined, it is quite difficult to frighten yourself in a Twin Otter.

On approach to the field at around eleven thirty, I thought I saw the Toyota in the car park. I landed and taxied up to the flight line and shut down. A striking looking woman in her early fifties or so was talking to one of the mine engineers. I went over to them. The similarity to Adelle was immediately obvious.

"Hello, you must be Doctor Helen." I said.

"And you must be Adelaide's pilot. Nice to meet you," We shook hands. "I brought the car back and Adelaide should be here shortly to take me home. Thanks for getting her up here so quickly, by the way. It usually takes her about twelve hours."

"It was great to have her company," I said. 'She's a lovely girl." I discovered that despite her faultless English, Doc was Portuguese. Adelle's father had been Australian and the family had lived in Africa for many years, both parents in the medical profession, working long hours for little money. Adelle turned up about ten minutes later to my great joy and gave me a quick hug.

"Doc hasn't been boring you to tears has she?" Adelle asked with a smile.

"Not at all, we've been talking about you most of the time."

Doc announced that they had better get back to town as time was getting on and I stood watching as they turned the corner out of the site.

I spent the next few days learning the odds and ends of my new job, how to find the mine strip in the dark, how to find the way back home in the rain, which can cause you to fly completely blind and most important, how to deal with the miners and their equipment. We had a couple of emergencies when one of the African mineworkers had his foot badly crushed by a mine trolley and another when one of the engineers was overcome by fumes. In both cases, the casualty was flown from the mine strip over to the Mission Hospital in Livingstone. We could, by stretching the shortfield performance of the Otter to the maximum, land in the three hundred and fifty meters of straight road near the hospital. This was always a big event in Livingstone and the police closed the road to all traffic so that we could get down. Such arrivals always attracted a large crowd and a successful landing (one that you can walk away from) was always greeted with applause. I had been at Morgan Mines for somewhere around four months and had been able to see Adelle on many occasions either down at Blantyre or up in Livingstone. We had formed a close relationship and I spent many ecstatically happy evenings with her and Doc Helen at their house near Livingstone,

Hogan had been moved by the company to a new mine somewhere in South Africa and two new pilots had joined our ranks. As I was the longest serving member of the flight department, I assumed the mantle of Chief Pilot. I had never previously been a Chief Pilot and I felt that I should at least assume an air of remoteness as befitted my status. However, both new men were experienced and good pilots so the remoteness bit didn't work. One day, right in the middle of the hot season, Miller, the senior mining engineer came into my shed—sorry, my office and put a wad of paper on the table.

"How much weight can that thing carry out from here?"

"That depends on temperature, fuel load and all sorts of things," I told him. "What's the problem?"

He told me that he had to get a major part of the drilling machinery over to the mine before evening. Work on one of the seams of bauxite had come to a halt, which was causing our German financial people great concern. We went outside to look at the machinery. It was certainly big, but not too big to physically go into the aircraft through the freight door. The weight, however, could be a problem. Miller and I devised a fairly accurate method of weighing the thing and discovered that the smallest assembly weighed almost six thousand pounds. With minimum fuel and a bit of luck there should be no problem. We set about stripping the seats out of the aircraft and fixing sheets of plywood on the floor to spread the load. Eventually, after a great deal of fussing with rollers, forklift trucks and so on, the major item was secured in the cabin.

Whilst I did some hard sums with fuel loads, Miller had the other smaller pieces brought over and secured them around the big machine. Eventually I decided that we were as ready as we would ever be and made the preparations for take-off. It was a blisteringly hot day and as always, I taxied with the small window open to take advantage of what breeze there was. At the end of the strip, I ran the engines up to full power, checked everything was operating correctly. Miller who was sitting in the right seat did appear a little concerned. I had never flown the Otter with this amount of weight before so I was also a little bit on edge, Putting my trust in God, DeHavilland and Pratt and Whitney, I ran the engines up to full power again and released the brakes.

Predictably, we gathered speed very very slowly. I hoped like hell that we had got the calculations about right. I hoped that both engines would keep going. I hoped that the temperature hadn't risen too much, and I hoped that Miller and the two other engineers in the back hadn't lied about their own weight. We were still only creeping along, still only forty-five knots and almost a third of the strip gone. Both engines were still in full song and, thank God, there was at last some feeling in the controls. Half the strip gone and still only fifty-five knots. Something was not right, The decision point came and went. Too late to stop now. Help me get this thing off the ground, Mr DeHavilland. Into the final third of the strip and only just fifty-five knots on the clock. She might just fly. I left it as late as I dared then eased back on the control column. Nothing. Still firmly on the ground. I hauled back hard. The nosewheel came off the ground and the Otter made a valiant attempt to fly and as the end of the strip went past us we were actually airborne. Not airborne enough however, to clear the scrub at the end. I had a momentary vision of an explosion of branches and shrubbery then a sickening crunch as the landing gear was ripped off. We sagged downwards as the speed decreased below stall. By some miracle, we were still almost flying and I even had some semblance of control. Perhaps even enough to get us to a safer place to crash. I shouted to the passengers to "Brace ! Brace !" but I suspect that they already had. Try as I might, I could not get us any more height and the heavier forest was only a very short distance away. No alternative, I had to get down quickly. I reached above my head and pulled all six levers for the engines, propellers and mixture fully closed and prayed.

We settled back on the ground with a deafening crunching, tearing noise, The Otter slid along the ground on her belly for what seemed like an eternity. The noise was deafening. The outer section of the right wing was torn off as it hit a tree and we swung violently to the right. The seat harness bit hard into my shoulders with the violent deceleration and the control column was wrenched from my hands. The nose of the aircraft ploughed into a large mound of earth and we at last came to a halt. Suddenly, all the noise had stopped and only the clicking of the cooling engines and the sounds of a fatally injured airplane could be heard. Gradually, the jungle recovered from its stunned silence and there was a screeching of frightened birds and animals angry and resentful of our intrusion into their domain. Because of the almost empty fuel tanks, there was now a real danger of fire. The two engineers in the back were moving so they had to be reasonably safe. Miller was slumped forward in his seat with blood running down his face. I had taken a nasty blow to the face from the control column and my right arm hurt a bit but otherwise, I seemed to be in one piece. I undid Miller's seat belt and leant him back. I tried to pull him from the seat but he opened his eyes and mumbled that he was all right. I helped him to his feet and we climbed over the cargo and fell out through the cargo door, which thankfully had come open in the crash. We got as far away from the wreckage as possible and slumped down on the ground.

We had all made it. Some minor injuries, perhaps, but we were all safe. The two engineers, although shaken were unhurt and set off in the direction of the strip to summon help. In the distance we could hear the sounds of shouting and of vehicles in four-wheel drive as the Land Rovers crashed their way through the scrub towards us. Before I got into the vehicle and left the maintenance people to make sure that the wreckage was not going to burst into flames, I looked sadly at the aircraft that had been my almost constant friend and companion for the last few months.

She was a very sad sight with fluid bleeding from the gaping wound in her broken wing, her landing gear ripped off and left somewhere behind her. Although I could not see her face as the nose was buried in earth, I could be fairly sure that the usual Twin Otter smile would have been totally disfigured for ever. Although I would have to take responsibility for the accident, which had almost certainly killed her, I hoped that she would forgive me.

With tears running down my face, I climbed into the back of one of Landrovers and was transported back to the camp

13

After the Otter

I can recall only vaguely the passage of the following twenty-four hours. Shortly after we got back to the camp, Helen, Adelle and a couple of medics from the hospital arrived in Adelles's car having covered the forty odd miles from Livingstone in less than an hour, which, considering the standard of the road, was almost RAC Rally standard. Doc Helen examined us all and pronounced that, although badly shaken, we had all come through our undignified arrival pretty well.

She insisted that Miller and I had to spend some time under observation and that I had to see her tame dentist as a matter of urgency as I now had a large hole where a front tooth had stayed with the aircraft, probably now an integral part of the control column. The reason for the accident had been spotted by one of the maintenance team. Whilst turning around to line up for take-off I had gone onto the rough ground at the start of the runway and had snagged a cable for the runway lights on the nose wheel. Apart from trying to take off with a large amount of weight, the poor Otter had also been trying to haul three hundred and some yards of heavy armoured cable into the air. A sort of arrester cable in reverse, hence the dire acceleration. As I had allowed the decision point to pass without aborting the take-off, the fault was clearly mine although everyone was at pains to avoid pointing the finger.

Miller and I were driven to Livingstone by Keith Dunkley, the more senior of our two new pilots. He dropped us at the hospital where Miller was admitted. Helen had insisted that my recovery would be supervised at her own house, claiming that I was a family friend, beds in the hospital were at a premium and anyway, Adelle had taken some leave to look after me.

Although the dentist had done his best, I was not a pretty sight even two days later.

"You look like you did ten rounds with Atilla the Hun." Adelle said with a laugh.

"I bloody well feel like it too!" I replied, carefully avoiding any word containing the letter S. I had absolutely refused to stay in bed and spent the days observing Adelle. As it was she who was supposed to be observing me, I remarked that this must be a mutual observation society.

One evening, Helen had been called to the hospital and we were sitting on a rug on the floor listening to a Blood, Sweat and Tears album. I turned to Adelle and kissed her gently. She responded by wrapping her arms around me and pulling me close. I felt her fingernails dig into my back and a strong sense of urgency overcame me as I felt her warm body press against my skin, She held me tightly and the kisses became even more passionate. Suddenly, she pulled away,

"I'm going to get hurt again aren't I," she said. "You'll have to go back to England and I'll be here."

"Couldn't you come back to UK and work? It'll be just as bad for me."

"Why could you not work here for Air Malawi? You could fly a Viscount couldn't you?"

I told her that respectable airlines usually avoided hiring pilots who had made catastrophically bad decisions and bent airplanes and that anyway, my licences were of doubtful value in Malawi. I was wondering if Gerry could pull any strings when she suddenly stood up and pulled me to my feet.

"One bad decision doesn't matter," she said. "This is probably another bad decision." She took my hand and led me across the room, through the hallway and into her bedroom. She kissed me again then stepped back and pulled her top over her head. She slipped off her skirt and stood naked in the moonlight. She was breathtakingly beautiful. Her fingers found the waistband of my shorts and pulled them down. I kicked them out of the way and reached for her. We collapsed onto her bed wrapped in each others arms, kissing passionately, legs intertwined. She crushed against me as I tenderly explored her body. The intensity of our caresses mounted to fever pitch until I though that my head was going to explode. Adelle moaned softly and turned to lie on her back. She looked straight into my eyes and flicked her tongue over her lips,

"I want you darling." she said softly. "I want you inside me. I want you so badly that I hurt."

She made soft animal noises as I slowly and gently kissed her from head to toe, then, when neither of us could wait any longer, we made love, slowly at first then with total abandonment as the intensity became unbearable. The explosion of climax was mutual and indescribably intense and we lay in each others arms for a long time afterwards, totally exhausted.

Some time later, Adelle giggled softly and said
"Aren't you supposed to ask how it was for me?"
"How was it for you?"
"Wonderful. What about you
"Unbelievable,"
"Do it again?"

I took her in my arms and held her close for a long time. We made love again more slowly this time savouring the sensations and finding experiences of mutual pleasure until at last we both fell into a deep sleep, totally exhausted.

The sun was already quite high in the sky when the bedroom door opened and Helen came in carrying two cups of coffee and a rack of toast, which she placed on a bedside table,

"Morning, you two. My, you've made a good recovery, Al!"

Adelle feigned a little cry of mock horror and buried her head in the pillow. Doc Helen smiled at me and gently closed the door behind her as she left the room.

Two days later, Helen pronounced me fit to return to work. Adelle had taken as much leave from the airline as she dared and also had to get back to work. We drove out to the camp together and said our goodbyes. She clung to me as I was getting out of the car.

"I'll be back as soon as I can. I'll call you from Blantyre as soon as I get there. You make sure that you miss me as much as I'm going to miss you!"

"Of course I'll miss you, darling. You will be in my thoughts every second of every minute of every hour of every day!" I said poetically.

"Smoothie!" Adelle said. "Please take care of yourself" I kissed her again and regretfully allowed her to leave.

The Otter had been removed from the jungle and was lying on the ground at the side of the strip. Two people from the Aviation Authority were looking at it wisely. I supposed that they were looking for clues to the reason for the crash. One of them came over to meet me as I walked towards the wreck.

"Name's Wilson. Civil Aviation Authority." he announced. "You were the pilot in command?"

"'Fraid so," I replied. "How bad is she?"

"In my estimation, the aircraft is a total loss. There's structural damage apart from the obvious damage you can see, There'll be an investigation, of course but was she flying properly before the accident?"

"Certainly. One of the nicest aircraft that I've flown."

"No engine problems? Nothing to suggest a power loss?"

"Absolutely not," I replied. "I apparently got hooked up on a power cable and the poor old girl was trying to lift the whole airfield into the air. She almost made it too."

"You did a good job getting down without hurting anybody Nice bit of flying."

"Thanks, but I just took it as it came."

Wilson grunted and went back to his examination. Keith had gone to Blantyre the previous day to collect the second Twin Otter from maintenance and whilst I was looking round the wreckage I heard the sound of approaching aircraft. The Islander and the Otter roared over the camp, low and in formation. They did a fighter break and started setting themselves up for landing.

"Bloody show-offs !" I remarked to my Otter, She didn't reply. Probably still mad at me. The two aircraft landed smoothly on the strip, separately, thank goodness and taxied up to the hangar. Keith waved at me from the flight deck of the Islander as he shut the engines down. He emerged from the aircraft and walked over to me.

"Surveying the wreckage?"

"They say she's a total loss."

"Yeah, can't see anybody fixing that up, can you?" he said. "Word is that they're looking at buying another aircraft pretty soon. Possibly a big single engined aircraft."

In my absence, Keith and Phil Moon, the other pilot had reorganised the daily trips between them which left me the three times weekly trip down to Blantyre in the Islander. This suited me very well because I wanted to work on getting a Viscount job with Air Malawi. It also meant that I could see Adelle much more frequently and we became more and more close although we both told each other and ourselves that there could be nothing in the way of long term commitment. I doubt whether either of us really believed that.

One day, when I was nearing the end of my contract a letter arrived from Air Malawi. They regretted that after carefully reviewing my application for employment, they did not, unfortunately, have any suitable vacancy for pilots of my experience level at that time. They would, however, keep my details on file and they thanked me for my interest in Air Malawi and wished me well in my search for suitable employment. Later that week I received another bombshell, this time from Adelle who had been offered a job with Qantas. As our relationship was obviously not now destined to be permanent, she had accepted and was to report in three weeks for line training.

We spent our final weekend together in Blantyre in the best hotel we could find. We laughed a lot and cried a lot. We walked together for hours on end. We ate and drank far too much and we made love over and over again.

And so, alas, my stay in Malawi came to an end. I had a lot to look back on, mostly very happy memories of a beautiful, warm woman, many new friends, wonderful scenery and several hundred hours of the most challenging and pleasurable flying that I had ever experienced.

14

Cropduster

Airplane manufacturers are a lot like automobile manufacturers in that they employ vast numbers of people whose sole function in life is to dream up wholly imaginative names for the company product. Piper, who make a substantial number of different light aircraft have a very imaginative series of names for their babies. Someone a long time back decided that North American Indian tribes have names which lend themselves to the aviation concept and so the Pawnee was born. The Pawnee's siblings include such names as Cherokee, Apache, Navajo, and Commanche. Quite what the Pawnee Indians have to do with crop spraying is uncertain, but that is the Piper Pawnee's primary role. It is hard to imagine a noisier or more uncomfortable aircraft. It is slow, cramped, has very limited fuel capacity and is certainly not a pretty airplane. Put a Pawnee in its correct element, however and it fulfills the function of carrying huge quantities of horrible chemicals from very short strips and delivering the chemical to the required crop.

The human element in the above mentioned chemical delivery chain is by necessity a somewhat strange person. He (or she) must have a Commercial Pilots License. The holder of such a license has undergone very rigorous training, taken countless examinations, been poked and prodded by medical people to ensure a satisfactory standard of fitness and above all, has had flight safety forced into him (or her) through every available orifice. Strange, then that to engage in crop dusting, almost all of those parameters are totally ignored. There is a requirement for any pilot who wishes to take part in the aerial application of agricultural materials to pass a tough course of instruction. This results in an Agricultural Rating. The typical crop duster pilot operates out of a tiny strip usually only just long enough to safely take off if the aircraft is empty. He stands by whilst the enormous hopper behind his seat is filled to the brim with really nasty horrible material which if inhaled would undoubtedly cause a terminal disease. He then fires up the engine and taxis carefully to the very end of the strip and runs the engine up to full power whilst holding the beast on the brakes. When he is satisfied that the engine is giving of its very best, he releases the brakes and starts to hope. No sudden lurch forward here! The thing is so heavy that it can hardly move. Painfully slowly, the contraption gathers speed and just as the pilot is about to give up all hope and resigns himself to becoming an integral part of the scenery, the critical speed is reached. Totally ignoring the stall warner, he hauls back on the control column and bullies the machine into the air.

The circus has only just begun. Keeping the airplane in the air once airborne is simple. Anyone who can walk and chew gum simultaneously can do that bit. Finding the correct field is marginally more difficult. There often exists a substantial difference of opinion between the crop spraying contractor and the farmer as to the exact size and location of the target area. The one thing that can be absolutely certain is that the target field is the one that is surrounded by high tension electricity pylons. There is usually no alternative other than to fly under the cables. On the approach to the spray run, that is a tolerably safe undertaking. Most cables are at least 35 feet off the ground and you get a lot lower than that when landing. The tricky bit is to be able to keep one eye on the cables at the far end, one eye on your spray pattern and one eye on the actual process of flying an overloaded airplane at a very low level. As most pilots only have two eyes, something has to give. Inevitably it is the flying that takes second place and most crop dusters trim the airplane for the so-called 'sneeze factor' so that in the event of a momentary lapse in concentration, the airplane will climb rather than plough into the ground. At the far end of the spray run, the spray valve is closed and the airplane has to be persuaded to climb at least enough to clear whatever obstructions exist at the far end. A very steep turn through one hundred and eighty degrees is then used to get into position for the reciprocal run and a steep descent initiated to get back down to spray height by the commencement of the run.

The observant reader will by now have deduced that crop spraying is not a job for the faint of heart. It is not considered by many to be a job for any other than certifiably insane pilots. That fine body of people, our Antipodean friends, are excellent ag pilots (ag being short for agricultural) This has probably something to do with their natural exuberance and saying "G'Day mate" all of the time. My own attempts to be an agricultural pilot lasted for a pitifully short time.

Having recently obtained the required rating and being somewhat short in flying hours on the Pawnee, my employer felt that I should get some experience of the airplane prior to actually using it for the purpose for which it was designed. The contract called for the spraying of many hundred acres of cotton in the Sudan and as the aircraft were in Essex, there was patently a small logistical problem. It was decided that three aircraft would go to the Sudan and that they would be flown there under their own power. A fairly obvious solution one might assume. The cruise speed of a Pawnee is in the region of 80 knots and the Sudan is absolutely miles away. Simple mathematics shows that the ferry trip was going to take a long time. Just to confuse an already confused issue, the maximum endurance of the Pawnee is approximately 4 hours. If a ferry fuel tank replaces the hopper, the range is increased to somewhere in the region of 6 hours at the cost of an increased all-up weight and resultant decrease in performance. The cramped conditions in the cockpit make a trip of longer than 30 minutes somewhat trying. Just to round things off nicely, most Pawnees are equipped with only the bare minimum of communications and navigational devices and we were to be provided with battery powered portable radios to satisfy the requirements of Air Traffic Control.

It was with some trepidation, therefore, that the three of us taxied out for take off one Sunday at the ungodly hour of five thirty in the morning. By careful taxiing, I had managed to be the last in turn for take off. I watched as the other two aircraft lurched off the short runway at Southend and lumbered up to something approaching a safe height. In turn, I opened the throttle and started the takeoff run. After what seemed like a week, the flying controls began to have some effect and I gingerly eased the aircraft off the ground and struggled for height. Once in the air, however, it felt a little better and had I not known otherwise, I would have sworn that we were actually flying. I joined the other two in a semblance of formation and we set course for the South coast. I discovered very shortly after take off that my radio had completely died. I attracted the attention of Frank Jolly who was flying the airplane on my left and held the dead radio up for him to see. He shrugged his shoulders and and we decided by means of some fairly complicated body language that communication between the three of us would be effected by a system of hand signals. Frank looked meaningfully at me and pointed forward to his engine then wiped imaginary sweat from his forehead. I took this to mean that his engine was overheating and wondered what action he proposed to take. Alas he took none, which left me in a great deal of doubt. Was he trying to tell me that it was my engine that was exhibiting signs of strain? He looked at me again and made the same sequence of signs. I anxiously consulted the gauges relevant to the engine and found nothing amiss. I made a question mark by drawing on the inside of my side window and pointing forward to my propeller. He threw his head back and laughed.

"No," he signaled. "Not your engine, and not my engine."

"What then?" I signed back.

"Don't worry!" came the signal. "Everything is fine."

We flew on serenely and eventually the coastline came into view. As we crossed the shore and got out of gliding range of land the engine did what all single engines do at such a time. It misfired. Not a bad misfire and not even enough to show on the instruments. Just enough to cause concern. I listened very carefully for a repeat performance but none came. I settled down and tried to ignore the little warning bell ringing in my brain. The engine roared healthily on and I concluded that my imagination had been playing tricks. Comforted, I allowed my thoughts to roam and consider the task ahead. We were to land in Brest for a comfort stop and to refuel for the next leg. We had decided to follow the French coast rather than take a long sea crossing, which I concluded was an excellent idea. Having spent many hundreds of hours over oceans in multi engined aircraft, I was not too convinced of the sanity of trusting to only one engine over water and out of sight of land.

The engine misfired again. This time it was quite unmistakable. The engine had definitely misfired. I switched between the two magnetos and scowled at the RPM indicator. The correct drop in rpm was there so both mags were functioning correctly. I pulled out the carburetor heat control in case ice had accumulated in the air intake. All was normal. I pushed the mixture control into the fully rich position. Again, all was normal. The engine seemed to have given up trying to frighten me and had returned to running sweetly again.

I relaxed again comforting myself with the thought that the French coast was now only about fifteen minutes away. Once again my thoughts drifted hither and thither, mainly thither and I became aware that certain parts of my anatomy were becoming rather numb, and that I needed to visit the toilet. Probably something to do with all the water a thousand feet below us. Thus occupied, I was letting my hands fly the airplane whilst I concentrated on other matters. The next misfire was so bad that I returned to the real world very suddenly and with a start. This time the engine had definitely missed at least three of its four firing cycles. Now considerably concerned, I started to prepare for the worst. I could, if necessary lighten the aircraft by pulling the emergency dump lever and jettisoning the extra fuel into the sea and damn the environment. This action, I concluded would extend the glide range by about 50 seconds. It would also improve the chances of floating were I fortunate enough to persuade the thing to settle on the sea and stay the right way up. The English Channel looked extremely cold and I tried to recall the details of the marine survival course which I had been obliged to take whilst in the Air Force. Alas all I could remember was that there was a fishing line somewhere in the life vest, and that there was a cute little whistle to attract attention. The engine continued to cough. I checked that my straps were tight and went through all of the checks that I had previously carried out. Looking across at Frank, I signed that I might have a small problem. He looked back at me and shrugged his shoulders, then carried on gazing straight ahead. The engine, being a contrary beast, resumed a healthy roar. The coast was now only about ten minutes away, maddeningly well out of glide range. I saw one of the cross channel ferries about a mile ahead and resolved to alter course towards it should the situation deteriorate again.

The engine reminded me of its presence by giving a discreet little cough then running sweetly again. Seven minutes out. Almost in glide range. Engine sounded fine again. I told myself not to sweat it, that everything would be just fine. Three minutes out. Now just within glide range. The engine could now do whatever it pleased. I could land this thing on the beach if necessary. Two minutes out. Got it made! I listened very carefully for any further signs of misbehavior from the engine. Running as sweetly as when it left the factory. All the temperatures and pressures were absolutely normal. The thing continued to run like a sewing machine all the way down the coast. It behaved impeccably when we made our approach to Brest. It responded magnificently when I applied extra power on the approach because I had miscalculated the sink rate. After landing, it positively refused to exhibit the smallest indication of discontent even when run up to full power on the ground.

As we taxied up to the fuelling area I parked alongside Frank's aircraft and shut down. We climbed out and I took off the heavy crash helmet.

"Thought I had a problem there, Frank," I said.

"What? a misfire?"

"Yeah, wondered if I was going to have to ditch for a minute back there."

"That's what I was trying to tell you just after we got airborne. The engines in these things seem to know when you're over water. Known as 'going into auto-rough' Get used to it in time. Happens over mountains too." He grinned. "It usually keeps going though. Usually." I fished around in the small box of spares that we carried and found a new battery pack for my radio causing the previously inert contraption to burst into life.

The trip from Brest to our next fuel stop in the Duchy of Luxembourg took forever. Frank and I played charades across the hundred feet or so that separated us. The time dragged on interminably and we blindly followed our leader who had been charged with the navigational duties. Frank looked across at me and made the sign for "Song" then "Film". He waggled the wings of his airplane then rotated his hand above his head. To complete the title he then held up his left arm and pointed to his watch. I didn't get it at all and had to leave a blank on my knee pad on which we had agreed to write the answers. Harry Keeling who was flying the lead airplane started turning right and descending slightly. We followed, trustingly. The turn tightened up and his descent became steeper. We had now turned through almost 180 degrees and had come down almost 700 feet. Frank looked startled and I quickly realised that all was not well. I heard Frank's voice on the radio.

"Harry what the hell is happening?" There was no response. We had now turned through 270 degrees and lost about 1000 feet.

"Harry this is Frank. Do you read?"

Harry's aircraft suddenly came out of the turn and started to climb. His voice came over the radio.

"Sorry guys, just dozed off there for a second. Where are we?"

"Don't you know?" I asked, unaware of the fact that my radio had now developed a disinclination to transmit. I was rather angry that none of us had any idea as to our exact position.

"Hey! I thought you were supposed to be leading." Said Frank.

"Stand by," he replied. "Looking at the map."

I thought that I could understand how Harry had fallen asleep. I didn't feel too well myself. In fact if I hadn't known better, I could have sworn that I was feeling air-sick. There was a very long silence. Eventually, he suggested that we were almost certainly only about ten miles north of track and that we fly south until we picked up the railroad tracks. I have to say that Harry was one of a disappearing breed of pilots, those who seem to know instinctively where they are to within a few miles. We flew south until, sure enough, railway lines appeared in front of us. I was perfectly happy to allow the other two to navigate as my supposed air-sickness was now making me quite dizzy. I opened up the small window and turned the fresh air vents to a full blast on my face.

We finally saw Luxembourg at around two in the afternoon. Harry made the radio call.

"Findel, Farmers 44, flight of three aircraft with you at 1500 feet ten miles west of the airfield" Farmers 44 was the somewhat pompous flight number selected by our revered leader.

"Farmers 44, Findel, we have your flight plan. Say again your aircraft type and persons on board."

"Findel, Farmers 44 is a flight of three Piper Pawnees inbound for night stop and fuel."

"Confirm that you are agricultural aircraft?"

"Affirmative Findel."

"And that you are not carrying chemicals of any description?"

"Farmers 44 negative."

Findel cleared us to the approach and I imagined the controller scratching his head wondering who in their right mind would want to travel halfway across Europe in a Pawnee. My numb extremities were in complete agreement with him. Harry, refreshed after his little snooze led us down the approach and we landed without incident one behind the other using only a tiny amount of Luxemburg's generous runway. I creaked my way out of the cramped cockpit and gingerly jumped off the trailing edge of the wing.

"That could have been interesting," said Frank pointing with his thumb at Harry.

"Yeah a formation crunch. Never done that before."

"By the way," I said, "I couldn't make sense of the last song and film."

"Ah ! That was Rock around the Clock," he said.

All of a sudden, I started to shake. Despite the warm afternoon sun, I felt cold.

"Are you all right?" said Frank.

"Just feel bloody cold." I could feel turmoil in my stomach. "And sick," I added. "In fact I don't feel too good at all."

Harry came over to join us. "Are you all right, Al," he asked. "You look terrible."

"I feel terrible," I replied.

Harry started towards my aircraft. "I hope like hell that I'm wrong," he said, "but this has happened before. Sometimes there is a chemical spill into the cockpit and sometimes it doesn't get properly neutralised. We better get you checked out."

My world turned upside down and Harry and Frank disappeared into a sort of greenish haze as the tarmac came rushing up to meet me.

I recovered consciousness briefly to find myself lying down on a long leather bench inside a building. I determined that I would prove to those people who were hovering over me that I was made of sterner stuff. I attempted to prop myself up on one elbow.

"Wunble dobble stog," I mumbled

Harry and Frank looked nonplussed.

"Zeggle spram?" Why could they not understand me? They just hovered there about six inches off the floor looking concerned.

"We think you've had some exposure to chemicals," said Harry. His white robes gave him a slightly angelic appearance. "We've called the medics and they should be here soon."

Two men dressed rather inappropriately in diving suits floated into the room and flew over to where I lay. One of the men bent over me and took my pulse.

"Mombey gloops," I told him. "Segool yamping."

"What did he say?" the man inquired. I concluded that he was not fluent in English as he patently was incapable of understanding even simple phrases.

"The stuff he has been inhaling must be hallucinogenic," said Frank. "We'd better get him to hospital and get him de-toxed." Frank flew across the room towards the door. I was full of admiration for Frank's ability to levitate and determined to communicate this appreciation to the medic who was trying to put an oxygen mask over my face.

"Globble devoil slumm," I said. I pushed the mask away and was violently sick. The room spun briefly before all the lights went out.

I spent the next two days in hospital surrounded by incredibly pretty nurses. On the second day, I was informed that another pilot had been flown in from England to continue the ferry of the aircraft to Sudan and that I was scheduled to return to UK on board a commercial flight as soon as they considered that I was sufficiently recovered. A very attractive lady doctor told me that I had been very fortunate in that the effect of the chemical with which the cockpit had been contaminated usually took at least two hours to have an effect. Had the flight been only thirty minutes longer, she told me, the end result would probably have been distinctly more messy.

And so, my first attempt at being an ag pilot was foiled. I returned to England by way of Rotterdam on a KLM Boeing, continuing to Southend on board a very ancient Carvair. The owner of the crop spraying company met me at Southend full of abject apologies and promises of an extended vacation. All expenses, he assured me, would be completely covered by the company. Such mistakes happened from time to time, he stated. I could confidently expect, he told me, to receive many further offers of work in the agricultural sector. With considerable dignity, I thanked him for his good wishes but suggested that he insert his offer into an appropriate orifice as I considered that my days of acting in the capacity of an ag pilot were well and truly over.

There were times later on when I felt inclined to regret that rather hasty decision as gainful employment in the aviation industry is somewhat elusive by nature. For that moment, however, I was in absolutely no doubt that alternative employment was mine for the asking. Ah well I had been wrong before.

15

Oostende

The Cherokee droned its erratic way through the sky of Southeast England, Slouched in the right hand seat, I was pondering the inability of my student to understand that this collection of cold metal could, if treated with appropriate respect and a quite insignificant degree of competence, transform this uncomfortable progress into sheer pleasure. He sat at the controls on the left side of the airplane and stared fixedly at the horizon, He appeared to be unaware of the fact that we were travelling in a manner befitting a porpoise. We were also, despite his clumsy efforts to point us in the direction which I had deemed suitable, lurching from side to side. This was not doing my abused digestive system a great deal of good. I comforted myself with the thought that at least he could only improve.

The song of the engine changed almost imperceptibly. My trained ear was immediately aware of the marginally lower note and I looked across at my fellow aviator and attempted to catch his eye. His forehead was covered in perspiration. His hands had a death grip on the yoke. He was sitting bolt upright and patently working very hard indeed. I must, however unjustly, increase his workload.

"Have you noticed the engine revs ?" He wrested his eyes from the swaying horizon and stared wildly amongst the instruments. I pointed to the RPM indicator which was informing us that all was not as it should be. He looked blank. "It would be as well to apply some carb heat" I advised him, "We have all the conditions for carb icing here, and if we don't clear the ice, then the engine will suffocate."

He frantically searched through his memory and, amazingly, came up with the correct solution. He looked across at me and with an unspoken question, touched the carb heat lever. I nodded wisely and he pulled out the lever, causing hot air to clear the accumulation of ice from the carburettor. The engine slowed down a little more, then, as the lever was restored to its rightful position, resumed its happy hum. A Piper PA28–140, known as the Cherokee, is the most kindly, forgiving and practical of all touring and training aircraft. However, all aircraft can bite if treated badly and Lima Tango (the phonetic pronunciation of the last two letters of her registration) was no exception. Whilst looking around for the RPM indicator, my pilot had inadvertently applied a significant amount of bank. We were now turning right and, because of the Laws of Aerodynamics, certain forces were now acting on the craft, which, if left unchecked, would develop into a spiral dive.

"We appear to be losing height," I remarked. He looked through the windshield.

"Oh God!" he muttered and set about the task of getting us straight and level again.

"Our height is supposed to be 1500 feet and we are actually meant to be flying over in that direction." I pointed to a position somewhere over his left shoulder.

"Sorry!" He turned to me and grinned. "I lost concentration for a sec there." His task of returning to the required height and heading completed with only minimal drama, he settled down again. I looked across at him. Behind the sweat and the grim concentration, I believe that he was actually enjoying this. If this was so, then I was ahead on points. Every pilot, irrespective of his experience has a passionate love affair with the sky. He feels at home in the sky. He knows that the sky can be a very harsh and unforgiving mistress but his love will not allow him to give her up willingly. He knows the joy of climbing up through a dark and overcast sky and coming out on top into the sunlight and looking down onto the snowfields of clouds below him. Up there, a pilot is king. He may feel pity for the scurrying masses below him. He possibly even feels sorry that the protagonists in the rat race cannot share the feeling of elation, of splendid isolation. He is free. My student still had most of this ahead of him. My task as a flying instructor was to teach this man how to achieve this euphoric state. I broke my reverie.

"Right, Terry, we'll head back now. Make your heading one six zero."

He looked uncomprehendingly at the gyro direction indicator, made a decision and started to turn the wrong way

"No, Terry," I said. "Don't forget, turn right to increase your heading."

"Aw shit!" At least he was becoming critical of his own performance. There may be a flyer in there yet.

With gentle prompting and a little assistance from me, we allowed the little airplane to drift down to 1,000 feet and I took the controls.

"Right. I will get us on the approach and when we are in a good position, I will ask you to actually carry out the landing."

The radio crackled into life as a Cessna in front of us requested and duly received permission to land. I waited for a space and then muttered the appropriate incantation into my microphone.

"Lima Tango, Southend," air traffic replied, "You're number two behind the Cessna on short finals"

The Cessna landed sweetly on the runway and trundled off at the intersection. The radio came to life again.

"Lima Tango, clear to land, surface wind 230 at 10." I acknowledged with a couple of clicks on my mic. At 700 feet I told Terry to take control and to place us gently on the ground. I cautioned him that I would not regard kindly any attempt on his part to break either the airplane, the instructor or the runway. Once again, I was favoured with the grin. He was happy. He was really doing quite well. We were as near as dammit in the right place and at the correct height. This would be a good landing, We would gently reunite our wheels with the solid ground and run smoothly along the runway I would soon be enjoying a chat with my fellow aviators over a cup of coffee. Soon, now, I would—

"Bloody Hell!" Terry was landing the bloody airplane twenty-five feet off the ground.

I have previously made reference to the kindly and forgiving nature of the Cherokee. Regrettably, even the most kindly and forgiving aircraft, when denied its lifeblood of airspeed, tends to succumb to the Laws of Gravity. Lima Tango, so deprived, dropped like a stone. Her stiff little legs bounced us back into the air Terry who was a big strong man thrust the yoke forwards to get the beast back on the ground. This time, we landed on the nosewheel. We bounced back into the air again. We were proceeding in a very undignified and life threatening series of bunnyhops, each of which, I am quite sure left a substantial indentation in the runway. I pushed the throttle all the way forward and lifted us back into the air. We droned around the circuit and although I should certainly have known better, I once again invited my student to effect the reunion with terra firma. To his elation, and to my own great surprise, the subsequent landing was quite passable. The airplane, with its ship's company of one intrepid aviator and one very relieved instructor turned smoothly down the intersection towards the clubhouse.

As we parked and shut down, I was aware of a sea of grinning faces from inside the building. I disentangled myself from the spider's web of seat harnesses, mic leads and headsets. Clutching my clipboard, the symbol of my instructor's status I made a practised and dignified descent from the Cherokee. Terry was not so accomplished. He emerged from the door with a mic lead wrapped around one ankle and somehow managed to get a seat belt wrapped around the other. I could not look. As I entered the clubhouse, he materialised beside me, glowing with elation. He obviously failed to appreciate that at the after flight debriefing, I must of necessity point out the deficiencies in his performance. This was a clear instance of buck passing. The responsibility for a safe arrival was mine alone, and I saw fit to delegate part of that responsibility to one who was insufficiently prepared. I was not, however, of a mind to admit to this.

"Terry," I said, "I'll write up the log and the landing time whilst you get us some coffee."

Ever anxious to please, Terry found some mugs that were almost clean and slopped coffee into them. I watched out of the corner of my eye. My God, how much sugar does this guy take? No wonder he's overweight.

We sat at the table and I fished a crumpled pack of Marlboro from my pocket, selected a reasonably undamaged cigarette and lit it,

"Those things kill ya!"

"Possibly, Terry, but so do lots of things, not least bloody awful landings. Now then." I launched into the post flight de—brief. This process is usually a relatively straightforward procedure, limited, in the main to straightening out any deficiencies which may have become manifest in the hour or so in the air. However, when that hour terminates in an adventurous landing, the interest of other aviators is inevitably aroused. It is invariably a cue for the entire population of the clubhouse to air their devastating and original wit.

"Air Traffic lost count of your landings and say they're only going to charge you for six"

"Goodyear are asking for your assessment on the kangaroo-skin tyres"

"The airport director wants the club to fill in the holes in the runway" Etcetera, etcetera—ha ha bloody ha!

Salvation came in the form of the Chief Flying Instructor who indicated that a quiet chat was required. I wound up our debriefing and left Terry to pay his bill and arrange his next lesson. I wandered into the CFI's office and collapsed into a dodgy armchair.

"So what gives, Ted?" I enquired.

"Seems we have a little problem, Al."

"Fuel bill again? Unpaid landing fees?"

He shook his head, making all of his several chins vibrate in close formation. It transpired that the owner of the flying school, one Charles Edward Smollett had trundled off to Oostende on the previous day with one of his lady friends and in spite of legislation to the contrary, had got uproariously legless and had decided to obstruct a Belgian police officer in the execution of his duty. He had therefore been arrested and was even now languishing in a Belgian slammer awaiting due process of law.

"Problem is that we desperately need the Arrow back here for tomorrow morning. I suppose you couldn't…?"

The chair creaked ominously as I wriggled uncomfortably. Despite my protestations and weak excuses, Ted used his ultimate weapon—money, so an hour later, we were in the air again heading for the RAF base at Manston or as it is more properly called—Kent International. The deal was, Ted would fly me to KI, I would then get to Ramsgate somehow, catch the 12.45 ferry to Oostende, pick up the Arrow and if possible, Charlie's girl friend and fly the complete assembly home. Sounds easy doesn't it? Very simple. Very straightforward. If you are the CFI.

As it happened, getting to Oostende on the ferry was the easy part. Getting out to the airport was relatively painless. Even stopping the Belgian taxi driver from robbing me blind was not that hard.

I walked into the airport office and as soon as I mentioned the Arrow, I was aware of the sort of hostile silence that only the Belgians and the French can produce.

"The aircraft is impounded M'sieu" said the little man behind the desk, barely able to conceal a generous measure of satisfaction. "The bill for the landing and for the navigation and for the parking is…" He treated me to a spirited performance of Bach's Toccata and Fugue in D Minor on an impressive desk calculator and produced a stream of paper with a figure at the bottom that looked like two months pay. He handed it to me with a European flourish.

"So" he said. "You will pay now please?"

"Yes." I replied "Or to put it another way—No. My boss will take care of that bill by wire transfer. I have the authority to give you that assurance." My lies were getting better, in fact so much better that I could almost believe them. Pierre or whatever his name was did not appear to be convinced. I was favoured with a Gallic shrug and he informed me that he would take advice on the matter. He did not indicate when and was not apparently prepared to give the matter any degree of urgency. The airport must make a living, after all, and an impounded aircraft accumulates fees like a London car park. Out of nowhere, I suddenly got one of my very rare bright ideas. Find Charlie's lady friend, She would probably be weighed down with credit cards. Most of Charlie's women were. She would be in a position to get us out of this. Two unresolved questions remained. Number one, who was she and number two, where was she?

Pierre was not inclined to offer a solution to either problem. I decided to leave the Arrow to accumulate another National Debt in fees and go to the Police Station.

"Where is the Police Station?" I enquired,

He generously pointed in the general direction of the town and suggested that, once there, there would be any number of people who would be able to assist me. I spent the next forty minutes aimlessly wandering round Oostende, The fact that nobody appeared to know where the police station was did not deter them from pointing the way. Finally, I came upon it by pure accident and ventured inside,

"I understand that you are holding a friend of mine, Charles Smollett" I stated. The young lady copper behind the desk told me that she would have to consult with M'sieu l'Inspector, gave me a five-hundred watt smile and vanished. She returned several minutes later in the trail of a florid man who instantly reminded me of Hercules Poirot. I was favoured with the look reserved for friends of arch criminals. He asked how he might be of assistance. I was tempted to suggest that an appropriate course of action would be to lock Charlie up for the rest of his natural life but wiser counsel prevailed.

"There are several matters which I must discuss with him." I said.

He looked me up and down and obviously decided that I was probably not going to take his police station apart.

"That may be possible," he said with an emphasis on the "may". "First, I must know what matters you will discuss, then we shall see."

"I need the keys to his aircraft, where his lady friend is and whether he has any money. There are charges made on the airplane which have to be settled."

"Ah!" He drew himself up to his full height in meters. "We, the Belgian Police have also several charges applying to M'sieu Smollett. He could, how you say—go down for twelve months. He pays for a meal with a forged credit card, he attempts to steal a car, he is drunk and disorderly in the streets of Oostende and he commits an assault upon the person of one of my officers"

Poirot patently considered that Charlie was one of the most dangerous criminals since Ghengis Khan.

"However, M'sieu," he continued, "I shall convey your questions to M'sieu Smollett and return to you presently."

He vanished into an inner sanctum, presumably leading to the dungeons. I settled down to wait.

Some time later, the door to the street opened and a girl entered. She was tall, very attractive with long black hair and a worried look on her face. As she reached the desk, her bag fell open and the contents spilled out onto the floor. Amongst the heap of junk my eyes lit on a familiar set of keys.

"Excuse me," I said "Are you Charlie Smollett's friend ?"

She gave a most unladylike snort.

"Not any more, I'm not. How did you know that ?'

"I've come to collect you and the Arrow and get you back to England."

"Thank God!" she exclaimed. "Let's get out of here!"

I carefully explained that, prior to our departure there were certain formalities to be taken care of, such as payment of the charges.

"Will they accept plastic?" she asked producing an impressive concertina of credit cards.

"Only if they're not forged. Charlie's in the joint for passing iffy credit cards,"

"These are real, dummy! So was Charlie's but the stupid sod was so drunk that he couldn't sign his name,"

I made an executive decision to discuss the other matters at a later date and in a more convenient location.

"OK, let's get out of here. Poirot is obviously not going to turn Charlie loose so I'll let somebody else worry about him."

Between us, we found enough Belgian francs for a taxi back to the airport.

"My name is Julia Hamilton" she told me. "I'm so glad you showed up. I had no idea how to get home."

I introduced myself and told her that once all the formalities were completed we should be back in Southend in about an hour. Julia conveyed the impression that this piece of information had hit the spot. As we found a taxi and wakened the driver I was considering the question of how such an attractive woman could possibly become involved with someone like Charlie. Always the master of subtlety, I tried an oblique question.

"Are you and Charlie……er…?"

"Are we what?"

"Well, you know—ah—Charlie doesn't seem your type."

"If you mean are we sleeping together the answer is no, if it's any of your damn business."

I wonder why I felt a wave of relief at this information. She was certainly a very attractive woman. I progressed to stage two.

"Does your husband know how you're getting back?"

"I don't have a husband."

Great. Now for the really clever question.

"If there's anyone you'd like to call we can do it from the airport before we go."

The shoot down was hard, fast and devastatingly effective.

"My name is Julia Elizabeth Hamilton, English, divorced, no kids, live on my own, no boyfriend, my own business and no repeat no intention of getting involved with anybody. Okay?"

I reached for the metaphorical ejection seat handle but stayed with the ship for the time being.

"Sorry. I didn't mean to pry," I lied. "You said something about business. Just wondered if anybody might be worried about you getting back."

"Look, Charlie and I have a little deal brewing. That's why the trip."

Charlie's 'little deals' usually involve ready cash, no paperwork and a very, very low profile. I started to worry ever so slightly.

"Look, Julia, I have to know whether there is anything on the aircraft that could land us in trouble."

She shook her head. I admired the way her hair moved. Almost like a TV shampoo commercial.

"Okay, I have to trust you. I hope I'm right."

Actually, I hoped like hell that I was right. The penalties inflicted on pilots who upset Her Majesty's Customs and Excise by introducing nasty substances into the Green and Pleasant Land do not bear thinking about. I had to concede that, despite her association with Charlie, Julia did not look like a drug smuggler so I elected to go along with her assurance.

The cab pulled up outside the terminal building with a screech of brakes and an odour of Michelin served well done, I paid the man and we got out. I idly speculated why Julia had apparently no luggage except for a large and impressive camera case. No immediate answer was forthcoming so I led the way to the control office and did the captain bit, paying the bills with Julia's Am-Ex, getting the weather, filing the flight plan and so on. We attracted a suspicious look from the customs man but he let us through and we walked out to the Arrow.

Julia followed me with interest as I carried out the external pre-flight inspection. This involves several procedures swathed in mystery and folk lore but it basically comprises counting the various bits such as wings and wheels, making sure that the bits which are supposed to flap do and the bits which are not supposed to flap don't. If the aircraft has been standing for a while, you take a fuel sample from the tanks via a device cunningly contrived for that very purpose and check that there is no water in the fuel. I pulled the prop over a couple of compressions to check that oil had not collected in the cylinder heads. Julia queried this.

"Charlie started it by turning the key inside,"

"I'm not trying to start it, just making sure that the engine doesn't break when I do start it."

"I'm not a bimbo," she snapped. "Don't patronise me."

"Sorry, love." Instant fury.

"Don't call me that!"

I was beginning to think that Julia was very concerned about something,

"Can you hurry it up? Let's get out of here."

That really made me worried.

"Okay, climb in then." I opened the door and jumped down. "You take the left seat, Julia."

As I was in command, I should, technically occupy the left seat but as most of my working day was spent in the right seat with a student in the left I was more comfortable there. I climbed in after her, closed and locked the door and zipped through the pre flight internal checks. Soon enough, I considered everything to be in order and about ready to go. I fired up the engine and whilst it warmed up, I announced our intentions on the radio.

"Oostende, Arrow Whiskey Golf radio check."

"Whiskey Golf, Oostende, loud and clear."

"Oostende, Whiskey Golf request taxi clearance for Southend, two on board."

"Whiskey Golf clear to taxi to holding point zero eight, QNH 1010."

I appreciate that this exchange of messages can be very confusing to those not used to it so I explained to Julia that I had checked with the control tower that they could hear us and that they had said it was okay with them if we waddled over to the end of the runway to await further clearance and that the QNH figure should be set on the altimeter so that it would accurately indicate our height above sea level.

Julia glared at me. I was obviously being patronising again. I decided to ignore Ms Hamilton for the rest of the trip. If possible. We arrived at the end of the runway and turned into wind. I wound the engine up to check that its several functions were all in order. It all appeared to be fairly satisfactory so I gave the flying controls a little wiggle and ensured that my passenger had her seat belt done up and that the door was locked. I announced to the tower that we were ready for take off,

"Whiskey Golf, Oostende," the tower replied, "you are clear to line up and take off, right turn after take off, surface wind is zero six zero at twelve knots. Call Approach on one two zero decimal six when airborne. Good day."

"Whiskey Golf right turn after take off and one two zero decimal six. Good day."

I taxied out onto the runway, set the directional gyro and started the take off procedure in one smooth, flowing professional manner. The engine bellowed at full power, the speed increased and I applied a little rudder to keep us on the centreline. Seventy-five miles per hour and I smoothly pulled the airplane off the ground. Brakes on and off again to stop the wheels spinning in the well and up came the landing gear at my command. Very smooth, Very competent. So why didn't she look impressed. After all, Charlie only gets to fly because he owns the bloody flying school. After him, I must have seemed like perfection. Why, incidentally, was Julia craning her head to look at the ground? The airport buildings were on her side of the airplane. Who or what was she looking for? I changed frequency to Approach and said hello. The answer to my question came over the radio.

"Whiskey Golf, Oostende Approach, you are required to land again immediately."

I ignored it.

"Okay, Julia, why?"

"Do we have to land? I'd really much rather that we didn't."

"I can delay them for a bit, but I have to know why. Now."

Julia was reluctant and I suspected that it was not only Charlie who had upset the local constabulary. The radio was persistent.

"Whiskey Golf, do you read Oostende Approach?"

I was running out of options so I went for the dead radio as a delaying tactic. I pretended that I was not receiving control's transmissions. After all, sometimes when you change frequencies, radios can act up a bit but it's never safe to assume that your transmitter has also failed. In that event, you transmit "blind", more or less saying that even if I can't hear you, I'm going to speak to you anyway. Rather like conversations with my ex-wife. I told Approach that as I could not hear them, I would change to Brussels Airways frequency, transmit blind and listen out. I hoped that Julia and Charlie hadn't done anything so bad that the Belgians would send up their Air Force to shoot us down. I hadn't been shot at in an aircraft for several years and I had no wish to re-live the experience.

"Right, Julia, what have you done and to whom and who is after you?"

"It's not what I've done, it's what I've got. It's not important who is after me but I assure you that it's not the police if that's what you're thinking." I told her firmly that I was not in the drugs business, the arms business, the illegal immigrants business nor any business which would lead to strife between the Authorities and myself so she better bloody well come clean or I'd turn this contraption around and she could take her chances with the Belgians, She might even get to share a cell with Charlie.

"My business is photography. What I have is a roll of film containing some very interesting shots of a rather important politician."

No further details were forthcoming but the indications were that governments might fall, economies might crumble and seas go dry unless the film was destroyed. Julia was not going to destroy the film. No way. No way at all. I gently pointed out that a career in blackmail tends to be rather brief and is not even pensionable. Hot denial.

"What's in it for you then?"

"Money. Lots of it."

She mentioned a tabloid newspaper for whom she did freelance work and who had expressed an interest in the extra curricular activities of the particular politician in question. The public have a right to know, didn't I agree. I didn't and said so. Icy glare. I pondered upon the probable length of time before Oostende managed to convey to Brussels their urgent desire to see us again and I decided to take a chance and give my world famous impression of a dodgy radio.

"Brussels, good day, Arrow Whiskey Golf with you, departed Oostende at…three thousand estimate mid channel at five five……ood day." All this was accompanied by the intermittent release of the transmit button giving a perfect (I hoped) example of a faulty radio. The reply from Brussels came back through my headset.

"Whiskey Golf, Brussels, be advised that your transmission is breaking up. Say your message again."

"Brussels Whiskey Golf, transmitting blind, Nothing heard, initiating radio failure procedu……proceeding as flight planned."

Julia, realising that I had no intention of returning to Oostende and the welcoming arms of the Single European Constabulary, started to look more at ease.

"We're not home and dry yet," I told her. "I need to know just how much of the brown and smelly is going to hit the fan when your pictures get to the streets."

"Well," she replied with a smug grin, "It's not going to win many friends at Westminster. Probably cause a by election."

I considered the implications of becoming involved in political intrigue. The cons far outweighed the pros.

"Julia, I don't want any part of this."

"Don't worry, you won't be involved."

"I'm bloody well involved already,"

Since I had ignored an air traffic instruction to return to Oostende and had claimed to have had a radio failure, which claim might well be refuted by the technicians, the customs bods at Southend would probably be all over the aircraft like a bad rash, we would probably both be strip searched, hopefully together (another icy glare) and because they would know by then what they are looking for, they would certainly find the film. This opinion was patently as popular as a fart in a spacesuit. Her features returned to Olympic glumness.

We droned on without further conversation until some time later the familiar coastline of Merrie England came into view. We were exactly on time. I announced this fact to my passenger and was rewarded with a "so what" look. I pointed out the various features of interest as we passed them, such as the rolling fields of Kent, the Medway, London, Tilbury the Thames even Canvey Island without raising so much as a glimmer of interest. I was wasting my time. At long last, the pier at Southend appeared through the haze and I decided to revive the radio.

"Southend, Whiskey Golf, do you read?"

"Whiskey Golf, Southend, read you fives. Thought you had radio problems."

"Southend, I assume that it was the headset. I found another one and this one seems to be okay—ahh, we're fifteen hundred feet over the pier, request right base for zero six."

"That's approved, Whiskey Golf, you're cleared to finals, no other traffic, call finals, QFE one zero one one."

"Whiskey Golf, rog."

I switched out the primitive autopilot, thanking it for its help and swung the little airplane into an elongated S turn to position us for our final approach to runway zero six. I expertly fiddled with the various knobs and switches to prepare the aircraft for landing. As we descended and the runway assumed its rightful place in front of us, I checked and rechecked as always, the several things that must be done to ensure a bloodless landing.

"Whiskey Golf, finals for zero six," I told the tower.

"Whiskey Golf, clear to land, surface wind zero three zero at ten."

What a wealth of information can be contained in just two cryptic sentences. I had informed those responsible for the dignified and orderly flow of traffic within the boundaries of their jurisdiction that I had positioned my aircraft in such a way that I was in precisely the correct position for landing on the correct runway and they had told me that, as far as they were concerned, it was safe for me to do so, and that, on landing, there would be a slight tendency for us to be moved to the right by a small amount of crosswind.

I made the appropriate alteration to our heading to ensure that when we landed, it would be on the nice black runway rather than on the nasty green grass to the right. I had a very swift re-check of the really important things like wheels down, brakes off, fuel, engine, flaps, prop in fine pitch and so on then gently raised the nose to reduce the airspeed.

Whiskey Golf settled on the runway with a gentle chirrup and was instantly transformed from a tolerably graceful airborne creature into a rather ungainly lumbering ground vehicle. I reminded myself that this transition was preferable to getting out whilst still airborne.

I got permission from the tower to leave the runway at the intersection and was told to park in the customs area. As I shut the engine down and switched off all the airplane's little functions, I was amazed to see that we were not surrounded by a detachment of the SAS nor even by the Essex Police Force. Nobody seemed interested. I submitted this observation to Julia for her consideration, She displayed a mixture of relief and curiosity. Patently, this was unexpected.

We passed almost unimpeded through Customs, immigration and air traffic and I invited my passenger to have coffee in the airport lounge. She accepted but had to make a phone call first. From my seat,

I could see that she was engaged in a very animated conversation after which she slammed the phone down in such a way that two elderly passengers bound for Jersey got airborne with fright three hours before departure. Julia returned to the table looking like a very unpleasant Cu-Nim. (Pilot talk for thundercloud.) I gently enquired as to what, if anything, was amiss. Ms Hamilton was spitting teeth as she told me that a certain political party had done a deal with her editor, the effect of which was that the photographs that she had taken so much trouble to produce would not be published either then or at any time in the foreseeable future.

Her discourse on this topic contained several generalisations about politics, politicians and political parties as a whole, and she cast some doubt as to the marital status of her editor's parents. I spotted a Club member stuffing a quarter pounder into his face and beckoned him over. I gave him Whiskey Golf's keys and asked him if he would be kind enough to return the aircraft to the flying club, leaving me clear to pursue the chase.

"Would you like to eat?" I ventured.

"I have to get back to London," she said, 'but thanks anyway, and many thanks for your help. I hope you don't get into too much trouble."

"Perhaps another time then?"

"Perhaps."

I walked with her to the car park where she laid claim to a current model Toyota. To my great astonishment, she leaned forward and gave me a quick kiss on the cheek, then started the engine and drove away.

I would have preferred at this time to relate that I went back to my Porsche, but instead I have to say that my transport was a tatty, rather elderly Ford which was, of course parked at the club, which was, of course a two day walk. Or at least it seemed like it by the time I got there. After a short wrestling match and a few well chosen words, I got the engine started and headed for the shambles of a place I called home. It's at times like those that I debate the wisdom of having simply walked away from the creature comforts of my former home to escape the daily traumas of existence with my ex. I suppose I had made my bed and now I was going to have to lie in it.

Alone.

16

Trial Lesson

The alarm on my watch started going off at seven-thirty. It was the sort of alarm which, if you didn't respond to it in milliseconds, got really shitty and increased in volume until, if it hadn't been such a hassle to get it off my arm, I'd have given it a really good throwing across the room. I settled for shutting it off and debated the possibility of getting up. I had a hangover which would probably have provided enough power to get a seven forty seven off the ground and, for God's sake, my teeth itched. I got out of bed and carefully set a dead reckoning course for the coffee maker. After some careful deliberation, I concluded that it was Thursday and that I was booked to fly with Terry again. I further concluded that such thoughts are not the stuff of which good days start and I postponed further mental processes. The coffee machine gurgled contentedly while I shaved and we both completed our appointed tasks at the same time. Two cups of Colombia's second favourite export later, I was starting—just starting—to feel like rejoining the human race. By the time I had dressed and had two more cigarettes, I was almost ready to face the day. Almost.

Just for once, the car forgot that it was supposed to have the early morning judders and behaved normally on the way to the airport. I pulled into the club car park at eight fifteen and lurched into the clubhouse. I filled in my logbook for the previous day and set fire to the end of another Marlboro. Hardly had I settled in the chair when the phone started demanding attention. I wondered who the hell was awake at this time in the morning.

"Flying club," I snarled into the thing.

A disembodied female voice asked for me by name.

"Yeah, you got him." I replied, totally ignoring the requirements of both grammar and syntax.

"It's Julia, Julia Hamilton, remember?"

How could I forget the ice maiden. After all she was the reason that I did terminal damage to a bottle of supermarket bourbon last night. Play it cool, Al.

"Yes, of course. How you doing ? Recovered from the trip?"

"I think I would like to learn to fly. Do you think that's possible? Could you fit me in sometime?"

"Yes, Julia, no problem at all. When would you like to come over?"

She told me she was free today but supposed that we were all terribly busy. I assured her that for her, I was never too busy and suggested that she got here as soon as she liked. I could almost see the arching of the eyebrows but we settled on eleven thirty. Terry was booked for an hour at nine so that would give us enough time for a preflight briefing.

Terry was, of course, late. His lesson was more straight and level practice. Regrettably, his perception of straight and level differed from mine by about twenty degrees and five hundred feet, but somehow we managed to complete the exercise without excessive loss of bodily fluids. Even his third ever attempt at a landing only dislodged two vertebrae. If I hadn't been so eagerly anticipating the arrival of my next student, I would probably have admitted, somewhat grudgingly that our Tel was making progress. I debriefed him and suggested kindly that he might care to read up on the stalling exercise because we would probably be trying that manoeuvre fairly soon as he was doing so well.

Terry glowed with pride. When a guy of his size glows it's about the candlepower of an airfield arc lamp. He was celebrating with a cup of coffee (four sugars) and a Danish or three when Julia's car pulled up outside. I swear that when she got out, a British Air Ferries Dart Herald stopped dead halfway down final approach. She was wearing what the night clubs would call "smart casual" but wore it like an advertisement in a fashion magazine.

Sally-Anne Bone, our only female instructor and given to quite unladylike comments remarked with considerable venom that wasn't that Charlie's bloody girl friend? What the bloody hell did she want? Didn't she know that the poor sod was still in bloody jail? I assured her that Julia was well aware of our Charlie's spot of bother and further offered the information that she was booked for some flying lessons. Yes, with me. No, I hadn't disgraced myself. Sally this is as much of a surprise for me as it will be to Charlie when he gets out. If he gets out. Yes, I suppose I should start looking for another job.

Sally-Anne was reputed to have a soft spot for Charlie. So had all of us in his employ. A very deep bog in Ireland seemed appropriate. However, since our lord and master tried to get inside her jeans at the airport Christmas thrash, Sally was firmly convinced that Charlie was her own, exclusive properly.

Julia came into the room and predictably, all conversation ceased. This happened momentarily on the entry of any stranger, but when someone who looked like she did came in the effect was doubled. Always the gentleman, I showed her to a nearly clean table, grabbed two cups of coffee and launched into the 'Flying is safer than driving" routine. I carefully neglected to mention the Twin Otter that didn't quite get airborne from a dirt strip in Malawi and cost me a front tooth and a significant amount of dignity.

She listened to me attentively. Were it not for certain other physical considerations, I might have concluded that she was all ears. This was getting decidedly dodgy. I was starting to get the wrong sort of ideas. Ideas which did not concern flying. With a superhuman effort I concentrated both active brain cells onto the mechanical contrivances which make flying machines perform and I finally pronounced that we might as well get airborne and see what sort of pilot she'd make.

Terry stalled in mid-chew as we passed. With his mouth half open, he was not a pretty sight. Our aircraft that morning was a Cessna 150. Julia accompanied me on the preflight inspection, known as the "walk round". I pointed out the various items of interest such as the elevators, rudder, flaps, engine, prop and so on and made learned pronouncements on the function of each. The Cessna is a high wing two seater and has an entrance door on each side. I opened the left hand door and watched as she climbed in. I shut the door and went round the front and got into the right hand seat. Maps and clipboard stowed in the door pocket, I manfully resisted the urge to help her with her seat belt and contented myself with checking her door and seat position. I quickly carried out the internal checks and ran through the starting sequence. The Cessna shook as the Lycoming engine burst into life. I looked across at Julia and grinned.

"Ready?"

She smiled back at me,

"As I'll ever be."

We put on our headsets and I fired up the radio.

"Southend Tower, Golf Alpha Victor Alpha Papa, good morning."

The tower acknowledged and on my request, authorised us to taxi to the holding point of runway two-four. I invited Julia to put her feet on the rudder pedals and "follow through" as I released the brakes and increased the power to move us off the grass and onto the taxiway. As we proceeded along the tarmac, I pointed out that steering is accomplished by use of the brakes and not by the yoke and invited her to try. To my surprise, after a few seconds of weaving, she had ft almost nailed down and we arrived at the widened part at the end of the taxiway known as the holding point. I turned us into the wind and applied the brakes. I ran the engine up to 2,400RPM and showed her the power checks and the other essential items necessary before committing ourselves to the air.

The tower asked if we were ready.

"Alpha Papa, affirmative." I replied. 'Checks complete and ready to go."

"Roger, Alpha Papa, you're clear to line up and take off, maintain VFR, not above two thousand feet. QFE is one zero one four, QNH one zero one six, surface wind two two zero at ten."

"Alpha Papa, one zero one four—one zero one six, maintain VFR, not above two thousand,"

I explained that "VFR" means that we had to have good visibility and that we were not allowed to go into cloud. We carried out the final checks of harnesses and hatches. We checked that we had full and free movement of controls and taxied onto the runway, lining up on the centreline. On my invitation, Julia placed her hands and feet on the controls and I opened the throttle. The Cessna leapt forward and I showed Julia how we had to compensate for the tendency to swing against the torque of the engine by pressure on the right rudder pedal. As we accelerated I pointed out the airspeed indicator's gradual approach to seventy miles per hour, at which point we would be in a position to leave the ground.

Actually, a Cessna can be hauled into the air at a speed considerably less than that but it's a lot safer and smoother to stay on the deck just that little bit longer. If you still have some deck left. Not at all like Malawi where I was still very firmly on the ground as the far end of the runway hurtled past.

When we reached flying speed, I pulled firmly back on the control column and we were flying. When we were climbing smoothly and I had the controls trimmed, I stole a glance at my student and noted that she looked relaxed and comfortable. Together, we swung the Cessna round to the right and settled on a heading that would take us to the training area.

"Just keep things exactly as they are for the moment" I told her. "We'll continue to climb to fifteen hundred feet and have a try at some straight and level flying."

She looked across at me and smiled. Today was definitely not an ice maiden day. We arrived at our chosen height and I re-trimmed the aircraft for level flight. I showed her that, hands off, the Cessna would not fall out of the sky or try any other life-threatening manoeuvre. I suggested that she experiment gently with the controls—a small amount of forward pressure on the yoke would lower the nose, a slight back pressure would raise it, turn the wheel slightly and the wing would drop and the airplane would start turning.

I have to say that nobody ever gets it right first time but Julia came as close as I'd ever seen. By the end of forty-five minutes or so, she could not only maintain straight and level but could also get us back to that state after some fairly drastic instructor induced departures.

I noted with regret that our time was almost up. I announced that we'd better be getting back and I helped her to point us back to the airport. She flew confidently while I did my Captain America bit on the radio and got us cleared to downwind right hand for runway two-four. I took over the controls and flew us round the pattern and lined up on the runway. Cessna makes an airplane which lands really sweetly and with Julia following the control movements we touched down smoothly and taxied back to the club.

As we drunk our post flight coffee she asked me what the next stage was. Was there anything she had to buy? What about logbooks? Didn't you have to have a logbook? And textbooks? I explained in my best "one thing at a time" voice that, yes, all of the aforementioned were useful and necessary but the next step was to have a medical by one of the Civil Aviation Authority approved doctors who knew which bits to prod, count, listen to and measure. By chance, I told her, one of our club members was appropriately approved.

It's a funny thing how you can feel somebody looking at you even when they are behind you. I was getting just such a feeling and I could tell by the intensity that it was Sally-Anne. I turned around and become the recipient of a withering glare that bounced off my Top Gun aviator sunglasses and killed the club's tame cheese plant. Sally-Anne was patently displeased. The subject of her displeasure was not likely to remain swathed in mystery. It seldom did. She was, however, cut off in mid glare as the phone rang. I should say, in fact, that the club phone did not ring. Not "ring" as in clear as a bell. Not "ring" as in gentle musical tones. Not since the last "first solo" celebration when the new first solo pilot and I gave it swimming lessons in the washing up bowl. Backtracking, then, the phone issued a disjointed series of clicks and half-hearted pings. Sally picked it up. As if by magic, her expression softened as she listened. After a little while, she replaced the receiver.

"Al, can I have a quick word?"

I excused myself and followed her into the flight planning room.

'That was Charlie. You better get her ladyship off the premises before I bring him back."

"Back? I thought he was still banged up. He got seven days, didn't he?"

"He got out last night and got a commercial into Luton this morning. I'm going to Luton to collect him. He's hopping bloody mad with you and her and anybody else who gets in his way."

I asked her how she was going to Luton. She told me she was taking the Arrow. I told her that she'd never find Luton and anyway the Arrow had got difficult things like a variable pitch propeller and wheels that go up and down, All jolly good inter-instructor banter. I returned to the table to issue the good news. I cannot, in fact, ever recall having actually seen a hair turn but this piece of good news did not cause Julia to turn one. She appeared unpreturbed and we discussed the various aspects of her proposed transformation into intrepid aviator and I helped her fill out the club membership forms.

Sally-Anne emerged triumphantly from the planning room festooned with an assortment of "going flying" accessories and grabbed the Arrow keys from the board.

"Luton is somewhere over that way," I said, pointing helpfully somewhere to the North. She stormed out of the club and Julia and I watched as she did the walk round at a brisk trot and taxied out toward the runway.

Funny things, airplanes. There are wise men, steeped in book learning and more than capable of doing all the hard sums necessary to design flying machines. They will confidently, and without fear of contradiction, tell you that, with a proper combination of gross weight, air temperature and density, engine power, propeller efficiency and so on, a certain aircraft will only be able to climb and fly at a given maximum speed. These facts are chiselled in stone. They do not take into account the enhancement in performance generated by the sheer mental power of a predatory female who has scented her prey. In Sally-Anne's hands, therefore, the Arrow hurtled down the runway and leapt into the air like jet fighter. The wheels were up and she was turning on course for Luton almost as soon as she was off the ground.

Julia did not seem to be at all concerned by the imminent return of her former partner and responded eagerly enough to my invitation to a spot of lunch. We got in her car and she drove out to a nearby pub where we could, coincidentally, see the whole airfield. We ordered a simple but wholesome meal and washed it down with toxin-free mineral water. OK, not quite true. We had hamburger and chips and a coke, but in these days where healthy eating has overtaken religion, you have to pretend sometimes. At least we had a side salad. Whilst we watched a procession of aircraft landing and taking off our conversation turned to personal matters. I discovered that Julia had a seriously interesting background, Sailing, for instance, and horse riding, both of which require the same gentle but firm measure of control as an aircraft. Hence the quick understanding of the flying controls. Hamilton was, I learned, her maiden name to which she reverted after a rather messy divorce from a property developer to whom she had been married for four years.

As we talked, I became aware of activity at the end of the runway. There was an airport fire tender parked at the holding point and another at the intersection of the two runways. There was also an ambulance and two airport police vehicles, all with pretty blue flashing lights.

"There's an emergency of some sort." I said.

"What sort of emergency?"

"Probably an aircraft with an engine out or something." I stood up. "I'd better get back to the club just in case."

I hurriedly settled the bill, hoping my credit card would not bounce and we exceeded the speed limit all the way back. As we got out of the car, I noted that the club had emptied and that everyone was watching an aircraft on final approach.

"It's the Arrow," one of the members said.

I looked at the approaching aircraft. I was reluctant to believe that it was our Arrow. Our Arrow had a wheel on each side and this aircraft had one only. I was aware that Ted, the CFI, had joined us. He told me that shortly after take-off Sally had an engine problem and decided to come back home. On her first crack at getting down, some observant guy in air traffic noticed that the landing gear was one wheel short of a full set and told her to go round again. Sally had then tried to re-cycle the landing gear and the end result was that not only did the offending leg still flatly refuse to lower, but the other side failed to retract, Add to this a by now, extremely sick engine and an airfield full of spectators and our Sally-Anne had got her hands full to capacity.

We stood and watched knowing that there was nothing whatsoever that we could do. The approach looked pretty good, though, she was as slow as she dared to go, perhaps just a little high even with a failing engine, but there was plenty of runway The Arrow crossed the boundary fence with the engine sounding like a sick cat and, as I wondered if (given my track record) any request to the CFI in the Sky would be effective, Sally plonked the good main wheel on the ground. For a little while things seemed to be pretty good. As the speed dropped, however, the legless wing sank towards the ground and Sally was holding it up with a massive amount of aileron. Things now started to happen very quickly. The aircraft started to swing tothe left and we saw the rudder kick hard over to the right in an attempt to keep the thing straight. There was an eruption of grass and dirt as the left wingtip dug into the grass at the edge of the runway. The tail came up as the noseleg decided that it had had enough. The prop and engine did a neat bit of trench digging and the whole assembly shuddered to a grinding halt. The airplane was immediately surrounded by the emergency vehicles who had been chasing it down the runway. The guy on the foam gun on top of the fire tender was ready to turn the whole scene into a Christmas card when we saw the door opening and Sally climbing out.

She walked a little way from the wreckage and stood to attention facing the crowd. She gave a Shakespearean bow then crumpled to the ground. She was immediately surrounded by medics but was clearly refusing to submit to their ministrations. She did, however climb into the ambulance which, to our surprise, headed for the clubhouse. I considered this most unfair because we had all run across the grass to see if we could help. The ambulance pulled up outside the club and Sally walked into the building. Before we could get back, she had re-emerged, got back into the ambulance and been whisked away.

We found that she had, however, written in the aircraft tech log.

1. Bad engine misfire.
2. Left main leg failed to extend. Unable to taxi after landing.
3. Hard landing checks required before next flight.
4. Sorry !
5. God save the Queen

17

Aerobatics

Every once in a while, aircraft designers scratch their collective heads and produce a gem of an airplane that not only flies beautifully but also looks just right. Notable amongst these successes are such aircraft as the Spitfire, the Hunter, the C47 Dakota and the Cl30 Hercules. The itchy scalp syndrome also affected the guys at Beagle Aircaft some few years ago resulting in the production of the Beagle Pup. This totally endearing little airplane is a pretty two seater, which, joy of joys, is aerobatic. Charlie had been persuaded to buy a Pup to satisfy the needs of club members who liked to spend summer afternoons upside down and as I was and still am very keen on silly manoeuvres in airplanes, I was nominated as aerobatic instructor for the club.

Julia had now been flying for a few weeks and was doing rather well and as her competence grew, some exposure to the upside down world seemed appropriate. When I made the suggestion that she might enjoy a few loops and rolls, she agreed avidly.

The day of her first aerobatic lesson was perfect. Not a cloud in the sky, visibility was magnificent and the airfield basked in the Spring sunshine, The sort of day when we used to let senior officers go flying alone. I had advised her to wear something comfortable and not too fussy. As always, when she arrived at the club, she looked positively stunning. She was wearing tight black jogging pants that did little to conceal her shapely rear end and a black roll neck sweater that not only did not conceal but accentuated her very shapely upper section. Her long hair was swept back and tied up and she had bought a pair of very expensive aviator sunglasses that completed the image.

As carefully as I could, under the circumstances, I went through the pre flight briefing, conscious of the fact that most of the male club members were almost drooling until at last we gathered up our various bits and pieces and made our way out to the Pup. Julia carefully and efficiently carried out the walk round and we climbed on board.

"It's very important to make absolutely sure that everything is properly secured," I said. "Last thing you need at the top of a loop is to be hit on the back of the head by a loose fire extinguisher." Julia smiled across at me.

"Whatever you say, captain, sir. You're the boss."

I made a mental note that this was going to be the day that I finally gather up enough nerve to ask this beautiful woman to come out with me. If she's still in this compliant, co-operative frame of mind, she might even agree. Checks completed, I started the engine and fired up the radio.

"Southend Tower, good morning, Golf Alfa X-Ray November Sierra, how do you read?"

"November Sierra, good morning, loud and clear."

'Tower, November Sierra, two on board, request taxi for the acrobatic area,"

"November Sierra, cleared to the holding point runway two four, QNH one zero one one."

I repeated the clearance and the QNH figure and opened the throttle to get us moving. I gave control to Julia and whilst she got used to the controls on the Pup, I set the altimeter to the QNH figure. Instead of a control wheel like Cessnas and Cherokees the Pup has a stick like a fighter aircraft and I showed Julia how to hold it for best control in the air.

"Gently but firmly, with the fingertips," I told her. "You'll get much more sensitivity that way."

She looked across at me and ever so slightly raised her eyebrows and a hint of a smile flickered over her face. I blushed furiously and fussed around with the map for a few seconds until my composure returned.

We arrived at the holding point and I carefully checked the engine performance and the two magnetos.

"Right, everything checks out just fine so let's get airborne," I said. I had discussed speeds with her earlier so I felt confident in Julia's ability to get us off the ground without undue incident.

"You do the take off then. Get us a clearance from the tower whenever you're ready."

She carefully did the pre take off vital actions then pressed the transmit button on the top of the control column.

"Tower, November Sierra at the holding point of two four," she said. "Checks complete, request take off clearance please."

"November Sierra, Tower, you're clear to take off, surface wind two three zero at ten, right turn when airborne, maintain VFR, not above one thousand feet initially Enjoy your flight ma'am."

"November Sierra, thank you."

I reminded her that one is supposed to repeat all clearances and instructions to avoid any possibility of confusion but that the tower people were probably overcome by her voice anyway so on this occasion it probably didn't matter. We turned onto the runway, Julia smoothly opened the throttle and the Pup bounded down the runway and Julia lifted us into the air.

"That was excellent, I told her. "Climb straight ahead to five hundred feet then come right to three three zero."

"Three three zero it is, captain!"

We climbed steadily upwards as the large reservoir appeared before us. The tower handed us over to Approach Control who cleared us up to two thousand feet. I told Julia to level off when we got there.

"Remember the sequence, attitude, power, trim," I said. Julia nodded and concentrated on her heading and speed. A bit of a perfectionist, she seemed to allow herself no leeway from absolute precision. I hoped that she wasn't working so hard that the pleasure was taking second place. Well, we would see about that!

We reached two thousand and in accordance with the Gospel According to Bramson (the author of a splendid series of pilot training manuals) Julia lowered the nose and reduced the power in a commendably smooth manner. As the speed built up, she rolled the trim wheel forward until the Pup would fly level, hands off."

Very nicely done," I told her. "Now we're almost in the aerobatic area, we'll carry out some safety checks." She nodded. "We'll check height, engine, fuel, and security and also make sure that we're in the right place and not about to hit anybody. Are your straps tight?"

She indicated that they were indeed tight and that her door was properly latched.

"Okay," I said. "We'll have a good look round to make sure there's nobody else near us. This will be a tight turn in both directions. We'll go your way first. Have a good look across and down and holler if you see another aircraft. Ready?"

"Ready!"

I moved the stick firmly to the left and pulled back firmly as I increased the power to the engine. The Pup dropped her left wing and we felt the tug of the G force as we pulled round in a steep turn. When we had completed the 180 degree turn, I levelled the wings then pointed the right wingtip at the ground for a steep turn to the right.

"My side is clear of traffic," I said. "Did you see anybody your side?"

"No," she replied. "All clear. That was brilliant."

"There's much better to come," I told her. "We'll just tell air traffic what we're doing then we'll do it." I pressed the transmit button. "Approach, November Sierra, we're in the aerobatic area, we'll be operating between two thousand and ground level for a while, give you a call when we want to come home."

"November Sierra, roger, you are clear up to two thousand five hundred if you wish. Listen out on this frequency Have fun!"

"We will, thanks. November Sierra standing by." I turned to Julia, "We'll do a stall first to get you used to the feel of the aircraft then a barrel roll, then a loop going into a stall turn and another loop to finish off. You may get a little disorientated but try to relax and follow through on the controls. If you feel ill, tell me and we'll stop immediately. Okay?"

"No problem, go to it, flyboy!"

I closed the throttle and firmly pulled the nose of the airplane up and pointed out the rapidly decreasing airspeed. The controls became very sloppy as they became less effective. The whole aircraft shuddered as the pre stall turbulence shook the wings then, for a second or two, we seemed to stand still. Suddenly, the nose dropped and we were pointing at the ground again. I pushed forward on the stick and opened up the throttle. As the speed increased, I pulled us out of the dive and back to level flight.

"All right, Julia?"

"Yes, fine. That was good."

"Okay, now a barrel roll."

Nose down, watch the airspeed build to 115 then stick back and to the left, a bootful of left rudder and over we went, As the horizon rotated in the windshield I saw Julia's eyes open wide and an expression of delight lit up her face, All the way round and power back a little. Push the nose down again, watch the speed increase to 120 then smoothly back on the stick until we were pointing straight up. Full power and a little more back pressure on the stick and a glance to the side to make sure we were straight as we became inverted at the top of the loop. I pulled the throttle closed as the nose dropped and dived straight at the earth, now filling the windshield. Full back pressure and the ground slowly moved down to where it should be. Once again the tug of G force as we pulled out of the dive and just as we levelled out, there was a most pleasing bump as we passed through the air that we had made turbulent at the start of the loop.

"A perfect loop," I remarked, "even though I say it myself!"

"I would have expected nothing less," Julia replied. 'That was great"

"Now, a stall turn," I said. "You may find this a little less pleasant,"

Down went the nose again. I checked the altimeter. We still had fifteen hundred feet. More than enough. Speed back up to 115, back on the stick until we were pointing almost vertically upwards. Bit more power and slight forward pressure to keep us pointing upwards then chop the power and just before we stop moving, hard left rudder. The Pup obediently sliced sideways through the air and her left wingtip pointed to the ground. We swung through 180 degrees vertically and once again the earth filled the windshield. As we pulled out of the dive, I let the speed build again to 120 and took us through another loop. As we levelled out at the bottom, I looked over at Julia.

"Well, what do you think?"

"That was, without question, the most exhilarating ride of my life!" she exclaimed "Can we do some more?"

"Sure," I replied. "Climb us back up to two and a half thousand and you can have a try on your own this time."

Julia competently set climb power and as we clawed our way back up, I ran through the speeds and procedures. With very little intervention and only minimal talking from me, she performed a pretty good barrel roll and a passable loop,

"I think I'm hooked!" she said.

"I think I'm hooked as well," I replied. "Would you like to go out for something to eat tonight?" She turned to me and I got the full impact of her big eyes,

"I was beginning to think you'd never ask. Yes, I'd love to go out with you. I'll have to change first but I have some stuff in the car. Can I change at your place?"

"Sure, no problem," I said. I took the controls. "I have control." I opened the throttle wide and as the speed increased pulled us through a flick roll and two consecutive loops and three turns of a spin to celebrate. The lovely Julia actually wanted my company. We turned towards the airport.

"Southend Approach, November Sierra," I said.

"November Sierra, go ahead."

"Southend, November Sierra, exercise complete, fifteen hundred feet and we are RTB."

"November Sierra, roger, maintain one thousand five hundred feet and call field in sight, join downwind right hand for two four, QFE one zero zero nine."

"November Sierra roger," I said and repeated the rest of the clearance. Julia was curious about RTB

"It means Returning to Base," I told her. "Did you understand the rest?"

"I think so, fly at one thousand five hundred until we see the airport then they want us to fly downwind, parallel to the runway with the runway on our right."

"For somebody with only a grand total of four hours instruction, you are certainly getting a good handle on things."

"Excuse me! Four hours and twenty minutes plus what we do today!"

I realised that Julia had indeed made very good progress. She was doing safe take offs and could very competently fly straight and level, climb and descend without a problem and carry out nicely balanced turns, Also she had completed quite a few circuit patterns without a problem. I wondered whether this was the day to let her try to put the bird on the ground unaided. A first landing is always a bit of a drama, Nothing you do appears to work as you expect. Every control input takes forever to take effect and external influences happen at the speed of light. One second you are going down like a dropped grand piano, the next, you are floating along, fifty feet off the ground and the little beast resolutely determines to stay in the air despite your valiant efforts to the contrary. On these early landing attempts, the final reunion with the runway is usually interesting, very occasionally dangerous and always nerve-racking. Especially for the instructor who must exercise restraint and allow his student to continue his attempts to transform airplane, runway and instructor into unrecognisable piles of smoking debris.

My train of thought was interrupted by Julia who was pointing out that the airfield was now visible and that it appeared to be exactly where we had left it.

"Tell air traffic, then," I said. "You're the pilot." She smiled at me and pressed the button.

"Southend Approach, November Sierra, we have the airfield in sight."

"November Sierra, roger, call tower now on one one nine decimal seven, good day."

I switched frequency for her and told her to carry on.

"Southend Tower, November Sierra......er...she lapsed into an uncomfortable silence. 'What am I supposed to say now?"

"The first thing to do is take your finger off the transmit button." She snatched her hand away as if the button was red hot. I grinned at her.

"Don't worry. We've all made unintentional broadcasts like that at one time or another." I pressed the switch. "Tower, November Sierra with you at fifteen hundred feet, four miles Northwest for landing."

"November Sierra, Tower, descend now to one thousand feet, join downwind right hand for two four, QFE one zero zero nine."

"November Sierra, down to one thousand and join right hand for two four, roger."

I reduced power and talked Julia into the circuit. As we settled on the base leg, the bit where you approach the runway at ninety degrees before you turn onto final approach, I called the tower.

"Tower, November Sierra is right base for two four."

"November Sierra, cleared to finals, number one."

"November Sierra, thank you."

Julia's first attempt at landing could not be described as faultless, She drifted way off track and got too low requiring a burst of power to stop us landing on the railway some five hundred yards short of the runway. However, after a landing rather bumpier than I would have preferred I had to admit that at least there was no blood and that the Pup would fly again.

During our post flight coffee, she chattered like a schoolgirl about how much she had enjoyed the experience and when could we do it again?

"You really should concentrate on the basics for a while," I counselled. "Aeros are a lot of fun and teach you to handle all kinds of unusual situations, but maybe we ought to work on your landings first."

"Whatever, but that was amazing."

I turned the conversation to another, more pressing matter,

"I have three more lessons to do today and then I'm free," I said. "Are you going to hang around, go into town or what?"

"I'll probably go shopping.

"Where are we going tonight?"

"Unless you'd prefer something else, I thought that a steak house might suit,"

"That would be good. I love steak."

I handed her my keys and wrote my address down.

"You might as well go straight to my place when you're finished," I said. "I should be back around four."

"I'll be waiting."

"I'll count the minutes."

The three lessons lasted for an eternity but at last I shut the last engine down for the last time, delivered my last after flight chat and made the last entries in the tech log.

"See you later, folks!" I shouted over my shoulder as I left the club doing about Mach 0.8. It was already four fifteen and I hoped that Julia would be waiting for me. As I screeched to a haft outside the house, the front door opened just a crack. I pushed it open and went inside,

"I hope you don't mind," said Julia from behind the door "I took a shower and borrowed one of you tee shirts."

"*Mi casa, su casa*" I said, exhausting my supply of Spanish. "My house is your house," I translated helpfully in case the significance should be lost. She pushed the door closed behind me and reached up to put her arms round my neck, She tilted her head back and her mouth found mine. I could feel the attraction of dinner slipping away fast but Julia pulled away from me and announced that really nice girls don't flounce around in other people's houses dressed only in a tee shirt. Not if they want to stay really nice girls. With that, she disappeared into my bedroom, firmly closing the door behind her.

"*Only* a tee shirt," I thought.

In a little while, she called out that she was now "decent" and should I feel inclined to chat whilst she applied her make up I was to feel free. "Decent" apparently meant the addition of underclothes as she was still wearing the tee shirt. We conversed intelligently on aeronautical matters for some time but I was becoming aware that time was pressing somewhat and that I also needed to get changed. I mentioned this fact and Julia inquired as to whether her continued presence would cause me embarrassment. Hell, no! I'd been round the block a few times and I was pretty quickly down to underwear myself. I had a swift shower and shave and returned to find Julia looking at a framed photograph.

"Who is this?" she asked.

"Just a girl I knew in Africa," I said. "Long time ago,"

"She's lovely, what's her name?"

"Adelle, short for Adelaide," I replied. 'She was a stew with Air Malawi."

"Did you screw her?" surprisingly forthright

"Umm…eventually."

"Did you love her?" I hesitated, unsure of what to say. "Hey, it's all right," she said. "You are allowed to have a past, you know. Anyway, I think you did love her and I also think she was a lucky girl. You're a nice guy."

"I think you're nice too."

"Let's get dressed," Julia said. "I'm starving." I picked up the phone and called a cab.

The meal was wonderful. Enormous steaks with all the trimmings and optional extras washed down with two bottles of red wine. Julia and I chatted non-stop as if we had known each other for years. She looked devastating in the soft candlelight. We rounded off the meal with coffee and Tia Maria then I asked the waiter to call a taxi.

As we were driven back, Julia leant her head on my shoulder.

"You realise that I've had far too much to drink, don't you?" she said. "There's no way I'm able to drive back tonight. Any suggestions?" I saw her smile in the dim light.

"If you don't mind sharing, you could stay at my place until you've sobered up. Shouldn't take more than three or four days."

"That's settled, then. Are you going to make love to me?" Forthright again

"If you play your cards right!"

Julia did play her cards right and I woke the following morning to the clink of bottles as my neighbours put their rubbish out. Julia was cradled in my arms, her long hair flowing over the pillows. I kissed her gently and she stirred.

"Whassa time?" she murmured sleepily.

"Almost eight thirty," I replied.

"Don't be difficult. Morning or night?"

"Morning."

She opened her eyes fully and a smile spread over her face.

"One of my most favourite times. Now where did we get to before you fell asleep?"

"If I remember correctly it was you who fell asleep after the third time, or was it the fourth?"

"Fourth. And we fell asleep together."

Her hands were doing indescribably wonderful things to me and further conversation seemed unnecessary as she moved to sit astride me. Around eleven, we got up and took a long shower together then reluctantly got dressed.

"I have a photo shoot in London tonight so I have to get back. Can I come back here when I'm finished? It'll be quite late but if you have a spare key, I'll try not to wake you."

Without a word, I retrieved a key from an empty ashtray and handed it to her.

"Can we go flying again tomorrow?" she asked.

"Sounds good to me. I'll organise an airplane. Hurry back, Julia."

"I will. Be sure, I will." She kissed me and was gone.

18

First Solo

Most people recognise the fact that the life of any human being is marked by milestones representing occurrences of significance. First day at school would, I suppose, be classed as a fairly significant incident. Ones first sexual encounter would presumably be another. In any event, these milestones are forever etched on the brain and are unlikely to be forgotten.

We aviators have an opportunity for another huge milestone denied to others. That particular milestone is the first time that you fly an airplane with nobody else on board. Ingeniously, this episode is known as "First Solo". This flight is usually of a very short duration, about seven or eight minutes but to the various participants who are firstly, the new solo pilot, secondly, the flying instructor who authorised the first solo, thirdly, the rest of the airport population, this period of time is perceived from the viewpoint of the participant. The third category can go to hell. They only want to be on the scene if there should be any blood. As far as the instructor is concerned, the flight lasts for about two hours. As far as the pilot is concerned, it lasts only twenty seconds. All three categories breathe a sigh of relief when it is all over and the triumphant pilot taxies back to the aircraft park. It says much for the standard of flying instruction that I truthfully cannot remember a serious incident happening during a first solo. Of course there have been slight mishaps. For instance, one first solo decided to go rather a long way round the circuit and got totally lost. He had to be rescued by gentle messages from air traffic who were able to overcome his rapidly increasing panic and got him to point the airplane in the right direction. To the student's great credit, he performed an absolutely faultless approach and landing.

I vividly remember my own first solo, although it is by now several thousand flying hours in the past. Aircraft have been a passion with me since as far back as I can remember and I had a fairly good understanding of the principles of flight at twelve years old, gained from the construction of countless flying model aircraft. The theory came to me quite readily and a subsequent exposure to gliding at sixteen years of age gave me experience in the control of the real thing. It was not, therefore entirely due to aptitude that my first solo took place at a very early stage in my instruction. It happened one afternoon when I had just undertaken a very grueling forty minutes at the mercy of Flight Lieutenant Mann who had made me perform a practice forced landing after take-off, a series of stalls and several touch and go approaches (we used to call them 'circuits and bumps' in those days). We rolled to a stop outside the line hut and Mann told me to keep the engine running. To my amazement, he climbed out of the aircraft and fastened the straps in the back seat.

"I have to go for a pee," he said. "Just take it round the circuit once and then come back here and stop. Don't break anything, lad. I'll see you here when you get back down."

The practice is not to allow the student to think for too long. I certainly had no time to become concerned.

"Okay, sir, once around the circuit then back here." I looked around for obstructions and seeing none, opened the throttle of the Chipmunk and carefully taxied out to the end of the runway. I requested and obtained permission from the Airfield Controller to line up and take off. I realised that I was a little nervous and counseled myself that I had already done this many times with the long suffering Mr. Mann in the back seat. We were lined up with seemingly miles of black runway in front of us. My brain was telling me that I should not open the throttle. It reasoned that it would be far better to just turn around and say the aircraft was u/s (unserviceable) than to finish up in the inevitable smoking heap on the ground. Discretion, it told me, was the better part of valour. My body, however, had other ideas. My left hand grasped the throttle lever and smoothly pushed it forward. My feet on the rudder pedals prepared themselves for the "Chipmunk lurch" as power came on. My right hand was feeling for the flying controls to come alive as the airplane bounded happily down the runway. My brain gave up the uneven struggle and agreed that as we were now committed to going flying, we might as well make the most of it.

As we soared into the air, I felt totally elated and could not resist bursting into song. I firmly believe that every student sings loudly on first solo. It's something to do with being totally out of reach of every other living thing on the planet. There is a feeling of absolute freedom and that nothing else matters. I sang a filthy song with some really bad words and I sang it loudly putting special emphasis on all of the bad words, simply because nobody could hear me.

I started my downwind turn. I carefully checked that I was the right distance from the airfield, that the height was correct and that everything about the aircraft was in order. Right, the downwind checks. Rather professionally, I considered, I carried out the downwind checks which ensure the best chance of a safe arrival. Things like making sure there is enough fuel in the tank in use, that the brakes are off, and that the landing gear (or undercarriage as the RAF call it) is in the best position for landing (i.e. not retracted.) It is also considered kindly to look after the engine by making sure that there is no carburettor ice. Better communicate, I thought.

"Tower, four four echo downwind," I called.

"Four four echo, cleared to final approach, no other traffic."

"Four four echo, roger."

I realised with a bit of a shock that whilst I had been on the radio I had allowed myself to gain some two hundred feet and had lost about twenty knots of airspeed. I corrected the deficiencies and determined to concentrate on the basics—*aviate, navigate, communicate.* in that order. The big test was now looming very close. Could I get this thing back on the ground in one piece. My mentor had told me many times that a good landing can only be made from a good approach and that, if the approach was sloppy, then an equally sloppy landing was inevitable. I would get this approach absolutely right. Nearing the end of the downwind leg, everything was looking reasonable, and as I turned base and started to lose height I imagined that I could hear my instructor behind me.

"A little on the fast side, laddie, remember, speed is controlled by raising or lowering the nose......watch your altitude......still a bit fast......aim for a descent rate of five hundred feet per minute......that's better......start your turn onto finals now...nice gentle bank...reduce power a little more, you're a bit high...runway nicely under the nose......that's a good rate of descent......keep it there......check harnesses one more time......height is fine now...that's good positioning...keep it coming......almost there......" Then, suddenly, the rear cockpit was empty again and I realised that this time I had to get it right on my own. I would not let Mr. Mann down.

"Four four echo final approach" I told the tower.

"Four four echo is clear to land. Surface wind is zero eight zero at ten knots"

As the runway threshold slipped under me, I closed the throttle and started to feel for the ground. I gently pulled the stick back to raise the nose for the flare. The Chipmunk settled on the ground on her two main wheels, and the tail wheel only a couple of seconds later. It had been a text book landing. I don't think I managed that degree of competence in a Chipmunk landing ever again. In a taildragger (an aircraft with a tail wheel) the landing is never over until the aircraft has come to a complete stop, so I maintained a high degree of concentration all the way back to the line. Flt/Lt Mann was waiting for me as I taxied in. He puffed furiously on his pipe and said

"Got it back in one piece, then. Seen worse landings too. Well done laddie."

"Thank you sir."

"Enjoy it ?"

"Very much."

"Now you can start learning to fly. Don't get the idea that you're something special just because you're the first one on the course to solo. You all have a lot to learn."

"Yes, sir, I know that, but I'll never have another first solo. That was special."

Mann gave me a curious look. He knew exactly how I felt.

"True, laddie, very true."

For precisely the same reasons, I knew exactly how Julia was going to feel in a very short time. She had done all the circuit training, the practice forced landings, the stalls, the spins, the control of the aircraft at low speeds and all of the other stuff. There was an obvious next stage and I knew that she was studiously avoiding asking the question for fear of getting an answer which she didn't want. As I was not the CFI, I was not in a position to make a decision about her readiness for going it alone, so I found an excuse to get Ted to fly with her. It was a perfect day. The sun was shining from an almost cloudless sky. There were a few small white cumulus clouds strategically placed by God to give the sky a bit of interest. A gentle wind blew from the west and visibility was unlimited. They took off in the Pup which had become a firm favourite with Julia and disappeared off to the northwest. After about an hour, the Pup returned and taxied in.

Ted got out and I watched with a mixture of pleasure and trepidation as Julia taxied the little aircraft back towards the runway. Ted came and stood beside me.

"She's pretty safe. A few rough edges but pretty safe. Don't worry, she'll be fine."

We watched as the Pup held short of the runway for the power checks then briskly taxied onto the runway, paused for a moment then full power and she was rolling. That was the longest take off of my life. Eventually, the airplane lifted gracefully off the ground and was climbing. I rushed over to one of the Cherokees and switched the radio on. The radio took an infuriatingly long time to warm up but then, at last, I heard Julia call downwind. Not a tremor in her voice. Not a trace of nerves. The Pup trudged slowly downwind. Surely she was flying too slowly. The circuit was taking forever. There has to be something wrong with the aircraft. A drop in power, perhaps.

"Stop fretting, Al," said Ted. "She's doing fine."

"I suppose so. Why is she flying so slowly ?"

"She's not. Actually her control of speed is very good. It's because you have a personal interest that you're seeing problems that don't exist. She's almost on base leg already."

Sure enough, we watched as the Pup turned and headed towards the airfield and a very short time later made another turn to line up with the runway.

"Tower, November Sierra is finals for two four" said the radio.

"November Sierra clear to land, surface wind is two four zero at twelve knots." At least there wasn't a crosswind. The Pup crawled slowly towards us, the wings rocking slightly in the turbulent air. From where I was sitting, it looked pretty good and I remembered the advice which I had been given all those years ago about a good landing coming from a good approach. This was certainly a good approach. Julia seemed to have the whole thing neatly sewn up. She crossed the runway threshold and as she neared the ground, the nose came up and the Pup neatly touched down. They rolled to the intersection of the runway and turned off.

"Tower, November Sierra's clear of the runway," said Julia.

"November Sierra, roger. Well done, that was a nice landing."

I breathed a huge sigh of relief and turned to grin at Ted.

"I think I was holding my breath for the whole of that circuit," I said.

"Like I said, you fret too much. She's pretty good." Ted started walking back to the clubhouse. I climbed out of the Cherokee and followed him. For some reason it seemed to be important that I didn't meet Julia at the aircraft as she taxied in. I suppose that would have insinuated some doubt as to her ability to get back safely.

With a burst of power, the little Pup turned off the taxiway and onto the grass of the club aircraft park. I watched from the window as she shut down and climbed out. She walked across the grass with a huge smile on her face. As always on these occasions, when she entered the club, the assembled multitude burst into spontaneous applause. If there had been more of us, it would have been quite deafening. As it was, four people can make quite a loud noise

"I did it!" she exclaimed, throwing her arms around me. "I went solo!"

"Yes you did," I said. "Congratulations. You realise that the drinks are on you tonight. You have to have a party in the club. It's a rule. Usually a barrel of beer for the instructional staff at least."

"I'd love to throw a party. Can we organise some food?" She paused. "I must call my dad. He'll be thrilled." Somehow it had never occurred to me that Julia had parents.

"Where do your folks live?" I enquired.

"Wroxham," she replied. "It's near Norwich."

"Yeah, I know where it is. I used to have some friends in Norwich. We could fly up to Coltishall if you like if you want to show off to your dad. The Air Force will let us land at Coltishall if we get prior permission"

Julia went into the office with Ted to get her logbook signed. In that logbook there was a grand total of eight hours and ten minutes. By any standards, that was a significant achievement. Julia emerged from the office smiling broadly.

"Ted says we can have one of the Cherokees all day Friday if we want. For the trip to Norfolk. If you like." I did some fast thinking. With a little bit of negotiating, I could arrange to have Friday off. It meant that some other poor soul would be lumbered with Terry, who had now logged over sixteen hours but still hadn't gone solo, primarily because of his insistence on landing twenty feet off the runway. Maybe a change of instructor would do him good. Sally-Anne had recovered from the accident in the Arrow and was back in the air. Maybe Sally could fly with Terry. I went into Ted's office.

"I know what you're thinking," he said. "Terry. I nodded. "I think I can persuade Sally to take him."

"That's what I thought. Might do them both good."

"Okay then, I'll ask her and if she agrees you can take Friday off."

"Thanks, Ted. Appreciate it."

Sally had been flying with another of our students and was just landing. Several minutes later, she walked in, said hello and busied herself with the tech log. Ted came out of the office.

"We have a new solo pilot, Sally."

"Have we? Who?" She looked round. "Have you gone solo, Julia?" Julia nodded, smiling. "Brilliant. Well done. When's the party?"

I felt somewhat bemused. Was this the same Sally who breathed fire every time she thought about Julia? Perhaps she's had a change of heart, I thought. Logically, it could only be because Sally no longer considered Julia as a rival in her never-ending quest for Charlie. That had to be it.

"Can you spare a minute, Sally," said Ted. "I'd like to discuss one of the students with you." Sally followed Ted into the office. When she emerged some minutes later she took me to one side.

"Look, I don't want you to get the wrong idea, but Ted and I think that Terry would benefit from a different instructor. If you don't mind, I'll fly with him on Friday. I know Terry doesn't want to fly with anybody else but maybe a different approach might get him landing properly."

"No, I don't mind at all," I said. "In fact, I could take the whole day off and go up to Norfolk with Julia."

"Quite an item, you two," Sally said. "Is it serious?"

"Sally, have you ever known me to be serious about anything?"

"Not until now."

So there it was. Sorted. Now just the party to organise. We spent the rest of the day buying nibbles and little sausage rolls, took the food back to the club then we went back to the flat to change.

"Tell me about your parents," I said.

"Not much to tell really. Dad retired last year and my mum does accountancy work from home for local business people. They have a house right by the river."

"What did your dad do?" I asked.

"He was in the Army. The Royal Engineers."

"So you were probably brought up on the move all the time?" I asked.

"We moved around quite a bit but we spent a long time in Germany. I went to the English School near Aachen," she said. "Then we came back to UK when dad had to go to the Falklands." She looked thoughtful. "My mum spent the whole time worrying herself into a heap. I somehow knew that dad would be fine. He's indestructible." She headed for my wardrobe. "What shall I wear? I suppose it's likely to be a rowdy affair?" I nodded.

It's your party," I said. "Wear what you like. My choice would be jeans and tee shirt."

Julia stepped back from the wardrobe and pulled her sweater over her head and stepped out of her jogging bottoms. "If you stand around looking like that," I remarked, "we're going to be late." She crossed the small room and put her arms round my neck.

"Don't care," she said. "Take things as they come. That's what my dad always says."

◆ ◆ ◆

We weren't really very late for the party but when we arrived, the clubhouse was already almost full but we eventually reached the bar, admittedly after a fair amount of pushing and shoving. Julia announced to a chorus of cheers that she was in the chair and of a mind to provide refreshment for everybody. I looked around. Everybody appeared to include almost the whole of the airport staff, most of the British Air Ferries crews and several spies from other clubs. I was shocked at the cost of the round but Julia took it in her stride. Photography obviously paid well. I was about halfway down my first Jack Daniels when Sally appeared at my elbow.

"Well done, Julia," she said, "that's the easy bit over with. You proved that you are an aviator, now you learn to be a pilot."

"That's very profound, Sally," I remarked, "but also very true. There are hundreds of people who blast around the sky in all sorts of airplanes who never really appreciate flying. They're too hung up on flying by the numbers."

"Coming from you, that's a joke," Sally retorted. "All you airline people run your lives by numbers."

"By numbers, ONE" I said in a military manner, raising my glass to the pre-drink position. "TWO!" I drained the contents. "THREE!" I passed the empty glass to Sally. The evening progressed and grew noisier and rowdier. Predictably, the real reason for the celebration was replaced by more and more outrageous flying stories and dirty jokes. One of the air traffic girls, a tall well built blonde, was propositioned by the rather drunk proprietor of an air taxi company with an interested audience of two flying instructors, one of whom was her husband. Although no actual blows were struck, the tense situation was relieved to a great extent when she threw her drink over her admirer, then took her husbands beer and poured it over his head and walked away. A spontaneous round of applause broke out as the two protagonists shambled over to the bar and bought each other drinks.

At around ten thirty, Julia detached herself from the group of impossible flying storytellers and joined my dirty joke group.

"I've just ordered a taxi," she whispered in my ear "I think we should make a move."

"That sounds like a good idea," I said. "If I have much more to drink I'll have to swim home." Julia looked concerned.

"Are you going to be all right?" she asked

"Right as rain," I assured her.

Some twenty minutes later, we were whisked across town to my official residence. I must confess to some slight difficulty in locating the keyhole but Julia, bless her, discovered where it had been moved to and let us in.

Alas, the liberal amount of Kentucky gold that I had consumed put bedroom frolics way out of reach so we simply collapsed into bed and fell into a deep sleep.

Friday morning dawned bright and fair. A perfect summer day and the two-day hangover that had followed Julia's party had finally disappeared. We performed our ablutions, snatched a hasty breakfast and set off for the airport.

"We'll make this one of your mandatory cross country navigation exercises, I think," I said. "That means you do all of the work, all of the flight planning and all of the flying, and I get to relax and enjoy the view."

We arrived at the Flying Club and Julia settled down with her new flight computer, an assortment of chinograph pencils, a navigation rule and the low level chart for South East England. I checked the printed forecast, which we had collected from Air Traffic on the way in.

"The two thousand foot wind is three one five at fifteen knots," I announced, proving that I could interpret the seemingly meaningless jumble of figures that constitute an aviation weather forecast. Julia entered the figures onto her computer. By today's standards, the term computer seems somewhat overstated. The device in question is more of a circular slide rule upon which one makes pencil marks and turns a circular panel to discover, for instance, the effect that the wind will have on the required course. Julia worked quietly for a little while, then passed the result of her efforts over to me.

"We should fly a heading of two nine five magnetic. Airspeed of one twenty will give us a groundspeed of one ten. I've put down three en-route checks and the trip should take one hour and five minutes."

I cast an authoritative eye over her calculations. "Looks okay to me. Let's go check the aircraft." I signed the flight authorisation sheet, Julia gathered up her map and flight log sheets and we walked out to the flight line. I untied the picketing ropes whilst Julia carried out the walk-round.

"It looks in pretty good shape," she said. "Might even fly."

"Right, then Captain, climb aboard," I said. She carried out the checks with a practised efficiency, her long slim fingers dancing gracefully over the switches then looked over at me.

"Clear to start?" I looked outside.

"No-one in sight my side."

"Nor mine." She opened the small window. "Clear prop!" she shouted and turned the key. The engine grumbled a little at being woken so early but finally burst into life.

Julia made the radio calls and we taxied out to the runway. There wasn't much activity on the airport at that time in the morning but as soon as we had arrived at the holding point and completed the pre-take off checks, the early morning BAF arrival from Belgium announced his presence.

"Lima Tango, Southend, are you ready for departure?" asked the tower.

"Lima Tango affirmative," I said.

"Lima Tango, cleared for immediate take-off, climb on runway heading to 1,000 feet, surface wind three zero zero less than five knots, break, BAF 3311, continue your approach, one Cherokee departing to the West."

"Lima Tango is rolling, maintain runway heading to 1,00 feet," said Julia.

We turned smoothly onto the runway and Julia opened the throttle to full power. As we lifted into the air, I said "That was very competent, but I wasn't too happy about you being rushed like that."

"I have to learn to fit into traffic sometime, It's like learning to drive and trying to get away from a road junction."

"Anyway, you handled that very well."

The flight proceeded without incident and the route checkpoints turned up roughly where she had predicted. As the Suffolk countryside rolled under us and Norwich appeared in the distance, Julia suggested that now might be a good time to make some radio calls.

"Go ahead, then," I said. "You're the pilot."

She keyed her mic. "Stansted Approach, Golf Lima Tango, 2000 feet abeam the radio mast at Eye, estimating Norwich zone boundary on the hour."

"Golf Lima Tango, contact Norwich Approach, now on 119.3, good day."

"With Norwich, 119.3, Golf Lima Tango, thank you, good day."

I was totally relaxed as Julia confidently flew the aircraft and made the radio calls to, firstly, Norwich and then RAF Coltishall who, in the custom of the Air Force constantly gave her headings to fly until the runway at Coltishall appeared in the windshield.

"Coltishall, Golf Lima tango has the runway in sight," said Julia.

The RAF controller cleared us to short finals. When Julia called on the final approach, she was told to confirm three greens. She looked across at me.

"Confirm *what*?" she asked.

I keyed my mic. "Golf Lima Tango, gear down and locked." I looked across. "The Air Force hasn't yet accepted that there are still aircraft without retractable landing gear, and as most RAF pilots try to land wheels-up at some time they always remind pilots to make sure their gear is down. It's a standard radio call." The controller cleared us to land and we flew down towards the runway making corrections for the crosswind. Julia pulled the power off as we crossed the threshold and held the nose up until the Cherokee settled onto the ground with a happy little chirrup from the mainwheels.

"Nice landing," I remarked. "Hope everybody was watching!" The radio came to life again.

"Golf Lima Tango, take the first exit and park beside the Dominie."

"Golf Lima Tango, roger," said Julia. She looked at me. "What the hell is a Dominie?"

"It's what the RAF call the HS125. That twin jet thingy over there."

We parked and shut down. Inside the control tower, we paid the landing fee and borrowed a phone.

"Hello mum, it's me. We're at Coltishall." She listened for a while, then, "No, at the RAF base. Can you or dad pick us up?" A pause "Don't know, I'll ask." She turned to the corporal behind the desk. "Can my dad bring his car onto the base?"

"'Fraid not, miss, but I can get you transport to the main gate."

"That would be great, thanks." She took her hand away from the mouthpiece. "Mum, we can get a lift to the main gate. We'll wait for you there………Okay, bye then." She put the phone down. "About ten minutes"

The corporal called through to another office.

"Just taking the Cherokee pilot to the main gate, Harry." He took a key from a hook on the wall. "Right then, this way. Did you lock your aircraft, miss?" Julia replied that she had and handed him the key. "Just in case we have to move it. Sometimes happens."

Some minutes later, we were standing by the main gate enjoying the morning sunshine. A dusty blue Volvo station wagon swung off the road towards us. Julia straightened up and walked towards the car. The passenger door swung open. Julia dived inside and warmly hugged the driver. The lady who got out was quite simply an older version of Julia. A striking woman whose appearance belied the fact that she must have been at least fifty or so, walked over to me and held out her hand.

"Hello, I'm Angela, nice to meet you at last."

"Nice to meet you too."

I climbed into the back seat and we set off towards the small town of Wroxham. Julia and her mother chatted non-stop for the whole ten minutes, neither one appearing to stop for breath nor listening to what the other was saying. We pulled into the driveway of a substantial house on the outskirts of the town. A man wearing gardening gloves and a white Panama hat emerged from a rose bed and walked towards the car.

"Daddy!!" Julia shouted. They wrapped their arms round each other and hugged as if they had been apart for years.

"Hello," he said to me, taking off his gloves and holding out his hand, "I'm Don Hamilton. Please excuse the attire. Damn greenfly. Place is infested with them. D'you know anything about roses, Al?"

"Only that you send them to girls," I said. He chuckled.

"Not a gardener, then. Me neither but Angie thinks that all retired people should garden. Only do it in self defence. I would have the whole place paved if I had my way." He waved a hand towards the house. "Can I get you a drink?" He looked at his wife. "Suppose it's too early for a real drink but perhaps coffee? Or tea?"

"Coffee would be great thanks," I said. "Beautiful house."

"Costs a bloody fortune to maintain. Like the situation though. Do you like boats?"

I replied that, next to airplanes, boats were my favourite form of transport. He beamed.

"When you've had your coffee, I'll show you my pride and joy. Got a mooring round the back. That's why we bought the place. Right on the river."

Julia and her mother chattered incessantly as they fussed around in the kitchen with coffee. Eventually, Julia came back outside carrying two mugs.

"Here you are then," she said. "Black, two sugars." She handed me a mug and beamed at me. "Has he tried to show you his boat yet? If he hasn't, he will." She reached up and kissed me on the cheek. "Don't bore him, dad, I need him awake on the way back in case I get lost." She grinned at me and retreated towards the kitchen. Don and I walked round to the rear of the house. Moored on the river was a beautiful thirty-something foot yacht. Gleaming white with a dark blue trimline and gleaming brass fittings.

"There she is. A picture, isn't she!" he said proudly. "She has a big Volvo inboard engine as well for when there's no wind." He stepped nimbly onto the deck. "Come on board, I'll show you round."

I climbed onto the boat and Don opened the cabin door. The saloon was spacious and well laid out with leather cushions and polished wood trim. He sat down and put his coffee on the table.

"So," he said. "Tell me about yourself."

"What would you like to know?" I asked. "There's not much to tell."

"How long have you and Julia known each other? She had quite a bad time with her ex and her mother and I were glad that she finally stopped moping around and started getting out again."

"Aren't you going to ask me if my intentions are honourable or something?" I asked with a grin.

"If they are, then you must be a saint," he laughed. "Just don't want to see her get hurt again."

I assured him that I had absolutely no intentions of hurting his daughter or anyone else for that matter, but that neither Julia nor I felt ready to settle down yet. That appeared to be the correct answer.

"What time do you have to go back?"

"We should get back before dark really, they need the aircraft first thing in the morning."

"That's a shame, still we'll have lunch and then maybe a trip up the river. How does that sound."

"Sounds good to me," I replied.

"Or perhaps Julia and you can go up to Coltishall on the boat and Angie and I will take the car up to the King's Head. We can have lunch there then take you two to your aircraft and I'll take the boat back."

"Sounds even better. Lunch is on me."

"Won't hear of it! You two are our guests."

An hour later, I was lying flat out on the polished timber of the deck, listening to the slap of the waves on the hull and the muted rumble of the big Volvo diesel as Julia steered us upstream. The four miles or so from Wroxham to Coltishall takes about an hour by boat. The really intelligent amongst you will be able to calculate that the speed, therefore is around 4 mph. This is the main attraction of a holiday on the rivers and broads of Norfolk. It is impossible to hurry anywhere and the result is a totally relaxing vacation. By the time we had reached Coltishall, I was so relaxed that I was fast asleep and I woke to the spectacle of Julia mooring the big boat single handed and with very considerable skill.

The afternoon passed very quickly in the company of these very pleasant people and it was very soon time to return to the aircraft. Don announced that as he had drunk far too much to drive home, he would return the boat to Wroxham and we would proceed to the airfield under the chauffership of Angela. Surprisingly, the Air Force had managed to avoid either losing our aircraft or loading it with nasty munitions, and we prepared for departure to the gentle rural noises of fighter aircraft thundering overhead. True to form, the Air Force gave us a departure groundcrew who stood at the front left hand side of the aircraft with a fire extinguisher until we indicated that we were ready to leave.

"Your folks are really nice," I remarked as we lifted off the runway.

"Glad you liked them," Julia said. "My mum thinks you're sweet." She grinned widely.

The return trip to Southend was marked only by a wide diversion around Stansted to avoid an untypical degree of traffic. In those days, that meant two aircraft within an hour. When we had landed and were rolling along the runway, I realised that Julia had exercised the same degree of natural talent when flying as she had with the boat. There was clearly a great future ahead of her in the Aviation Industry, I reasoned and said as much.

"I want to learn to fly so that other things become possible," she told me later on that evening as we partook of the joys of the Bombay Curry House. "I really wouldn't want to live the sort of life that you lead, never knowing where you're going to be tomorrow or how long you're going to be away." She paused and looked thoughtful. "I don't know how you see the future, but I fully intend to continue my career along the present lines. I would like to become a good pilot but I belong behind a camera."

"So settling down with me isn't an option?"

"'Fraid not, sweetheart. But I do love you lots and we do have a lot of fun, don't we!"

I reflected that my chosen career did not appear to encourage long and fruitful relationships. Still, we *were* having a lot of fun and there was no question of a termination of the relationship, at least not in the short term.

Eventually, we went home to my apartment and had fun. A lot of fun.

19

The Circus

Sometime after I had returned from Malawi, having discovered that the salary of an assistant flying instructor was insufficient to support my required lifestyle, I got a flying job with a fairly reputable cargo airline. They operated antiquated CL44 aircraft, mainly to Africa and Hong Kong, carrying whatever cargo could be found. The CL44 was a development of the Bristol Britannia, which for many years was the passenger workhorse of the Royal Air Force. The CL44 however was longer, heavier and had Rolls Royce Tyne engines. She carried a crew of two pilots, a flight engineer, sometimes a navigator plus one or two loadmasters and an aircraft technician referred to as the "flying spanner" in case we went unserviceable away from base. Unusually, access to the freight bay was gained by swinging the tail assembly complete with fin, rudder and tailplane to the side, thereby exposing the complete cross section of the airplane. When pressurised in flight, air pressure used to escape through the seals of this swinging section and the flight engineers used to carry blankets, which they would soak in water and stuff into the joint whilst in flight. Although very crude, this solution was quite effective and the aircraft, although obsolescent, gave very few major problems in service.

I soon learned not to be surprised at the strange variety of freight, which arrived at Stansted to be loaded onto the aircraft. However, there was a buzz of excitement when we learned that several of our aircraft had been chartered by a wealthy Arab nobleman to transport a complete circus to the Middle East to give a performance for his son's birthday.

Trailer after trailer, brightly painted in circus colours began to appear in the cargo area. The aircraft had been already prepared to carry the unusual loads. The heavy stuff like the big top and equipment for the trapeze artistes and the tightrope walkers was fairly easy and were loaded up without problems. As we were accustomed to carrying various species of animal, no real problems were expected. As a matter of course, we carried racehorses, cattle, pigs and police dogs so our sales office foresaw no difficulty in transporting Shetland Ponies, lions, tigers and elephants. Elephants? The engineers expressed concern about the sheer physical volume of corrosive fluid escaping from an elephant when it takes a leak. With considerable ingenuity, they lined the interior of the cargo hold with heavy gauge polythene up to head height and welded the joints with a heat gun to make a sort of giant polythene bag. They fixed one inch thick marine ply boards to the floor and covered the whole floor area with innumerable bales of peat until the stuff was about nine inches deep. It all appeared very cosy and safe.

Then the inevitable happened. One of the celebrated Stansted fogs descended on the airfield, reducing visibility to just a few yards. There was absolutely no chance of moving out, so arrangements had to be made to house the animals until the weather cleared.

The cargo hangar was completely cleared and the circus people started setting up the cages for the animals as the transit cages were too cramped for prolonged occupancy. When they had finished, we had our own private zoo and people from all over the airport suddenly found pressing and urgent reasons to visit us. It has always made me uneasy to see magnificent beasts confined in cages but I had to acknowledge the genuine affectionate bond between the keepers and their charges. The three beautiful tigers fascinated me and I spent a long time close to their cages and got into deep conversation with their trainer.

Late in the afternoon when the meteorological office had decided that the fog was going to be with us for some time, all the aircrews were stood down as we were all running out of maximum permissible duty hours. I watched with fascination as the animals were fed, marvelling at the immensely powerful jaws as the big moggies effortlessly crunched through huge chunks of raw meat, bones and all. The spectacle had attracted a fairly large and appreciative audience of engineers, aircrew, storemen and office staff who stood around making "nice pussy" comments. When the tigers had finished eating, one of them started to become very agitated and paced up and down her cage making noises like a vintage Bentley on the starting grid of a race. Thinking that something was amiss, I went to tell Sammy, the trainer who came back to the cage with me.

"She's all right," he said. "Just wants some exercise. You ever take a big cat for a walk?"

"No," I said. "Am I going to?"

He took a strong leather collar and two chains from a locker under the cage and unlocked the cage door. Suddenly the audience melted away. Fast. Very fast. The hangar had emptied of people faster than at four o' clock on a Friday before a Bank Holiday. The tiger by this time was giving the impression of one very pissed-off big cat but Sammy went into the cage and right up to her. He put his arm round her neck and stroked her head.

"He's bloody mad," I thought.

As soon as the collar was round her neck, the tiger calmed down. Sammy clipped one chain to the collar and she followed him to the door of the cage like a large amiable dog. He clipped the other chain to the collar and handed the other end to me.

"She won't pull or misbehave, but as she doesn't know you, just keep the chain tight and you'll be fine."

The idea of the two chains is to keep the animal securely out of striking distance of the handlers, the theory being that if the animal tries to attack one handler, the other can prevent it. Nice theory. I certainly did not feel confident in my ability to restrain a very large and powerful carnivore if her sights were set on an extra meal. Neither was

I sure that the slightly built Sammy could prevent the big cat from chomping through my carcass with the consummate ease that she had demonstrated at dinner.

With some trepidation, at least on my part, we walked the superb animal out of the hangar and into the fog. The moisture in the air glistened on her beautiful coat as she sniffed the air, hoping, no doubt to catch the scent of the wild Yak or Antelope which abound in that area of Essex. To my surprise and relief, taking a tiger for an evening stroll turned out to be far less trying than exercising a Springer Spaniel. At least she didn't want to dig holes everywhere. By the time we returned to the hangar, I was getting quite brave and letting the chain go ever so slightly slack. Very courageous. When the tiger was back in her cage, Sammy suggested that I help him to rub her dry.

"She loves being dried," he told me. "She'll roll over on her back and behave like a house cat. Just watch out for her feet."

Rather warily, I helped Sammy towel the animal dry. He was right. The tiger loved it. If you've never heard a tiger purr, try standing next to a big diesel at idle and you'll get the idea.

"She'll be quite happy for you to stroke her head now if you like," Sammy said. "Just below her eyes. She likes that."

After a few minutes of stroking, I was getting quite relaxed and was totally unprepared for the friendly cuff from a massive paw, which sent me sprawling to the floor.

"Told you, didn't I," Sammy chuckled. "I said to watch out for the feet."

The following morning saw the fog even thicker. The airport weather man proclaimed that the visibility would not improve for at least another twenty four hours so I spent the day playing with Sacha the baby elephant who was a most delightful creature, talking to 'my' tiger and generally getting in everybody's way and making a complete nuisance of myself. Eventually, after another night, the weather improved and the decision was made to saddle up and ship out.

All of the cats, ponies and zebras were loaded without any problems. The only blip on the horizon occurred when the elephants were invited to board their flight for the Middle East. The loading crew had decided to use the ramp normally used to board horses and cattle. The tail of the aircraft is swung open and the ramp is wheeled up to the freight bay and the top end of the ramp is held in place by quick release pins. At the top, the ramp narrows so that the cattle are admitted to the aircraft one at a time. Nobody had thought, however, to take the waist measurements of the adult elephants. Bad mistake. Sacha, the baby, always ready for a jolly game, romped up the ramp after her keeper. Mum lumbered up the ramp after her. Sacha slipped easily through the gap at the top but mum was a bit too broad in the beam and her progress in pursuit of her offspring was brought to a shuddering halt by the restriction.

There was no alternative but to bring her back down and have the ramp made wider. Regrettably, nobody had told us that elephants will not walk backward down a slope and Tania flatly refused to budge despite the threats and pleading of her trainer. To further compound matters there was not enough room to turn the enormous lady round. Eventually it was decided to call on the services of the mobile crane and the ramp was unhitched and the legs dismantled. The whole assembly was then lowered, complete with protesting elephant to the ground. Frantically the engineers widened the gap at the top and the ramp was lifted up to the aircraft. Tania was once again invited to join her flight and after some initial resistance, climbed up the ramp. A joyful mother and child reunion took place accompanied by loud trumpeting, probably heard all over the airport.

When all of the animals and trainers had been safely loaded and secured, (no—we didn't chain the trainers down) and all of the odds and ends had been loaded, the crews boarded, preparations were made for departure and engines started. On this trip to Oman, I was rostered to fly as first officer with John Akehurst as captain. As I carried out the long pre-departure check list, the loadmaster came forward to tell us that our animal passengers, the Shetland Ponies, had been safely secured in their stalls and that, as far as he was able to determine, seemed ready for take off. He complained that, like every other airline passenger in the world, they had totally ignored his pre-flight briefing regarding the positions of emergency exits and the methods of using life vests.

One by one the four Tyne turboprop engines whined into life and our departure commenced. Take off and climb out passed without incident and a little later I went back to the freight bay to find our equine passengers contentedly munching hay, apparently totally unperturbed by the sensation of flight.

The long flight to the Middle East was tedious but uneventful and our landing in Oman was only three minutes late on our estimate. We got out of the aircraft to see that the first arrival, the aircraft carrying the elephants was surrounded by very worried looking engineers Estimates of how many gallons of elephant pee could be absorbed by the peat had, apparently, been woefully inaccurate. The floor of the aircraft was a soggy swamp and it was anybody's guess as to how much damage had been done to the structure under the floor. Indeed, some of the electrics had already started to show problems. It was decided to clean out the whole freight bay and leave the doors and tail open in the forlorn hope that the heat would dry it out enough for the trip home.

As we were de-briefing, one of the air traffic people approached us waving a telex message in the air.

"Captain Akehurst?" he called.

A prerequisite for promotion to the giddy rank of captain is the ability to instantly recall ones name. John confirmed his own right to the rank by responding without a second's hesitation.

"Yeah, that's me," he said confidently. He took the flimsy sheet and read it out loud "Proceed as soon as practicable to Bahrain to await cargo. Further details follow." He sighed. "Looks like we're on our way again, I'm afraid."

We had enough duty time left to carry out the trip to Bahrain and the flight engineer and the flying spanner went off to organise refuelling and get us in shape for the trip whilst our loadmaster clucked like a mother hen as the Omani loading crew off-loaded the ponies. Our departure from Oman and the two-hour trip to Bahrain were uneventful apart from John sleeping soundly through the whole flight. I woke him up to carry out the pre landing checks and we landed smoothly which is not an easy thing to do in an empty CL44. As we taxied in, John remarked on the unusually large number of aircraft on the apron.

"If there's a lot of other crews here tonight, I feel a party coming on," he said.

We reported our arrival to anyone that seemed interested and then booked into the International in town. Another of our own crews was already there as were a Qantas crew, a British Airways crew and some people from Cargolux. None of us had to fly the next day, so a party seemed inevitable.

It was a usual hotel practice to accommodate all aircrews on the same floor so drinks and food were easily arranged. As it was predictable that this gathering of flying people would get noisy, rowdy and totally out of control, nobody was going to dress in anything other than drinking in and throwing up in clothes. Shorts and tee shorts seemed to be the appropriate dress code. That thought had occurred to everybody except of course the BA crew who turned up in dresses, blazers, shirts and ties. In fairness, it was only the girls who turned up in dresses despite the rather dubious sexual inclinations of one of the stewards. By twenty-two fifteen, (that's pilot talk for quarter past ten) the revels were approaching the rather silly level. The music was getting louder and the Qantas stewardesses who only drank to be sociable had become so sociable that two of them had crashed out in a corner hugging a fire extinguisher which had been specially stolen from the corridor. John was happily dancing with a floor mop and whispering sweet nothings into its ear. The rather pompous BA captain had expressed his disgust about the unseemly behaviour of so-called professionals and had led his crew towards beddy-byes about an hour previously.

It was clearly now the time for silly games. One of the Aussies suggested a corridor race. This traditional Australian sport, according to our Antipodean friend, involved stripping naked and running the length of the corridor and back timed against a stop watch. It seemed easy enough so we agreed. The Australian captain announced that, as he was superbly fit, he would carry out the first run to set the standard. Off came the Aussie dinner jacket (shorts and tee shirt) and he sprinted down to the end of the corridor and back. The stopwatch read twenty-two seconds. Not bad. His second officer went next and recorded a time of twenty-four seconds.

John suggested that both times seemed rather slow and suggested that I go next. I stripped off my clothes and on the signal to go, fairly blasted down the corridor to the end, counting off seconds in my head. As I reached the end, my time was certainly not more than nine seconds. Boy was I ever fast. Show those Aussies! I executed a racing turn against the wall and headed back towards the room travelling like a missile. Why did I suspect nothing? At about five seconds into my return journey I noticed that the corridor was strangely empty. At about seven seconds, I heard the door slam shut. I leave you imagine the thought of being alone, naked in the corridor of a large busy international hotel. The feeling sunk even further when the elevator stopped. The emerging occupants were the BA captain and a young flashy blonde. The captain gave a disgusted snort and flashy blonde giggled like a schoolgirl as I ineffectively tried to take cover behind a fire extinguisher. As soon as they were out of sight, I banged on the door. They let me in eventually but I have never, since then, been able to fully trust an Aussie.

20

The Dove

Much as I might have wished otherwise, my time in the air was not totally spent instructing. I was employed by the cargo airline as a CL44 pilot. On occasions, therefore, I had to drop everything and tear off to Stansted and fly to places like Lagos and Hong Kong. Technically, I suppose I should not have flown for anyone else, but the company was quite easygoing as far as moonlighting as a flying instructor was concerned.

As well as the CL44 s the company also owned two smaller twin engined aircraft, a Cessna 421 and a De Havilland Dove. The former was a beautifully equipped aircraft, the latter, an elderly rather tatty piece of aviation history. The 421 was fast, smooth and scrupulously clean. It was maintained regardless of expense as it was the chairman's personal chariot. The Dove, on the other hand, received the barest minimum of care and attention, just enough to keep the old lady reasonably safe. I loved the Dove dearly as one loves an elderly, rather dotty aunt. Together we bumbled around the skies to the accompaniment of creaks, groans and unidentifiable internal rumblings. The Dove was wont to make strange noises too.

One morning I was awakened at some ungodly hour by the insistent ringing of the telephone.

"If that's for me, let the bloody thing ring!" Julia was never at her most logical in the mornings. I picked the phone up.

"Good morning, Al," said the voice at the other end. "It's Fozzie at Stansted. Need you to do a trip in the Dove."

"What, today?"

"Yup, it's a charter. Full uniform, clean underwear and highly polished shoes." I groaned inwardly.

"What time?"

"Depart Stansted at 10.00 local to Gatwick. Load and depart Gatwick at 11.30 for RAF Leuchars in Scotland."

"Good God, that's miles away. How many passengers?"

"Only two."

"Can I take my lady friend along?"

"Don't see why not. Is this the famous Julia?"

"Yes it is."

"She's a pilot isn't she?" Fozzie asked.

"Almost," I said. "She's good."

"In that case, she can go on the manifest as First Officer. Make sure she wears something appropriate."

"We'll be there soon, Foz. Thanks."

"You're welcome. Bye."

I replaced the receiver and went to start the temperamental coffee maker Julia opened one eye.

"What's happening? Come back to bed."

"We're going flying. You can get some time in a twin."

She woke instantly. Any prospect of flying was guaranteed to make her sit up and take notice.

"A twin? Did you say a twin?"

"I have a charter to Scotland with two passengers, probably very rich or VIP. I've got you on the crew manifest as First Officer so you'll have to wear a uniform of some sort."

"Like what?"

"Wear your black trousers and one of my crew shirts and you'll be fine."

Whilst we had coffee, I found a brand new crew shirt that was too small for me but fitted Julia perfectly. She tied her hair up and with her black trousers and sunglasses looked ready to fly Concorde.

We set off in Julia's car and called into the Little Chef for breakfast. Whilst we ate, I explained some of the differences between flying an airplane with two engines instead of one.

"There's a lot more to go wrong," I said, "and any problem tends to be a little more critical. For instance, before you lift off, you have to have reached at least single engine climb speed so that if you lose an engine, you won't go back down. I'll explain a bit more on the flight down to Gatwick. You'll soon get the hang of it."

Ian Foster, the Operations manager, commonly known as Fozzie, met us in the operations office and handed me the flight briefing folder with the flight plans, weather briefing, the aircraft tech log and load manifest. He didn't spend much time looking at me but concentrated on Julia.

"Nice to meet you, I'm Ian Foster, and you must be Julia."

"Your memory's improving, Foz." I remarked. "Who are the passengers?"

Fozzie told me that our client was a very famous boxer and his wife, off to St. Andrews for a celebrity golf tournament. We sat down at the table and I scanned carefully through the various pieces of paper and explained what we might expect in the way of weather.

"There's a bit of bad weather over the Borders but it shouldn't get too nasty. We're filing for 8,000 feet so we should be above a lot of it."

We walked over to Air Traffic, filed the flight plan and read the NOTAMS—Notices to Airmen—which is a sort of airborne road report giving details of minor inconveniences like runways being closed for maintenance, Royal Flights, unserviceable navigation aids and so on.

At last we were ready to go out to the aircraft. As I carried out the externals, I left Julia inside the Dove to familiarize herself with the control panel and get comfortable in the right hand seat. The flight deck of a Dove can be best described as cozy but in Julia's eyes, compared with a Cherokee, it was probably like a 747. I quickly carried out the pre start checks from memory and called the tower.

"Stansted Ground, good morning, Golf Alfa Victor November Uniform, radio check and start up please"

"November Uniform, loud and clear. Clear to start, temperature is plus 18."

"November Uniform, thank you"

I started the two Gypsy Queen engines and watched for the pressures and temperatures to stabilize whilst we did the pre-taxi checks.

"Stansted, November Uniform ready to taxi."

"November Uniform, call the Tower now on one one eight decimal one five for taxi clearance."

"November Uniform to the tower, thanks."

Julia spun the frequency selector for me.

"Stansted Tower, November Uniform at the Terminal Building, request taxi for Gatwick, two on board." I said.

"November Uniform, Stansted, clear to taxi via northern perimeter to the holding point runway two three, QNH 1016"

"November Uniform, holding point two three via northern perimeter QNH1016."

Taxiing a Dove is rather like rhinoceros mating It is accomplished with a great deal of noise, effort and lurching and takes for ever to produce a result. Eventually, however, we snorted and weaved our way to the holding point and I ran both engines up for pre take-off checks.

"Tower, November Uniform is ready for departure."

"November Uniform, cleared to line up and take off, surface wind 245 at 10 knots."

"November Uniform, Roger."

We moved onto the runway and lined up the nosewheel on the centreline. I told Julia to take the controls.

"I'll take care of the power, flaps and landing gear, you fly the airplane." She looked at me doubtfully. "Go on, I'll talk you through it. You'll be fine." I opened the throttles and told the tower that we were rolling. As we gathered speed I noticed that Julia was very tense.

"Try to relax, you're doing fine. We're straight on the runway, the speed's coming up nicely…now, just a little bit of back pressure to take the weight off the nosewheel……little bit more……that's fine. Still another fifteen knots to lift-off speed…keep it there…now firm back pressure…more…she's quite heavy on the elevators. Pull back a bit more…bit more…right, hold it there. There you are, we're flying !" Julia grinned widely. I went through the after take off rituals of landing gear, prop pitch, boost and flaps.

"November Uniform," said the tower, "Airborne at zero five. Call London now on one two four decimal six. Good day."

"One two four decimal six thanks. November Uniform, good day." I left Julia to turn to a heading for Gatwick and called London. They cleared us to fly at two and a half thousand on visual flight rules—VFR. Time for a little instructing.

"Take us up to two and a half thousand feet on this heading" I told her, "then level off. I'll show you some of the things that you have to be aware of in a twin." She leveled off at the top of the climb and I re-set the power and adjusted the props to cruise settings.

"Lets look at what happens if one of the engines quits," I said. I reduced power on the left engine to idle. "What I've done here is taken all of the power off one engine, just as if it had failed." The Dove started to drop the left wing and tried to turn to the left because all of the power was now being produced on the right side. "You're going to need to keep us straight by using the rudder. When you do that, you'll find that all of the effort is on one leg. That way you can positively identify which engine has failed. Dead leg equals dead engine. Your left leg isn't doing any work, therefore neither is the left engine." She nodded, concentrating hard on keeping straight. "I'll compensate for the loss of power by opening up the good engine to full power which is going to make it even harder for you to keep us straight. In a real situation, we would shut off the fuel to the dead engine and feather the prop." I explained that feathering the prop meant turning the blades edge on into the airstream to create less drag. "Now adjust the rudder trim so that you don't have to push so hard."

She turned the trim wheel and started to look more comfortable as the pressure came off her right leg.

"In the event of a real engine failure, there's a lot more things that we would do. The main thing is to positively identify which engine has failed. You'd be amazed how many high time pilots have inadvertently shut down a good engine." I restored the power and re-trimmed. "How are you enjoying flying a bigger aircraft?" I asked her.

"Not much different really. This is nice"

"When we get to Gatwick, things may get a little busy but you do the flying and I'll do the rest unless you get into trouble."

We didn't get into any trouble and Julia flew the Dove competently right into the Gatwick zone when I took over for the final approach and landing. I could see that she was nervous as we took our place in a procession of landing aircraft, slotted in behind a BAC1–11 and in front of a DC8.

"When we land, it'll be a good way down the strip," I told her. "We have to clear the runway pretty quickly for the DC8 to land. He's about three minutes behind us." We landed and turned off down one of the high speed exits. The tower handed us over to ground control who told us to park at the General Aviation Terminal. When I had shut the engines down, we got out and went inside the building. Our passengers had not yet arrived, so we helped ourselves to coffee from the machine and went to get an update on the weather.

"Not much to trouble you, captain," said the weather man, blinking owlishly at Julia through his thick glasses. "Just a lot of nimbo stratus around Newcastle. Cloud base there is about five hundred feet but it tops out at about nine thousand then it's clear up to eighteen. We had a report of a bit of severe turbulence in the area as well and a Dan Air flight diverted to Manchester with an injured passenger. All in all not a bad day so far."

I collected copies of the latest weather charts and we made our way back to the lounge to await our passengers. We had only been waiting about ten minutes when a car pulled up outside and a very large man and a tiny Mediterranean woman got out and walked into the building. Both Julia and I recognized the boxer immediately and we went over to greet them.

"Hello," I said, "We're your flight crew. I'm Allen Hall and this is my first officer, Julia Hamilton." The big man stuck out his hand to Julia.

"Pleased to meet you. I'm Henry and this is my wife, Maria."

"Nice to meet you, sir," said Julia "and you too ma'am."

"Henry," he said. "Just call me Henry."

"Okay Henry, nice to meet you."

"Pilots have got a lot better looking than when I was a lad," he said, attracting an icy glare from his wife. Feeling somewhat left out, I suggested that when we were ready for departure, we could walk out to the aircraft. Whilst I did the pre-start checks, Julia fussed over our passengers with seat belts and cushions, then came forward and wriggled into her seat.

Gatwick cleared us to start up and taxi then asked us if we were ready to copy our airways clearance. An airways clearance more or less details the route and height that Air Traffic Control would like the aircraft to fly. It is important to copy all the details down correctly because the controller will ask that the clearance will be repeated to him. One of the Ten Commandments in the Controlling Industry is

'Thou shalt not trust any pilot. Nor shall ye trust anyone who setteth his foot on the flight deck of an airplane, for verily they are ignorant and can neither hear nor obey. So ye shall command any of such to repeat verbatim any clearance which thou hast given unto him.'

When I had correctly repeated the clearances, I showed Julia on the chart that we would be routing by Airway Blue Four to Pole Hill then turning slightly right to Talla and Grice.

"All airways are numbered," I told her. "Usually a colour and a number. Pole Hill is a radio beacon up in the North, and so is Talla. We'll be tuning the radio navigational aids to the beacons to keep us on track."

We got our take-off clearance and this time, because we had paying passengers on board, I did the flying and Julia looked after the radios and did the hard time/speed/distance sums. As we got farther north the ride became more bumpy and I switched on the Dove's pretence of being a real airliner—the "fasten seat belts" sign. I asked Julia to go into the cabin to make sure that our passengers had in fact chained themselves down.

"If they ask why, tell them that we're experiencing a little mild turbulence and that we don't expect it to get too uncomfortable."

In the distance, however, the sky had turned a very unbecoming shade of dark grey, stretching right across our intended track. Going round the sides did not appear to be feasible, as the forecast had indicated that the band of weather stretched from coast to coast and we couldn't climb high enough to get over the top. It seemed likely that we were either going to have to turn around or penetrate the murk and take whatever beating was handed out to us. Julia came back and slid into the seat.

"Looks a bit nasty up ahead," I remarked.

"Are we going through that?" Julia queried.

"Yes, I think so unless it gets really rough. If we absolutely have to, we'll land at Leeds Bradford but I don't really want to do that." She looked concerned. "Don't worry," I told her. "This old girl has been through a lot worse than that. Anyway, you need some time on instruments"

"I'll probably crash us."

"No you won't. Just concentrate and do what I tell you and you'll be fine."

The dark cloud was very close and now the rain was starting to patter on the windshield. The turbulence was now becoming quite uncomfortable and I double checked our escape heading for Leeds just in case it became necessary to call it a day and divert. Julia had taken the controls and was visibly tense.

"Relax, Jules, I won't let anything happen to you."

"I'm not at all sure that this was one of your better ideas."

The great wall of cloud raced towards us and suddenly, everything went dark. We were now taking quite a spanking as the turbulent air shook the airplane. I reached overhead and turned the cabin lights on then opened the flight deck door to see how the passengers were faring. To my surprise, they were both fast asleep, apparently oblivious to our rough passage. The turbulence did not seem to be getting any worse and Julia was coping very well keeping us on height and heading.

"I told you the aerobatics would help," I said. "You're doing very well."

"I don't have a clue what I'm doing," she said. "Remind me where it is we're heading for."

"A radio beacon called Talla. It's a VOR station." I pointed to the instrument. "Keep the vertical needle in the centre. If it deviates, fly the airplane towards the needle." She looked doubtful. "If the needle drifts to the right, it means that the VOR station is to our right and we have to turn to the right to get back on track."

Okay," she said, "I think I've got that."

"There's a bit more to it than just that, but that'll be enough for the moment."

As the VOR station got closer, the weather started to improve and we suddenly flew out of the murk into daylight. The VOR needle started swinging from side to side and Julia started to look confused. I explained that as we were now very close to the beacon, even small variations on track would produce a violent reaction from the instrument.

"Just ignore the needle for the moment and hold your heading. You'll see the little flag at the side change from "TO" to "FROM" as we pass over the VOR. After that, we turn onto a new heading for Leuchars." Julia turned smoothly onto our new course and I requested and received permission to change frequency to the tower at RAF Leuchars. As always, the RAF people were very helpful and polite. They steered us by radar onto the final approach for runway zero nine. Julia was doing so well that I only took over on the turn to finals. We landed smoothly and turned off the runway halfway down.

"Dove November Uniform, please hold your position," said the tower, "and await the escort vehicle."

"Dove November Uniform, roger."

Julia asked me why we had to have an escort because we could already see the visiting aircraft park over by the control tower.

"This is a front line fighter station and they're very security conscious," I told her. "They won't take a chance on us taxiing near their warbirds in case we scratch the paintwork." A Landrover with a "Follow Me" sign on the back arrived to lead us over to the parking area. As we taxied, a pair of F4 Phantoms thundered down the runway and lifted off into the now clear sky. We were met at Station Flight, the visiting aircraft park by an RAF marshaller who guided us into our allotted space and signalled me to shut down. As I shut down the systems, Julia went to supervise the disembarkation of Henry and Mrs Henry. The big man was waiting for me as I got out of the aircraft.

"That was a very pleasant trip, thanks very much." he said.

"It was nice meeting you. I hope the weather wasn't too rough for you," I replied.

"No, it was fine. Slept all the way."

We all went into the office where the sergeant in charge offered us coffee, fuel or anything else that the Air Force had to offer. I declined the fuel, but coffee would be great. A bit of up-to-date weather would be nice too, if possible. Almost as soon as he had gone to satisfy our every whim, a car pulled up outside.

"That'll be for you, sir. It's from the R and A," (Royal and Ancient Golf Club) our marshall said to Henry.

"Okay, thanks, we'll be out in a minute." He turned to me "Thanks again for the flight. It was very nice."

"My pleasure." We said our good-byes and the big man and his diminutive lady went out to their car. I used the phone in the office to file a flight plan back to Stansted then we went out to do a careful pre-flight on the Dove to make sure that nothing important had fallen off. Julia and I climbed in and started the engines. The tower gave us taxi clearance and Julia, now competent in taxiing the bird, took us to the holding point of zero nine, past the QRA (Quick Reaction Aircraft) hangars where two F4s, fully armed, hid behind the closed doors ready to go to war at a minute's notice. We held short of the runway as a pair of Phantoms landed with puffs of smoke from their tyres, then announced to the tower that we were ready to go.

"Dove November Uniform is clear to line up and take off, surface wind is zero one zero at ten knots, right turn after take off and avoid overflying St Andrews. Contact Leuchars Approach on 126.5 when airborne."

"Dove November Uniform, roger." I released the brakes and lined up on the runway.

"You have control." I said to Julia.

"I have control." She curled her fingers around the throttle levers and smoothly pushed them halfway forward. Brakes off and we rolled forward. Full throttle and we gathered speed. All systems functioning, speed coming up and I called the speeds out to her.

"Twenty knots to lift-off, start the back pressure,…fifteen to go…ten to go…more back pressure…five to go…pull back…we're airborne. Well done. Brakes on and off and landing gear coming up………three hundred feet flaps coming up and throttles back a little to reduce manifold pressure……that's fine. We're going to have to go out to sea a little way otherwise we'll be over St Andrews, so keep as you are for the moment and climb."Julia was working very hard in the still unfamiliar cockpit but despite the variety of tasks I threw at her, she was coping very well.

We reached 1200 feet and started our right turn to the south. I pulled the propeller pitch levers back to coarsen the pitch to cruise settings, settled back in my seat and lit a cigarette. There was a loud bang from the left engine and the airplane shook violently.

"What the...!" I shouted. Julia gave a little cry as she tried to correct the swing to the left.

"I have control!"

"You have control." She lifted her hands a few inches above the yoke. I pushed hard on the right rudder pedal and quickly pulled the throttle and pitch levers for the left engine to the closed position. I went through the failed engine procedure out loud.

"Identify failed engine, throttle closed, mixture to cut-off, prop to feather, hit feathering button, fuel off, ignition off, check for fire—no fire warning, full power on good engine, trim aircraft, assess situation." I paused and crushed my cigarette into the ashtray.

"Okay, we're still flying and there's no cause for alarm, but we have to turn back." I thumbed the transmit button. "Pan,Pan,Pan, Leuchars tower this is Dove November Uniform, five miles to the east, one thousand feet, left engine failure, returning asymetric, over."

"Pan Dove November Uniform, you are cleared for priority landing runway zero nine. Remain on this frequency. Break. RAFJET flight two one orbit your present position we have an emergency in progress"

"Two one standing by, break, good luck November U" said the flight leader of the two Phantoms comprising flight two one.

"Thanks fellas. Pan November Uniform now turning downwind right hand for zero nine. Aircraft is handling okay and this will be a standard asymetric landing and we should be able to clear the runway"

"Pan November Uniform, roger, clear to land at your discretion, no other traffic, QFE is 1010, surface wind still 010 at 15. Crash One is standing by, call final approach, over."

There are two points that I should clarify before proceeding. First, when there are messages over air traffic radio, aimed at different people, the messages are separated by the word "break". The prefix "Pan" is an indication that the sender is in a situation which has the potential of developing into an emergency. Emergency messages understandably take priority over other radio traffic. Okay, end of lecture. Back to the story.

I acknowledged the tower's message and concentrated on keeping the airplane flying. A Dove flies reasonably well on one engine. It loses a little sprightliness, not that there's an awful lot of that to lose, and the flying controls respond rather reluctantly. The secret is to anticipate, keep the turns as gentle as possible and keep plenty of height in the bank. When we arrived at the turning point, we were still at 900 feet and I started a gentle turn to the right to line us up with the runway with plenty of height. I eased a little flap down and gingerly started to reduce power. Once again, I talked myself through the procedures.

"Speed, ninety, flaps, set for landing, gear, down and locked,......speed still good at ninety, brakes off,...correct the drift,...speed still fine...a little bit high...about two miles to go...check harnesses..." I pressed the transmit button, "Tower Pan November Uniform, final approach."

"November Uniform, cleared to land, wind zero one zero at fifteen." Right, this is it. I smiled at Julia who returned the smile rather nervously. Reduce the speed a little and increase the rate of descent by pulling a little more power off the engine. We're going to make the runway with no problem, speed down to eighty, five hundred feet per minute descent, about a mile to go, check harnesses again

"Check your seat belts Julia."

She pulled hard at her already tight harness and nodded at me. I grinned reassuringly.

"Don't worry, we'll be fine."

Runway threshold coming up...half a mile to go...two hundred feet,...over the threshold, the black and white zebra crossing flashed by under us...one hundred feet...over the tyre marks left by hundreds of landing jets...let the speed bleed off...nose up a bit more...fifty feet...forty...thirty...nose up a bit more...twenty feet and pull back on the yoke to flare...feel for the ground...

A double bump as we landed, first the right wheel then the left. I closed the remaining throttle and let the Dove trundle along to the exit where we turned off the runway and stopped. I looked across at Julia who beamed at me.

"That was brilliant."

"Why, because I got us down in one piece?"

"You never seemed to get worried. Just did the business like you did this sort of thing every day."

"Now may not be the best time to tell you this, but that was a first time for me too and I came real close to committing a serious stomach offence when the engine blew up."

"You didn't show it."

A small tractor came charging towards us with a towing arm behind. The driver expertly backed the towing arm up to the nosewheel and he and his mate fixed it to the Dove. The driver looked up at us.

"Okay, sir?" I gave the thumbs up sign. "Brakes off then, sir." properly respectful, these RAF types. I released the brakes and we were towed back to the aircraft park looking and feeling rather sorry for ourselves. The tractor and the Dove pulled to a stop. I applied the brakes and the towing crew put wheel chocks under the mainwheels. Julia and I got out of the airplane.

"Nice landing, sir, ma'am," said the driver.

"Thanks for your help, corporal," I said. "Better than being in the AA!"

We were greeted by a flight sergeant who told us that the SATCO (Senior Air Traffic Control Officer) was anxious to see us and that the corporal would drive us across. We had a hair raising drive across the airfield and screeched to a halt outside the tower. Once inside, we were escorted to the SATCO's office.

"Hello, I'm squadron leader Dave Ward. Please sit down. Coffee?"

"Yes please," I said. "We could use it."

"You did a nice job getting down, folks. I have to say, though, that if you had burst a tyre on the runway your aircraft would have immediately become bulldozer fodder We had two Phantoms waiting to land and we don't ever allow anything to block the runway." He got up to pour coffee from a jug. "How do you take your coffee, miss?"

"Black, please, no sugar." said Julia

"Black with two, please." I added.

"I just need you to fill in a couple of forms if you wouldn't mind. You know what the RAF is like for paperwork." He put our coffee down on the desk and pulled some forms out of a drawer. "Basically, date and time, type and registration of aircraft, captain's name, and damage to aircraft, persons and property."

Whilst I scribbled on the forms, the SATCO asked Julia what our plans were. If we planned to stay at Leuchars tonight, would we care for dinner in the Officers' Mess? Presumably we should phone the company? Use his phone, he suggested. Would we like him to arrange overnight accommodation? He knew of a very nice hotel in Cupar not ten miles away. He would be delighted to make the arrangements. Typical. One smile from Julia and every male within miles is falling over himself to please her. The phone rang.

"Squadron Leader Ward." A pause, then "I see. Okay, I'll tell the captain. Thanks, flight." He put the phone down. "That was flight sergeant Watson over on Station Flight. They've had a look down the front of your engine and it seems that a piston has come through the side of the engine for a bit of fresh air. Basket case, I'm afraid."

"I'd better tell our Ops, if I may. That'll make their day."

Foz, I have to admit was not happy. Why, he demanded to know, did bloody ratty old airplanes seem determined to make his life a misery. Did I not realise that he had better and more important things to do than to rescue hapless pilots who were incapable of keeping even a toy aeroplane like the Dove in the air for more than a few lousy hours at a time. Could I not have brought it back to Stansted? Yes, why not on one engine? What did I suppose the Chairman was going to say? He supposed that I was now about to check into some outrageously expensive hotel and expect the company to foot the bill. I needn't think that the company was going to pay for Julia. That was my problem. I inquired as to whether he had finished. He admitted that he had and told us well done anyway. Now could he please speak to someone in the Air Force? I handed the phone to the SATCO who listened for a while then gave Foz a phone number and put the phone down.

"Looks like you just walk away from the wreckage," he said. "Mr Foster is arranging for a spare engine and a team to come up here to mend the aircraft. Now, may I expect you both for dinner? Say seven thirty?" I looked at Julia and nodded.

"Yes, thanks very much. That would be great."

"In the meantime, you can use the guest rooms in the mess to clean up if you wish. Or would one room do?" he asked with a smile.

"One will be fine, thanks," Julia said.

"Good, I'll get one of my lads to drive you over and I'll see you both in the bar at seven thirty."

After we had freshened up, I phoned the hotel and booked a double room and arranged for us to hitch a ride on the Air Anglia (Later to become Air UK, later still KLM/UK) flight from Edinburgh to Norwich on the following day. I figured that we could get from Norwich to Stansted easily enough.

Dinner with Dave Ward in the mess was fun. The food was excellent and Julia was sparkling company and had most of the young officers dancing attendance on her. Our taxi arrived to take us to the hotel and we reluctantly said good-bye to our host.

When we checked in, the elderly night receptionist sniffed suspiciously at the absence of a ring on Julia's finger. Julia giggled as we went upstairs.

"She's probably wetting herself at the thought of naughty goings-on in her hotel."

"She's probably more annoyed that she's only managed to get rid of one room instead of two." Just before we finally fell asleep, Julia said,

"You were brilliant."

"So were you."

"I meant today. In the Dove. And just now." I held her close. "I think you're brilliant all the time, Julia."
"Al," she said, "I think I love you."
"I think I love you too." With that, we drifted off to sleep.

21

Skytrucker

Life as a cargo hauler wasn't always fun. Like professional soldiers, a lot of our time was spent simply hanging around waiting to hear what was going to happen next. The maritime expression for our way of life is "tramping". That is, we would go where the work could be found and carry whatever cargo needed to be transported to wherever it was required to go.

Although we would sometimes wait for days in some outlandish hole for a cargo to turn up, there were also times when we were so busy that we would be away from base for fourteen days at a time, flying to our legal limits and occasionally, somewhat in excess of them. A very strong bond of loyalty existed between members of a crew and we almost ceased to have individual names and were referred to as "John Akehurst's first officer" or "Robin Dawson's flying spanner" and so on.

A captain was jealous of the proficiencies of his crew and would go to great lengths to prevent good crew members being "head hunted" by other captains. Our own spanner, a fiery red headed Welshman called Taff Evans was reputedly the best in the business and certainly had absolute empathy with the aircraft. He was also a world champion sleeper and could go into a deep sleep at will, irrespective of time, place or situation. I recall vividly that on one trip from the Middle East to Norway, carrying some military aircraft spares, we were faced with some really violent weather systems and John and I were using our combined skills to pick a relatively clear path through the storms. We had climbed to 25,000 feet to try to get over the top without success and a detour around the edge would have added another two hours or so to the trip.

We elected, perhaps unwisely, to try to penetrate the storm using our somewhat unreliable weather radar. The first ten minutes or so were uncomfortable but unremarkable and it looked as if our decision had been reasonable. Then the buffeting became worse. The aircraft was shaking like a leaf and we were being thrown around violently. It became so dark outside that we turned the flight deck lighting up full.

"It's blacker than the inside of a cow!" said John. I was more than prepared to accept his assessment as I had never seen the inside of a cow. "I think we're in for a rough ride." Hardly had he finished the sentence when one of the Heavenly Hosts turned a fire hose on the windshield. I had never before experienced such a volume of water. It battered against the glass in front of me and ran like a river over the nose of the airplane. John lowered his seat and tightened his shoulder harness.

"I advise you to do the same," he said. "I think there's worse to come."

Simon Bell, our flight engineer was anxiously scanning his gauges, looking for the first signs of trouble. So far the airplane was in good shape despite the beating that she was taking. As suddenly as it had begun, the rain stopped and we were flying in reasonably smooth air. For no reason that was apparent to me, John called for reduced power and trimmed the aircraft for a slower speed. I looked across at him with an unspoken question.

"You'll see!" he said. Some fifteen seconds later, we dropped like a stone. I watched in total disbelief as my altimeter unwound. We were going downhill like an express elevator leaving our stomachs far behind. We lost something like five thousand feet in an impossibly short space of time and the airspeed was increasing rapidly towards the 'never exceed' figure beyond which damage to the airframe is liable to occur. John was pulling back on the control column but his efforts to slow us down were to no avail and our terrifying descent into Hell continued unchecked.

At last our downward plunge slowed and we were able to restore a sensible airspeed. We were once again in an area of smooth air.

"What goes down will probably go back up," our captain said wisely. I thought of the chicken vindaloo that I had eaten the previous night and agreed with him. We flew along serenely for several minutes and I was starting to believe that John's concerns were without foundation. Without warning, the bottom fell out of our world. If we had been dropping fast before, now we were really on a bobsled to hell. Manuals, charts, coffee cups and pencils floated around the flight deck as we literally fell out of the sky. The whole aircraft shuddered and creaked and the wings and engines flexed violently as the downdrafts tried to tear us apart. There were blinding flashes of lightning and immense flat sounding booms of thunder and we took at least one major lightning strike on the nose of the aircraft. I was now totally convinced that we were all going to die, thrown to the ground like a broken toy by some huge contemptuous hand. How could any aircraft survive this appalling treatment?

Thankfully, our rate of descent was slowing and we were at last able to regain some semblance of control. Although we were still being tossed around in the turbulence, we were able to confirm that at the very least, all the engines were still with us and operating normally, all the flying controls were intact and most of the aircraft systems were intact with the exception of the radar which had fallen prey to the lightning strike. Then the hail started. We were bombarded by hailstones the size of golf balls. Millions of them. I was afraid that the windshield would be smashed. Certainly the outer skin of the aircraft was taking a beating. The noise was unbearable. When people talk about all hell being let loose, they should fly through a real hailstorm. Then they would know what they're talking about. The noise of the hail was augmented by the noise of the continuing thunder. Thunder, when heard in close proximity in an aircraft sounds nothing like thunder heard on the ground. As there is nothing to reflect the sound, the natural reverberations do not occur and the boom sounds very flat almost as if it were inside your head.

Without warning, we were suddenly snatched into a searing, heart-stopping climb. We were gaining height faster than an Apollo moonshot. The G force pushed us down in our seats and even John was starting to look worried.

"Nose down!" he shouted. "Help me get the nose down!" The airspeed was now decreasing and approaching the stall speed. The stick shaker which gives the pilot warning of an impending stall by vibrating the control column was making our arms shake violently and although we managed to correct our nose high attitude to one where we were pointing downhill, we were still going up at an incredible rate. To compound our problems, it was almost certain that we had collected a good deal of ice on the airframe. Certainly there was ice on the flight deck windows despite the strenuous efforts of the screen heaters. Simon started to express concern about his engines.

"We have a vibration on number two," he said. "Could be just ice on the prop but I think we lost a turbine blade in the hail."

"I'll live with that for the moment," said John. "I think we're going to need all the power we can get very soon."

The giant forces that were playing with us were getting tired of the game and eventually threw us out into clear air. Our frantic ascent had stopped and we were once again flying almost normally. Some two hundred feet below us, we looked down on the top of the massive cu-nim. Our altimeters read an incredible 33,000 feet, at which height, given our weight, we would not be able to prevent a gradual descent back down into the appalling weather system. We opened up all four engines to take off power and, despite the now severe vibration from the injured number two engine, we were just able to maintain our height. After an agonisingly long period we flew clear of the storm and were able to descend to a more appropriate level. As John, Simon and I breathed more easily and started to assess the damage, the flight deck door opened and Taff came through, hair ruffled and rubbing his eyes.

"It's bloody freezing back there," he complained. "Why is it so cold?" I explained that during our little encounter with Mother Nature, we had experienced severe turbulence and violent updraughts which had propelled us to the giddy height of thirty plus at which height the temperature does tend to drop just a little. Now would he please be good enough to examine the airplane and determine what, if anything had fallen off.

"What encounter with Mother Nature?" Taff asked.

John and I exchanged incredulous glances then burst into laughter. Taff had slept peacefully through the whole episode without a care in the world.

The remainder of the trip was thankfully uneventful although the vibration from the damaged engine became worse and we shut it down as a precaution. When we landed at our destination, Orland, a Norwegian AirForce base at the edge of the Trondheim fjord, we were able to see the extent of the damage. There were great dents in the skin of the aircraft caused by the hail and the radome (the black pointy bit on the nose of the airplane that usually hides the radar) had two neat holes caused by lightning strikes. Add to that the damaged number two engine and it seemed probable that we would be on the ground for at least two or three days.

The Norwegians are superb hosts. They have a very smooth and quite lethal tipple tasting rather like Peach Schnapps which they drink in vast quantities at every conceivable opportunity. Not surprisingly, then, we had some riotous evenings in the mess during which we learnt some of their mess games and taught them a few of our own. We introduced them to corridor racing which they enjoyed immensely as the Scandinavian peoples revel in mixed gender nudity, and we taught them Deck Landings. The conduct and rules of Deck Landings require all participants to strip to the waist. Two or three long tables are set up end to end to simulate the deck of an aircraft carrier. The 'flight deck' is copiously lubricated with beer and the 'pilots' run around the room with their arms outstretched making engine noises. They run towards the end of the flight deck and at the appropriate point, launch themselves into the air so that they land on their stomachs and slide the length of the tables. A good landing requires that the pilot slides the complete length of the table and stops at the end. Failure to execute a good landing invokes a forfeit. This invariably requires the offender to empty a full glass and buy a round of drinks for the assembled company. When everybody is suitably inebriated, the rules change. Each pilot selects a partner to be his 'controller'. The game now becomes Night Deck Landings. The pilot is blindfolded and runs a complicated circuit around the room, responding to instructions given by his controller who guides him to the end of the flight deck and at the appropriate moment, issues instructions to 'land'. As this process is deemed to be very simple, the other pilots and controllers shout conflicting instructions to confuse the issue. The secret of success is to be able to isolate the voice of your own controller and to be able to ignore all the others. Although this game frequently results in a little blood, I have never known any injury more serious than a cracked rib. The Norwegians, bless them, loved the game and probably still play it.

At the end of the second day, another of our CL44s landed at Orland bringing a spare engine and a team of fitters to effect repairs to our aircraft. Despite the cold biting wind sweeping off the fjord, the work was completed by three the following afternoon and we carried out an air test with about half the people on the base on board. They stood or sat in the freight bay hanging on to whatever they could find to hang on to. Totally illegal of course, even in Norway but nobody seemed to be terribly worried that there was no seating in the aircraft. As a salute to our hosts, after we had satisfied ourselves that the airplane and the new engine functioned correctly, we returned to the airfield and thundered over the base in a high speed very low level pass followed by a steep climbing turn and a short field landing. Not a comfortable procedure after a night on the Peach Schnapps.

As darkness fell, we said our good-byes and set off for Stansted with the lights of Norway sparkling like diamonds in the crystal clear air behind us. John and I had decided that as Orland was a military base, we should have a military call-sign. We had decided on something appropriate. I keyed my microphone.

"Orland Tower, this is SKYTRUCKER. We are departing your zone to the west at nine thousand feet. Thanks for your help and your hospitality. Hope to see you all soon."

"Skytrucker, this is Orland Tower. Nice to have met you. You're cleared to Stansted as flight planned. Good luck and goodnight. Orland Out."

Nice people, the Norwegians.

22

Lagos

There are some exceedingly wise sayings in the aviation industry. For instance, "Take-offs are optional but landings are mandatory", "You never see an old helicopter nor an old helicopter pilot" and "It's better to be on the ground wishing you were flying than to be flying and wishing you were on the ground." I feel that there should be at least one pearl of wisdom that cautions pilots against flying into a certain country in West Africa without adequate provision for the greasing of the sweaty palms of authority.

Whether through lack of warning, foresight or indeed intelligence, I found myself, a newly promoted and still probationary captain willing to be rostered to exercise my newly attained command status on a trip from Stansted to Nigeria The country was noted for its negligent attitude to human rights, its wide spread corruption and its depressing attitude towards the rest of the world. When I rather self-consciously signed out my first commercial flight as captain, I was allocated "Big Jim" Potter as first officer. Big Jim had been a first officer since Gladiator was a rank and not an aircraft but for some reason he had been passed over for command time and time again. Slow moving and slow talking, Big Jim had lightning swift reactions when required and had an intimate knowledge of the CL44, having been an engineer at some stage of his long career. An amiable companion and a fine pilot, I felt easier in my first command at the prospect of his company.

Our crew, consisting of Big Jim, Pete Davenport, our flight engineer, Sam Wells, our flying spanner and me drove down to the aircraft. Jim and I completed the externals and agreed that the ship was in reasonable shape and might well succeed in getting off the ground. We climbed the metal stairs to the entry door. As I entered behind Jim, I found Pete standing by the flight deck door From somewhere he had found a penny whistle with which he proceeded to "pipe me aboard." When the appalling noise terminated, he saluted smartly.

"Cap'n's on the bridge" he said to the accompaniment of raucous laughter from the rest of the crew. Obviously this was going to be a good trip.

Loaded with twenty-seven tonnes of bagged Portland Cement, we roared down the runway and lifted off at 0920. It was a great day to be flying. As the old girl creaked and groaned her way up to a breathless 22,000 feet, the usual CL44 in-flight routines like stuffing wet blanket into the gap where the swing tail didn't quite meet the rest of the airplane, and nursing the inevitably recalcitrant "hot-cup" coffee maker proceeded as usual. I felt relaxed and happy. My relationship with Julia was intimate although not in any way possessive. She spent many nights at my place but still retained her own flat in London. We flew together a lot and she was fast becoming a proficient pilot. Our episode in the Dove had brought us very close and we both cherished the time we spent together. I had achieved a job with a high degree of responsibility and had a reasonably good income. All in all, I told myself, things were looking decidedly rosy. I decided that I would buy myself a Toyota. Probably a Celica. That would impress the hell out of the people at the Club.

We crossed the English coast at Dover and turned almost due south over the English Channel. We spent the few hours in idle chatter mainly exchanging flying stories and tales of reckless abandon at far-flung corners of the world. As we neared our destination, we gradually became busier. Communication between African countries leaves a lot to be desired and a wise aviator keeps his eyes and ears wide open. The local food opens any other orifice which modesty forbids me to mention. We were able to relax a little when we finally had the airport in sight and we had descended to a few thousand feet. I determined that this landing was going to be a "greaser". I would set us down so gently that even Jim would be impressed. I maintain even to this day, that the landing would indeed have been one of my better ones. The power was right, the rate of descent was spot on, I had corrected the drift, all the correct procedures had been followed and all the rituals, like putting the landing gear down had been observed. Everything was indisputably in the right place. Everything, that is, except the bloody Peugeot pick-up truck which was waiting to cross the runway. The driver waited until we were almost right on top of him, and then decided to wait no longer and cross anyway when we were on the point of touchdown.

A large airplane in landing configuration cannot be described as a nimble machine. Sudden demands for a climb made upon it by the pilot result in a somewhat lukewarm response and little else. Realising what had happened at literally the last moment, I hauled back on the control column. The nose of the aircraft lifted slightly and despite all theories to the contrary, I believe that we gained almost six feet. Whether or not we did, two facts are inarguable. Firstly, we missed the truck and secondly we fell out of the sky and crunched down on the runway with a jolt that could have loosened teeth.

"Where the bloody hell did that come from?" I said as we rolled out.

"He was stopped on the taxiway as we approached, then decided to make a run for it," Jim said. "He must have a bloody death wish."

"He nearly got his wish" I said. "Don't know how we missed the bastard." I turned to the rest of the crew. "Sorry about the landing. They're not always that smooth." Pete looked up from his panel.

"It's only ten points for hitting vehicles anyway"

We taxied over to the transit aircraft park and shut down. We left Pete and the loadmaster on board to do the housework and went into the office. The man seated behind the desk seemed disinclined to acknowledge our presence and made a great show of being busy by shuffling papers around. Finally, he lit a cigarette and leaned back in his chair.

"Yes?"

I told him that we were the arrival from UK and that we required fuel, parking and off-loading facilities if he would be so kind. It is rather obvious to me now that the code of practice which would ensure speedy and effective results necessitated some measure of private and personal reward to the appropriate official. It was regrettably not obvious to me then, and I merely stood and waited with a rapidly diminishing stock of patience whilst he shuffled through his wads of paper, all the while shaking his head and looking at me with apparently genuine sorrow.

"It seems, captain, that only the unloading area at the far side of the airfield would be available. I don't think that I can offer you anything better."

"But there's no lighting or anything over there," I protested. He shrugged eloquently and smirked.

"Sorry captain, that's the way it goes," he said. "Take it or leave it."

"Can we leave the aircraft where it is until another area is free? There's a Cargolux almost ready for departure right there," I said, pointing to a spot not half a mile from where we stood. "Why can't we have his bay?"

He carefully cleared a space in the centre on his desk and rustled around until he found an empty A4 manila envelope, which he placed in the centre of the clearing.

"That might be a possibility," he said. He edged the envelope fractionally in my direction. "Why don't you come back in an hour, maybe and we see what we can do for you." At last, the penny dropped. I took the envelope and left the office. About an hour later, I took fifty US Dollars from the flight imprest and went over to the bank in the terminal building and changed it into the local currency. I put the money in the envelope and went back to the agent's office. I put the envelope on his desk. He grinned and put it in a drawer.

"I think the Cargolux plane is going to the transit park soon. You can have his spot over there."

"Thank you very much."

"Glad to help, captain." I walked back to the aircraft. Big Jim and the rest of the crew were sitting on the steps of the access stairs. Jim got to his feet.

"Have you sorted it?"

"Yeah, we can move onto the Cargolux DC8 spot as soon as he moves out. We'll refuel over there," I told him.

"The return cargo won't be here until tomorrow, according to this," said Jim waving a piece of paper in the air. "Maybe we should go to the hotel. I could use a shower and a bite to eat."

Pete remarked that he was so hungry that he could eat the ass off a dead hippo. Pete was always hungry. Our discussion was interrupted by the sound of the DC8 firing up its engines. We got on board leaving the loadmaster and spanner to pull the steps away and I got into the seat whilst Pete started up the two inboard engines. The DC8 taxied out of the bay and we moved slowly into the vacant spot and shut down. Although we were able to lock the door to the flight deck, I took not only my own bag but also the bag containing the flight imprest, some sixty thousand US Dollars in cash. We carried this sort of money in case we were required to go to a place where our credit was no good. (For practical purposes, that was most of the civilized world!) and needed fuel or the like. As we walked towards crew immigration, Jim asked me if I had given the agent "a drink". I replied in the affirmative. Jim said he had thought as much and wondered as to the amount.

"I figured about fifty US. I changed it into local at the bank."

"You did what?"

"Changed it into local money. Why?"

"Their own money's worthless. You should have left it in dollars. Didn't he say anything?"

"He didn't look. Just stuffed it into a drawer."

"Christ! Now it'll hit the fan. We better watch out"

We entered the crew immigration area. The Customs man carefully examined our crew licenses and passports. Did I have anything to declare? I told him that I did not.

"No electronic goods? No cameras?" Again, negative. "Drugs of any sort?" he inquired. Talk about carrying coals to Newcastle!

"No thanks," I replied with a feeble attempt at humour which went right over his head, "I'm flying tomorrow."

"You will be kind enough to open your bag please." I opened my bag. He looked sad. Only flying stuff. "Open the holdall please." Only spare clothing. He looked even sadder. "And the other case." Not even a "please" this time." I unlocked the briefcase containing the money. His eyes lit up.

"This is your money, captain?"

"I wish! No, of course not. It's the company's money. For emergency use." I was careful not to elaborate on the exact definition of the word "emergency".

"It is illegal to bring large amounts of foreign currency into this country without prior permission." he said.

"What was I to do? Leave it on the aircraft? I'm responsible for it."

"That is your problem. I asked you if you had anything to declare and you said no."

"Well, I'll stay airside with it until we go." I said. Airside is the piece of the airport which is still technically outside the country. "I'm not leaving it."

"Captain, you have committed an offence by attempting to smuggle foreign currency into our country. The matter is now out of my hands." He looked pleased with himself. "I regret that I must detain you and your fellow officers until the matter is settled."

"You mean you're arresting the whole crew?"

"Yes."

"But that's ridiculous. It's only me you're accusing."

"We must detain all of you until we can determine just who is involved." He beckoned to the two police officers who were leaning against a wall, smoking."We will, of course, keep this case as evidence. You will get a receipt in due course." He pointed to the two policemen.

"These officers will take you to the detention area." He turned away trying not to let us see that he was smiling smugly.

They took us down a long corridor and a flight of stairs into a small room, which had two chairs and a metal table. There was only one window set high on the wall. The walls had at one time been light blue but little of the original colour remained.

"Wait here," said the larger of the two policemen. "Mistuh Jone' come to speak to you soon." Pete asked if there were any more chairs. "I go see," said the man. They left, closing the door behind them. Big Jim leant against the grimy wall.

"I don't think we're under arrest, otherwise they would have left one of the knuckle draggers in here with us. I didn't hear them lock the door." Pete went over and tried the handle. It spun freely without moving the latch.

"The bastards *have* locked us in," he said. "You can't open the door from the inside."

As we considered our plight, the door opened and a short black man wearing steel rimmed glasses came in with the knuckle draggers behind him.

"My name is Mister Jones," he announced. "Police Department. You have an engineer on your crew, I believe?"

"Yes," said Pete, "I'm the flight engineer."

"And your name?"

"Peter Davenport."

"Well, Peter Davenport, you will go with the officer to your aeroplane where some of my people will conduct a thorough search of the plane. You will do your utmost to be of assistance and you will open any panels as they require. Understood?"

"Understood. What are you looking for?"

"Perhaps nothing, perhaps much. We shall see." He turned to Jim. "And you are?"

"Potter, James, First Officer. What the hell is all this about? I want the British Consul over here. Now."

"Mr James, you will come with me."

"Please!" said Jim

"Please." They went out, leaving Sam and me in the room.

"How long do you think they'll keep us here?" Sam asked.

"Who knows? We haven't done anything illegal as far as I know. They have to let us phone the Company," I replied. "I hope!"

Sam and I settled down to wait. We waited for about forty-five minutes, then the door opened and Jim came back in. Jones stood in the doorway and indicated that Sam should follow him. Sam looked at me and shrugged his shoulders as he left the room. I asked Jim what had happened.

"He was asking about the cargo. He said if there was anything to find then we better tell him before his apes tear the aircraft apart. He reckons the money was either to buy drugs or was money got from selling drugs. I don't think he's ever seen sixty grand in cash before. He was almost wetting himself." He paused. "He also assured me that somebody from the Consul's office is coming over, but I'm not that convinced."

"Did you get any idea how long we're likely to be kept here?"

"All he would say is 'As long as it takes' however long that'll be."

The small room was dark and stunk of God knows what. There were cockroaches and other creepy crawlies on the floor and walls. As the time was now approaching five in the afternoon it was starting to get dark. In that part of the world, night falls very suddenly. It's as if daylight couldn't wait to clock off and get the hell out of there. The twilight is very short lived, about ten minutes or so. The single electric light mounted in the ceiling in a shatterproof housing came on, presumably activated by a time switch. About fifteen minutes later, Sam came back in.

"They're letting me go," he said. Jones is apparently going home and they've told me to go to the hotel and wait there."

"Phone the company," I said. "Tell them what's happened Get the MD out of bed if you have to but tell them that we're rotting in the slammer and tomorrow could be the day they bring out the rubber hoses."

"I'll phone the Consul as well. See if anybody knows what's going on. I'm going to the airplane to see if Pete's okay. I think we're in the clear. Jones seems to think he's got the wrong aircraft. You should be out pretty soon."

Jim and I waited. Then, when we got bored with that, we waited some more. Between us we must have waited for about three hours. Then the door opened and one of the gorillas came in.

"You come wid me," he said. He took us along the corridor and into another room. My heart sank. This room was darker, dirtier and smelt worse than the other one, and even worse, had no window at all. There were wooden benches fixed to the floor against three of the walls and on each bench was a rather dubious looking blanket. The steel door had a spy hole covered by a flap. Have I described a prison cell?

"How long do you intend to keep us here?" I demanded. The gorilla shook its head.

"No unnastan'" it said.

"Looks like close of play for today," said Jim. "Do you suppose we'll get anything to eat?"

"Would you eat here?" I said, knowing full well that Pete would.

"Point taken."

It seemed likely that we were going to be detained at least until morning so we carefully threw the filthy blankets into a corner and sat down on a bench to debate the probable outcome. I must have dozed off because I woke with a start at around three in the morning to find a large rat sniffing around my right foot. I kicked out at it and it scurried away under the door whilst I was looking around for something to clobber it with. Jim laughed and said

"Now you know why my feet are off the floor."

"Never mind that," I said noticing a lack of glitter on my left wrist. "Those bastards have nicked my watch."

"No they haven't. I took it off when you fell asleep in case they did take a liking to it," he said. "It's around 3.15 in the morning."

"Hopefully, something will start happening soon. This is definitely not my idea of a good time." Jim gave me my watch back with the advice to put it in an inside pocket. We sat around very uncomfortable and quite cold until around six in the morning, there was a jangle of keys and the door opened. Jones came in wearing a supercilious smile and the same clothes he had on the previous day.

"We have finished searching your aeroplane," he said. "We have found nothing." He looked sad but brightened up as he continued, "However, I have several questions which I must ask you." He looked at me. "You will come with me please." He turned to Jim. "You, Mr James, you may go to your hotel. For the moment, I have finished with you. However, do not leave the hotel." He walked out, leaving the door open. Jim said

"Don't worry, Al, I'll do whatever it takes."

"Thanks. See you soon."

Jones led me into another room, much cleaner and more pleasant where he sat behind a desk and leant back in the chair. He motioned me to sit. I sat.

"At last, captain, we come to you."

"I demand to know why we are being kept here. What are we being accused of? You have absolutely no right to detain my crew and me. Where is the Consul? Has anybody actually called the Consul?" He cut me off in mid flow.

"We have a long standing problem here with aircrews from Europe taking drugs into the country. Our government is determined to stamp it out and I suspect that your aircraft is or was carrying drugs. What do you say to that?"

"That is absolute rubbish. If anybody in this country can get high on sniffing cement, they're welcome to sniff the whole bloody cargo. Bags and all We are not and do not carry drugs. Ever." I stood up.

"Please sit down. As I said, we found nothing on your plane but I need to know why you were carrying so much money."

"I told you at the desk. It's in case we get stuck somewhere and need fuel or something."

"Your company will confirm this?" he looked thoughtful." We have had a telephone call from your chairman. He was very angry."

"I'm not bloody surprised. So am I."

"However, until I am completely satisfied on the question of drugs, then you will remain in custody."

"You mean, locked up? That is disgraceful."

"I am prepared to release you but you will surrender your passport and your licence. You will report to me here as I may require. Other than that, you are free to do as you please. We are not barbarians here."

"And the money?"

"We will, of course, retain the money."

"Then I must have a receipt." He pulled a sheet of paper towards him and started to write in a rather laborious hand. I was amused to see his lips move as he wrote. He looked up.

"How much money, captain?"

"Sixty thousand dollars—no fifty nine, fifty." As if he hadn't already counted it.

"We counted only fifty eight thousand." I though fast. This must be the way the game is played.

"You may be correct."

"Yes, I think so." He finished writing. "Here is your receipt. I'm sure my suspicions will be resolved shortly."

"Now may I go to my hotel?"

"Yes, of course. We will speak again tomorrow, say three in the afternoon."

"Whatever."

"Good-bye, captain. Until tomorrow."

"Good-bye." I walked out with as much dignity as I could muster.

I managed to coerce one of the gorillas into driving me to the hotel. I checked in and had one of the longest showers I have ever had in my life. I was awakened by the phone at around eleven. As the fog in my brain cleared a little, I realised that the voice belonged to Pete. He told me that the return cargo had arrived and did I know whether they could start loading. As far as I knew, Jones had finished with the aircraft, I told him, and therefore, as far as we were concerned, the cargo could go on board and all of the paperwork could be done.

"There's been a phone call from Stansted too," said Pete. They want you to call the chairman as soon as possible."

"Okay, I'll do that now. Have you seen anything of Jones today?"

"He was sniffing around earlier but he left us alone."

"Okay, get loaded up and I'll find Jim and the rest and we'll get the hell out of here." Pete said that suited him fine and put the phone down. I put in a call to Stansted and after some shuffling around, got through to the chairman.

"They let you out, then?"

"Yes, sir, eventually. I'm afraid the flight imprest took a bit of stick."

"How much stick?"

"Around two grand, I'm afraid."

"The last time this happened, it cost us five. You got away light."

"Didn't feel it. The slammer here ain't the Hilton."

"Do you good. Fine character forming stuff. Anyway, glad you're okay. That was your first trip as skipper wasn't it?"

"Yes, sir, it was."

"We'll talk some more when you get back. Did you get the consulate involved?"

"We tried but nobody showed."

"Not surprised. Bloody useless, they are. Anyway, go and bring my aeroplane home."

"Okay, good-bye sir."

"Bye."

Late that afternoon, I retrieved my treasures from Jones and, to his obvious annoyance, insisted on counting the money in his presence. He was full of assurances that it had all been a dreadful mistake and that he hoped we bore him no ill will. Common sense demanded that I keep my mouth shut so I didn't tell him my innermost feelings about him, his police, his country and his prisons. I contented myself by saying that we would all be happy to get back into the air and away from here. He smiled sadly.

"You may possibly return here, captain. I trust your next visit may be more pleasant."

"I'll know the score next time."

"Hopefully," he said, "hopefully."

And then, happily, we all went home.

23

Eleven Minutes

Captain Bill Reid had not slept well. Even at five fifteen on that September morning, the humidity in his Hong Kong hotel room was insufferable despite the air conditioning. He looked at his watch and groaned, concluding that it was pointless trying to go back to sleep. He turned the bedside light on and reached for the phone.

"Reception, good morning," a disembodied voice said.

"Hello, this is Bill Reid in three-fourteen. I ordered continental breakfast for five forty-five. Could you have it sent up now please? Oh, and would you call the rest of my people and make sure they're awake."

"Certainly Captain. You go away today?"

"Yep, we certainly do!" Reid chuckled, "I'll be glad to get back to a sensible temperature." He thanked the girl on the front desk and put the receiver back in the cradle.

Two doors along the corridor, in room three one six, Tony Dean, the Flight Engineer was having absolutely no trouble sleeping. It was a matter of four hours since his delightful Chinese companion had quietly let herself out of his room and returned, soft footed to her own room. Tony was enjoying a very erotic dream when the insistent ringing of the phone disrupted his sleep. He picked up the offending instrument and listened to the instructions from his Captain relayed to him by the front desk. He mumbled his thanks and asked for coffee and orange juice to be delivered as soon as possible.

Terry White the First Officer occupied a room on the floor below. He had eaten at a local restaurant the previous evening and had returned to the hotel early. Despite the temperature, he had slept well and woke refreshed, ready for the flight which was the first stage of their return to England. Terry's young wife was expecting their first child in November and he was eagerly anticipating the return to England for the seemingly endless round of preparatory shopping for all the accoutrements that accompany the arrival of a new baby.

The three crewmembers of the CL44 cargo aircraft met, as arranged in the hotel lobby at six thirty am. Surrounded by their baggage and flight bags, they waited for the arrival of the taxi that was to convey them to Kai Tak Airport. In the view of most operational aircrew, Hong Kong's Airport was not without its difficulties. It was said that, on the convoluted approach over Kowloon and Mongok to runway 13, flightcrew could see not only whether the occupants of the apartments were watching television, but that they were close enough to see which channel was selected. The final approach on the infamous 'Kai Tak Curve' approach to runway 13 started with a huge red and white checkerboard positioned on the side of a hill and both metaphorically and literally, everything went downhill from that point. The final approach had been likened to an approach to an aircraft carrier and most crews breathed a communal sigh of relief when the wheels touched the ground.

A battered Mercedes taxi screeched to a halt outside the hotel. Bill picked up his flight bag with a sigh.

"I wish those little sods would learn to drive," he said. "Come on then guys, home to England for tea and medals." The Chinese taxi driver reluctantly helped them stow the baggage in the trunk of the car, then swung the Mercedes out into the traffic without a rearward glance. In Hong Kong, like most other Asian countries, the traffic right of way seems to depend mainly on strength of the survival instinct of the drivers. The drive out to Kai Tak International Airport consisted of fierce acceleration, sudden braking and violent avoiding action, punctuated by prolonged blasts on the horn.

Reid threw his flight bag in a corner of the air-conditioned operations room. He addressed the weather briefer.

"What do we have in the way of weather today?"

"Nothing much for you, Bill. Just a few frontal systems over Europe. You should have a pretty good ride I think." Terry White was busying himself on a table, surrounded by performance graphs and fuelling sheets. From time to time he spun the wheel on his CRP5 navigation computer and scribbled a few figures on the Navigation Log. Finally he stood up and surveyed the result of his labours.

"All done skipper, I think we're ready to blast off."

"Right then, lets go count the wings."

The three men hitched a ride to their aircraft on the freight agent's pick-up truck. Tony Dean, as Flight Engineer slowly and meticulously walked around the big aircraft, examining the lower surfaces of the wings for possible fuel leaks and peering up into the cavernous wheel wells for signs of damage. Being an engineer, his pre-flight inspection of the airplane was based on his detailed knowledge of the CL44 and was therefore lengthy and very thorough. When he finally climbed up the metal stairs and took his seat behind the two pilots, the internal checks and pre-flight briefing were almost complete.

"Anything fallen off Tony?"

"After me, you'll be the first to find out, Terry," he grinned.

The Captain picked up his headset.

"Doors closed please and steps away."

Tony stood by the open doorway and signalled for the groundcrew to wheel the big mobile access stairs clear of the aircraft. He thanked them, heaved the big door closed and pulled the locking bar into the safe position.

"Steps clear and door closed and locked Skipper."

"Thanks, Tony." He pushed the transmit button on his control column. "Hong Kong Ground, Good morning. Freighter Kilo Kilo…" He released the button and turned to the First Officer. "What the fuck is our call-sign Terry?"

"KK3751"

"Sorry Hong Kong, Freighter Kilo Kilo three seven five one for start-up and taxi please."

"Five one, Hong Kong, clear to start, temperature is plus twenty. Call ready to taxi."

"Five one roger." Reid stretched his legs against the rudder pedals. "Okay Tony, crank them up." As the four engines slowly picked up speed the aircraft came to life. Dean scanned his instruments.

"Temperatures and pressures all in the green," he reported. "RPMs stabilised."

The long rituals of checking and cross-checking, of challenges and responses, of the final checking of doors, harnesses, windows and, once on the move, of brake testing proceeded without incident and the big aircraft lumbered towards the runway.

Reid looked around the crew.

"All set? Let's go home." He clicked his radio switch. "Hong Kong Tower, KK three seven five one is ready for departure."

"Five one, Hong Kong Tower, you are clear for take-off. Surface wind is zero nine zero degrees and eight knots."

"Roger, Understand clear to line up and take off."

"Affirmative."

Terry looked doubtful. There would be a lot of runway behind them if they were to line up for take-off from their present position.

"Do we really want to go from here, Bill?" The radio came to life.

"Five one, if you line up where you are, you lose about one thousand feet of your take-off run."

"One thousand feet?"

"One thousand feet approximately five one."

Bill Reid and Terry White looked at each other. Bill pressed the transmit switch.

"Okay, we'll go down to the end, thank you."

"Five one roger."

Slowly and sedately the CL44 trundled along the runway towards the City. All the pre take-off checks had been completed and the three flightdeck crew chatted idly, making the sort of small talk which men who spend seemingly endless hours in each other's company are wont to do. They reached the end of the long strip and turned slowly through one hundred and eighty degrees. Terry pushed all four engines up to full power and held the shuddering aircraft on the brakes.

"Ready?"

"All set." Reid pressed the transmit switch again.

"Tower, Five one is rolling."

"Five one roger." The huge aircraft slowly gathered speed. The crew checked and crosschecked the instrument readings as the airspeed increased. As the First Officer was the handling pilot, the Captain was calling the speeds.

"One hundred knots," he said.

"Cross checked."

"Vee one." Terry started to raise the nosewheel off the ground.

"Rotate!" Smoothly, the freighter rose into the air.

"Positive climb, gear up please." As Bill moved the selector into the 'up' position, the fire warning bell started clanging loudly.

"Engine fire number four!" shouted Tony. As the crew carried out the fire drill, shutting the engine down and feathering the propeller quickly but without panic, the Tower controller called.

"Kilo Kilo five one, you have smoke from your number four engine."

"Yeah, we shut it down," Reid transmitted. "Roger, Kilo Kilo five one, we have had an engine failure." Tony Dean was looking worried.

"We should get this thing back on the ground," he said. The Tower called again.

"Kilo Kilo Five one, what are your intentions?" Terry looked across at the Captain.

"We're too heavy to land. We're going to have to get rid of some of this fuel."

"I agree." To the tower, Bill said, "Five one will go out and dump fuel then return to Hong Kong."

"Five one, roger." The CL44 slowly climbed through seven hundred feet, grasping for height on the reduced power provided by the remaining engines. Tony was trying to look out through the right hand flight deck window to examine the failed engine.

"It's still churning out smoke," he said.

"Do you see any flames, Tony?"

"No, only smoke."

The Tower controller spoke again.

"Five one, be advised that Tathong Point straight ahead is eight hundred and seven feet," referring to the elevated VOR facility set on high ground.

"Thank you," said Bill, "We are visual."

"Roger." A few seconds later, the Tower said, "Kilo Kilo five one, contact Hong Kong Approach on one one nine decimal one."

"Hong Kong Approach on one one nine decimal one. Roger." They climbed steadily in a cautious silence for a few moments, then the Captain changed to the second communications radio.

"Hong Kong Approach, this is Kilo five one on one one nine one," he said.

"Five one, go ahead."

"Approach, we are just climbing through one thousand feet. We'll be dumping fuel shortly."

The Approach controller picked up his powerful binoculars and focussed on the CL44. Even although the aircraft was now some miles away the trail of smoke from the right hand outboard engine was clearly visible. He considered the options for a few seconds. He consulted a colleague and decided to steer the crippled aircraft into a safe area for the hazardous procedure of dumping excess fuel.

"Kilo five one, from the outer marker, I suggest you turn onto an easterly heading and climb to about four thousand feet before commencing dumping fuel."

"Roger," said Bill, "We'll turn east and climb to four thousand."

"How long do you need for fuel dump?"

The two pilots looked at each other.

"About ten and a half minutes?" Terry nodded. Reid transmitted the information to the ground. The Controller picked up the telephone on his desk to his supervisor.

"We have an aircraft with an engine out and trailing a lot of smoke. I've sent him out east to dump fuel then he will be returning here. I think we should have the emergency services on stand-by just in case." He listened for a few seconds. "He will be returning in around ten minutes or so. I will bring him straight in on runway three one." A pause, then "Okay, thanks." He put the phone down just as the radio came to life again. Bill Reid's voice icily calm came from the speaker.

"Hong Kong Approach, Five one, we won't be able to dump. We have an engine on fire at this time and we have to come back and land with the fuel on board."

The controller reacted instantly.

"Roger, five one, make a right turn, I say again, a right turn onto heading of three one five." That was a heading that would take the aircraft directly towards the airfield although the resultant landing would be in the direction opposite to the take off. As the big freighter descended towards the airfield, the controller gave the crew small corrections to their heading.

"Five one, make your heading now two niner five. You are twelve miles to the east of the airfield. If you are visual at any time, you are cleared to continue visually. The surface wind is zero nine zero degrees and six knots."

"Tower from five one, you better stand by with the fire cover. We don't see flames any more but there's still a lot of smoke."

"Roger, five one. We are ready."

On the flight deck, Tony Dean suddenly shouted

"Flames! Flames! The fire is going again!"

"Fire the second shot. Give it the second shot." Bill Reid pulled the fire handle again, firing the second extinguisher.

"It's no good," Dean shouted. "Flames all over the trailing edge. The fuel is feeding the fire." Reid keyed the radio.

"We're losing it, Approach, We're going in!" Terry White was fighting to keep the aircraft level.

"I'm losing it, Bill! I'm losing control."

"Hold it up Terry," shouted Reid. "Hold the wing up." With a noise that could be heard over the roar of the flames, the stricken engine lurched downwards. The mounting bolts, weakened by the intense heat of the fire fractured, allowing the huge Tyne engine to tear itself from the wing and plunge towards the ocean below. When it separated from the wing it ripped away fuel lines and the outboard section of the wing and the aileron. Fuel gushed from the broken pipe work allowing fuel to feed the hungry fire.

In the Tower some ten miles away, the controller listened helplessly to the final transmission from the doomed aircraft.

"Approach, the engine has come off. We're going in! The engine has come……" Silence, apart from the hiss of static. The controller keyed his microphone.

"Kilo Kilo Five one do you read?"

"Kilo Kilo three seven five one, do you read me?"

He continued to call for several minutes without response, realising that the worst had happened and that there was very little that could be done. Eventually, he handed his position over to his supervisor and sadly walked away to start on the endless form filling that inevitably follows tragedy.

It will be obvious that the foregoing narrative was not and could not be written from a personal perspective. The events described are based on the transcript of Air Traffic recordings of the incident which tragically took the lives of three of my colleagues. I hope that I have not conveyed any sense of panic in the portrayal of the events. The crew were true professionals in every sense of the word and I am certain that they handled the emergency in a calm and measured manner. Such men and women remain rational and cockpit voice recordings generally convey great dignity and little profanity as they attempt to control the machine that is carrying them to their deaths. In respect for the privacy of the families who were left behind, and because the accident had a profound effect on all of us who worked for the company, the names and identities of the crew have been changed. On that terrible day in September 1977, the three crewmembers plunged to their deaths in a fiercely burning aircraft into the sea off Hong Kong eleven minutes after take off. Only the body of the Flight Engineer was ever recovered. The company held a service of Remembrance in the church in Stansted village that was attended by almost every employee.

May they rest in peace.

24

British Air Ferries

I sat uncomfortably outside the Chairman's office, on the top floor of the Company office building on the upper-class side of the airport. It had seemed fairly normal whilst in the Air Force to have to carry out a bit of Axminster drill in the Station Commander's office, due, no doubt to the fact that my friends and I were seldom out of trouble of some description. 'Hat and No Coffee' interviews were taken as an acceptable part of Service life, but this was civvy street. I had absolutely no reason to be apprehensive on this occasion as the forthcoming interview had been arranged at my behest. Still, our Chairman, a self-made millionaire and an ex sergeant pilot was a man to be treated with the utmost caution. Somewhat eccentric, he was given to peremptorily sacking people who had incurred his displeasure. On one occasion, he had sacked the Chief Engineer twice in the same meeting On the credit side, however, the dismissed employee was expected to resume work the following day. He had bought the airline in a very shaky financial condition and with exceptional shrewdness, had turned the shambles into a profitable concern. One of his first moves had been to issue an edict that the keys to each and every company car were to be on his desk by nine one morning. He then issued a directive that any employee who felt able to justify having a company car should report to his office and plead their case in person. By the end of that day, some twenty-seven cars had been offered for sale in the local car auction.

The reason for my request of a personal interview stemmed from the fact that Rumour Control had indicated a possible sale of the Company to a very famous shipping line. The potential buyer was known to have a reputation for converting the viable parts of target acquisitions into cash and simply scrapping the rest of the company. As we had recently acquired three shiny DC8 freighters it seemed to us that a bit of asset stripping would inevitably take place if we were taken over. The DC8s would stay as would the DC8 trained crews but the rest of us, still condemned to wander the skies in our old CL44 turboprops would become surplus to requirements. Mr Chairman also owned a small passenger airline, which operated twin engined Dart Herald aircraft to France, Holland, Switzerland and Belgium from Southend Airport. The object of my interview was to request a transfer to that airline.

I attempted to engage his secretary in idle conversation to little or no effect. Dressed in a low-cut top and a skirt, which, had it been any longer, might have passed for a belt, she appeared to be typing a letter. Her typing skills certainly appeared to require some honing, as she divided her time equally between the typewriter keys and a bottle of correction fluid. Eventually, the telephone on her desk buzzed. She picked it up and listened.

"You can go in now," she intimated. I went in.

The meeting progressed smoothly enough, although the boss was sceptical about my fears and concerns.

"If the company were to be sold," he said, "it would be unthinkable to get rid of the 44s. We have built up a good customer base with them and there is no reason to suppose that anything would change." He stared at me for an eternity.

"They are becoming rather difficult to maintain though," I said. "Spares are very hard to come by."

"And you think you would like to fly Heralds?"

"Yes, I think I would like to give it a shot." He looked down at some notes on his desk.

"You only just got a command on the CL44. Are you sure you want to go back to being a co-pilot again?"

"Better than being an unemployed captain," I said.

"Anything you might have heard about redundancies is only rumour at this stage. However, I actually do need more crews at Southend so if that is really what you want, I suppose we can consider it." He stared at me for a few seconds. "I suppose I can put a few cards on the table. I am seriously considering selling and there is a very good offer on the table for the company as a going concern, so there is no prospect of shedding crews or aircraft." He picked up a pen and absentmindedly doodled some kind of insect on his blotter. I waited patiently. One did not interrupt the chairman whilst meditating.

"I know what you're thinking," he said. This was the first intimation that our revered leader had telepathic powers. "If the company is doing well, then why am I selling it?" I didn't know, and mumbled something to that effect. "We are buying all of the Malaysian Air Force Dart Heralds and converting them to passenger configuration. That takes a lot of money and I want to concentrate on that part of the business." His pen put some stripes on the insect. He added a pair of antennae and put a smile on the face. There was a prolonged pause then eventually he broke the pregnant silence.

"Okay then, if that's what you want to do, finish off your current roster then ask Foster to get you on the next Herald ground school."

"Thanks very much," I said and stood up. I pointed to the insect on the blotter. "You just re-designed the bumblebee!"

"It's high time the airline business got its head out of its arse," he said. "Every piece of advertising is so serious. I'm thinking of changing all that." He reached into a drawer and produced a folder covered with clear film. "What do you think?" The picture was a bumblebee with wings and a tailplane in vivid black and yellow. Written in a circle around the happy bee was the legend "Buzz Off With BAF"

"Probably the new advertisement. Stickers for car windscreens, mugs, pens, tee shirts. The lot."

I had visions of the happy little insect appearing on cars and desks all over the county.

"That will probably do as much for bumblebees as it will for British Air Ferries," I remarked. The great man grinned.

"Both need a bit of a lift," he said. "Enjoy yourself at Southend. I'm hoping that we'll be able to give one or two of the established airlines a bit of a shock."

"I'm sure I will," I replied and took my leave.

◆ ◆ ◆

It was very pleasant to be based at Southend. As the more attentive reader will recall, it was in Southend that I settled after leaving the Air Force. I had many friends there and a fairly comfortable residence which had the advantage of being only a mile or so from the airport. An additional benefit was that I could resume my musical activities although the band had long since found a replacement keyboard player. Because of the ability to forecast my working schedule several weeks ahead with a reasonable degree of accuracy, I scanned the Musicians Wanted columns of the local paper After a couple of weeks of either rejecting or of being rejected by various bands, a fairly active band playing a wide mixture of music decided that they and I could muddle along together.

Charlie Smollett shook his head with a passable impression of sadness when I visited him at the flying club. The club, he remarked, was not doing too well. There didn't seem to be so much money around these days. Fuel prices had gone through the roof and of course those bloody highwaymen who ran the airport were taking hard-working flying club owners to the cleaners over landing and parking fees. When he learned that I didn't want a full time job, however, he brightened up considerably.

"Can always use a part-time instructor," he remarked.

"Especially if they come cheap, Charlie?" I added. He looked hurt. "You have my phone number as and when the need arises," I said. In actual fact, I was much more interested in the social side of the club than the meagre amount of instruction that I would conceivably be doing. Instructors enjoyed the benefits of the club facilities without having to pay the membership fees. Although the lovely Julia was now only a distant memory and Sally-Anne had departed to fly Viscounts up in East Midlands, there was still a more than adequate supply of potential female companionship.

Ground school for the Herald was not particularly mind stretching, as I was fairly well versed in the art of handling turboprop engines and the aircraft itself was an uncomplicated machine. The intricacies of the various systems were painstakingly explained to us by an ancient engineer who lovingly traced the paths of fuel and oils around the airplane on coloured charts pinned to an easel. As far as the actual flying was concerned, we flew on actual passenger flights, seated on fold down jump seats behind the operating crews so that we could become accustomed to the attitudes of the aircraft on the various stages of a flight. The jump seats were a fine trap for the unwary. Preparing the jump seat for occupancy was similar to erecting a deck chair in a hurricane and there were several stages in the procedure where unwary fingers might become inexorably tangled in the folding metalwork. Eventually, after several such flights, we took over the co-pilots position for at least a part of the trip in order that we might get the feel of the aircraft. As time progressed, we were allowed more and more time at the controls until at last, we were tested by the training captain and pronounced capable of forming part of the flight crew.

Some of my colleagues expressed wonder at my apparently illogical move from a command of a large, four engined aircraft to a first officer's position on a much smaller aircraft. The wisdom of my move became apparent when, some three months after my move to Southend, the Stansted operation ceased trading accompanied by many redundancies both in engineering and aircrew. The simple fact was that the short sectors, most lasting only an hour or so, and the regularity of work schedules suited me far better than the nine hour flogs down to Africa. It was also entirely unlikely that I would be locked up as had happened in the past. Our usual passenger load consisted mainly of businessmen and families travelling to the Continent for a spot of duty-free shopping. It was altogether a much more relaxed operation. The chairman, now free from the pressures of the Stansted operation, found ample time to make a complete nuisance of himself. He had the terrifying habit of suddenly turning up when and where he was least expected and if he was to see something that caused him displeasure, strong men would turn pale and mothers would gather their children around them and take cover.

Predictably, he was on the airfield on the morning when the driver of a forklift truck loading baggage, totally misjudged the height of the freight door. The captain and I were preparing the flight plan whilst generally discussing the news of the day when we became aware of a group of people standing around the rear of our proposed aircraft. From the window of the operations room, we were unable to determine the source of their keen interest in the side of the fuselage but it was evident that something was amiss. We arrived at the aircraft to find that the tines of the fork lift truck were buried in the skin of the fuselage to a depth of at least six inches. The Chief Engineer was visibly shaking as he surveyed the damage.

"God only knows what Mike is going to say about this," he wailed. "He'll have my guts for garters even though I was in the hangar at the time."

"Does he know yet?" I enquired.

"Yes, more or less. He's on the other side of the airport and the tower called him on the radio."

I should mention that any vehicle travelling in the aircraft movement area was required to carry a radio to communicate with the tower just in case they were liable to come into conflict with a taxying aircraft or needed to cross the active runway. Messages, however, were kept brief and the chairman had not been advised of the exact reason for the necessity of his immediate return. As he had been engaged in supervising the polishing of his private Cessna Golden Eagle, it was predictable that he would be somewhat irritated at being dragged away.

As we stared at the fork lift being slowly and carefully disentangled from the aircraft, I looked across the airfield to see Mike's Jensen Interceptor totally ignoring the taxiway and bouncing across the grass at high speed, heading for us. He screeched to a halt and leapt from the car almost before it had stopped. He looked at the two neat holes in the skin of the aircraft. He looked at the ends of the forks, which had made the holes. Slowly, he looked around the assembled company until he identified the person whom he rightly assumed had been the driver.

"Was this your doing?" he thundered.

"Yeah, I was driving the forks."

"You are fuckin' fired!" he roared.

"You can't fire me," the man responded.

"Watch me. Collect your cards from personnel. Now."

"You can't fire me because I don't work for you. I work for the airport." Mike hopped from one foot to the other whilst he rationalised this catastrophe. He turned to search amongst the faces of the spectators. Finally, he settled on a face he recognised, a junior operations clerk who had simply come out to see the show.

"You! Get over to Airport Admin and tell them that this moron here gets sacked right now." He turned to the chief engineer. "Wally," he said, "Stay here. I want a word with you." Wally turned visibly paler as the Chairman propelled him by the arm away from the carnage. At some distance from us and certainly out of earshot a long and serious conversation took place during which Wally did a great deal of listening and very little speaking. When the monologue ended, Mike got into the Jensen and drove sedately towards the terminal building. Wally trudged over to join us at the aircraft.

"Did he fire you?" someone asked.

"Surprisingly, no," he said. "All he said was that we could easily have done without this. Then he asked me how long it would take to repair. I was sure I would get the bullet for this!"

Our own problems were not over, however as we had fifty-two passengers expecting to fly to Rotterdam and we did not appear to have an aircraft for them. We returned to operations to await developments. The two men behind the desks were frantically phoning around, presumably as a result of the accident. Through the ringing of telephones and the clatter of telex machines came a triumphant shout.

"Fixed it. Got it sorted. Air Anglia has an uncommitted F27. Shall I confirm it?"

"If they can get it here right away, yes, do it. Where is it? Norwich?"

I concluded that as our passengers were now going to travel to their destination on board another aircraft chartered from another airline, our services would not be required.

"Cup of coffee, I reckon, Bob," I remarked to the captain.

"Yep, that would do it for me," came the reply. The operations officer confirmed that there was no reason for our continued presence, so, at my suggestion, we made our way over to the flying club where the coffee was almost drinkable. Dave Wilkinson, who had replaced Ted as Chief Flying Instructor waved a greeting as we entered the room and headed for the coffee machine.

"You working today?" he asked.

"We were but the aircraft is broken," Bob replied.

"If you're interested, this young lady," he indicated a dark haired girl sitting at a table, immersed in a text book, "needs a pre-GFT trip. You wanna do it?" The General Flying Test is the final assessment of the capabilities of a student pilot. If successfully carried out, the full Private Pilot's Licence is then issued. It is customary for the candidate to have a kind of mock GFT prior to the actual test and this can be done by any instructor, whereas the actual test proper can only be administered by the CFI.

"Yes, Dave," I said looking at the girl. "I'll be happy to do that." She gathered up her books and I signed the authorisation sheet for the flight. I despatched her to the Cherokee to do the pre-flight whilst I finished my coffee. When I saw her climbing into the aircraft I went out to join her.

"Hello again," I said brightly, "My name is Allen."

"Jane," she said.

"Right, Jane, I'd like you to start up and taxi out. We'll go out to the Northeast, around two thousand feet and we should be up for around forty minutes or so. Okay?" She nodded her understanding. "I shall just sit here, fat dumb and happy except that I will be asking you to carry out a few exercises that they will ask you to do on the real GFT. Otherwise, I shall take no part in the handling of the aircraft unless you ask me to. Unless, of course I think that you are going to kill us." She smiled. A beautiful smile that lit up her whole face. She efficiently carried out the internal checks and started the engine. She asked for and received the required clearances from the tower and started to taxi towards the runway.

"How many hours have you got, Jane?" I enquired.

"Forty two and a few minutes," she replied. "I should have done the GFT last week but the weather was too bad." For a PPL, the minimum amount of flying time before the issue of a licence was forty hours, of which at least ten had to be solo.

Jane's forty-two hours and the few minutes of instruction seemed to me to have been pretty effective. Her handling of the aircraft was smooth and her radio procedures clear and effective. I was quite relaxed as she took off and climbed out towards the coast. She levelled off at the required two thousand feet and we droned onwards for a few minutes.

"I would like you to reduce the speed to eighty please Jane, and maintain two thousand feet." With a minimum of fuss, she reduced the power and held the nose up to reduce the speed to comply with my request.

"*Satisfactory*", I thought. I asked her to carry out a few more exercises before hitting her with the big one. She handled everything that I threw at her with a calm efficiency. I concluded that she would have little trouble passing the real GFT, provided she could handle the forced landing. I reached forward and pulled the throttle fully closed.

"You have engine failure," I said. Her reaction and subsequent handling of the simulated engine failure was straight out of the textbook. Her choice of field was fine, and the approach, although a little fast would have resulted in a successful landing. I told her to restore full power and climb back up to our original height.

"Who was your instructor?" I asked her.

"Sally most of the time, but I did the stalls and spins with Ted."

As we climbed back up, I felt completely relaxed. The sun shone in through the window on my side and in the distance, the sea sparkled in the sunshine. It was a beautiful day for flying with excellent visibility and very little in the way of turbulence. The Cherokee was flying well and Jane was a competent pilot. Indeed, all was well in the world.

An ear-splitting scream abruptly brought me back to reality. There was a flurry of activity by my side.

"Oh my God! Oh my God!" Another scream, followed by a whimper. I saw a flurry of seat belts as Jane frantically unbuckled her harness.

"What the hell is the matter?" Jane, now free of the restraining seat harness was rapidly clambering into the back seat of the aircraft.

"Jane, what the hell is wrong? What's the matter?"

"Kill it! Kill the bastard!" she cried from the back seat.

"Kill what?"

"Spider," she whimpered. "Kill that spider." I looked around and saw a fairly innocuous looking spider trudging on a north-easterly heading across the instrument panel. I reached across and scooped it up in my hand. Opening the small direct vision window I ejected the arachnid into the slipstream. I supposed that the poor creature would eventually return to earth safely.

"Right, Jane," I said, "It's gone." She examined the instrument panel from the safety of the rear seat.

"I suppose you think I'm a baby. I am terrified of the things. It's the way they...*scuttle*. Can't stand being anywhere near them." I persuaded her to return to the front seat and fly us back to Southend. Her handling of the aircraft had gone to pieces and I had to rescue the landing before we dashed ourselves to pieces on the runway. Before we shut down, I said that we should go to the terminal and have a chat over a cup of coffee.

As kindly as I was able, I said that there was no way that I could allow her to continue solo flying with a phobia that could endanger not only herself but also any passengers that she might carry as a private pilot. Through tears, she agreed reluctantly. I suggested that she should suddenly develop a bad cold which would provide a reason to delay her GFT until she was able to control her fear.

"You might be able to get some kind of therapy to alleviate your problem," I suggested. "Maybe you should see your doctor. There are courses that would help. I will keep quiet about today if you promise not to put yourself in danger." She nodded, wiping her eyes.

"Scout's honour?"

"Dyb dyb dyb," she said.

"I'm sure you will be fine. You are a good pilot and if it hadn't been for your little excursion, I would have laid odds on a good result. Stick with it."

With the benefit of hindsight, I am happy to relate that Jane not only successfully overcame her dread of spiders but also went on to become a commercial pilot. The last I heard, she was commanding a Boeing 737 in Germany. I am quite sure, however that she vividly recalls the day when she relinquished the controls and hid in the back of the Cherokee.

25

The Ferry Pilot

I can recall, with absolute clarity, precisely where I was when I learned of the death of King George VI. Most people, who were around at the time, can remember where they were when President John Kennedy was assassinated. I do not need to refer to my logbook to remember the date of the incidents that follow. It was the second day of April in the year of our Lord nineteen hundred and eighty-two, the day that Argentinean forces invaded the Falkland Islands and the Falklands War commenced. On that day, I had transported some forty passengers on a scheduled flight to Marseilles and we had spent almost four hours on the ground whilst engineers sorted out a problem with our right hand propeller.

The twenty or so passengers who had arrived for the flight back to Southend accepted the delay with a commendable degree of equanimity. Although it was still fairly early in the day, the sunshine was warm as we waited for the technicians to complete the work. Steve Roper, the First Officer was absorbed in the departure procedures charts, trying to guess which departure procedure Air Traffic Control would require of us. Marseilles, being a rather posh part of France, operates extremely strict noise control in order to cause the minimum of disturbance to the local residents and although the Dart Herald, which we were flying, was a very quiet aircraft, the procedures applied equally to our flight.

"Trying to learn them all, Steve?" I asked in a feeble attempt at humour.

"We have to expedite our climb to 2,500 feet whichever departure they give us," he said. Steve was fairly new, not only to the aircraft, but also fairly new to commercial flying, having only recently acquired a Commercial Pilot's Licence. He had been trained by British Airways and then had joined the hundreds of fully trained pilots, type rated on jet aircraft for whom British Airways had no crew positions. Those unfortunates were given the option of either carrying out only the minimum of crew training flights and staying at home for the rest of the time, or being released from the airline to take up crew positions with other companies until a British Airways position became available. Steve had opted for the latter course and had joined us only three weeks previously. Although he initially sneered at the slow flying Herald, with *propellers* for Gods sake, he had very quickly come to realise that most airplanes are quite easy to love and I am sure that he enjoyed his work. They teach them well at Hamble, the British Airways training school, and Steve was a fairly competent pilot with an ability to absorb information like a sponge.

Our two flight attendants were chattering in the way that only young women can chatter. I lit a cigarette and leaned back in my chair.

"Somebody should find out how much longer they're going to be," I remarked, making it quite clear that I, as Captain, considered that such a quest for information should be delegated to others. Steve looked up from his study of the charts.

"Do you want me to go?"

"Yes, if you like. If you learn anything of interest, you could tell the desk so that they can advise our customers." He stood up and buttoned his jacket.

"I won't be long," he said and strode purposefully towards the aircraft. I watched his progress and hoped that he would treat the engineers with proper respect. There is little more irritating for an engineer with many years of experience being told his business by a youthful pilot.

He reached the aircraft and I saw him speak to one of the two technicians. His answer came in a rapid series of gesticulations, punctuated by frequent pointing at the offending prop. To my astonishment, Steve then shook hands with the Frenchman and walked away. I waited with some impatience as he strolled back towards us, then noticed that all of the ground equipment had been cleared away and one of the engineers was on the flight deck about to ground run the engine. Steve walked up to us.

"Well?" I said.

"They are pretty sure they found the problem. They're going to do a quick ground run then we should be clear to go." I noticed our station manager approaching with the definite air of a harbinger of glad tidings.

"Capitaine," he said, "your propeller is fix-ed." I stifled a snigger. The poor man sounded precisely like Inspector Clouseau in the Pink Panther films.

"Thank you very much, Claude," I replied. "When can we start boarding?"

"They do the ground runs on the engine, then if all is well, ten minutes more."

I listened as the engineers put the prop through its paces. The Rolls-Royce Dart engine fitted to the Herald has a very distinctive sound, and experienced people can detect the various stages of power selection from a distance. I sent Steve off to the control tower to request the next available departure slot and gathered up my bag. Having prised the two girls away from their table, the three of us arrived at the aircraft just as the engine was shut down. I climbed up the stairs and stood in the doorway of the flight deck.

"I can find no fault M'sieu," the man said. "There was, within the electrical system, some dampness. We have corrected this and all is well."

"The pitch lights were okay?" He nodded vigorously,

"*Mais oui*! All is totally in order."

"*Merci bien,*" I said in a truly disgraceful assault on the French language.

"We shall remove, from the environment of your aeroplane, all of our ground equipments, then I wish you a pleasant flight." Although somewhat quaint, his command of English was miles ahead of my command of French. I felt inclined to compliment him to which he shrugged his shoulders and said,

"But English is the language of the airlines m'sieu." He appeared somewhat unhappy at this state of affairs. Although his remark was accurate, French controllers have the endearing habit of talking to French aircraft in French and to the rest of the world in English. The result is that, unless one understands French, one has little idea of the nature of instructions given to other aircraft in the vicinity. This can be a very worrying situation.

Steve arrived back at the airplane and I sent him to carry out the external inspection whilst I busied myself with the internal checks. The passengers arrived, relieved that their extended wait seemed to be at an end and in a remarkably short time, we had the engines running and were ready to leave. I called the tower.

"Marignane Ground, BAF461 on stand Delta four, requesting taxi clearance."

"BAF461, Ground, clear to taxi to the holding point runway one four left, via taxiway two alpha. The QNH is 1008. Expect an Alpha Victor November two echo departure."

"Ground, BAF461, to the hold runway one four left, QNH 1008 and AVN2East." I nodded to Steve who released the brakes and increased the power. We completed the few remaining items on the check list which included an assurance that we were both familiar with the departure procedure.

"The departure will be a left turn as soon as we get to five hundred feet onto a heading of three two zero then climb like hell. We pick up the zero four six radial from Martiques at Vello. Okay so far?"

"Yes thanks, I had a chance to study the plates earlier.

"Ready for the taxi checklist?"

"Ready when you are."

"The nosewheel steering and brakes are checked. Instrument response is normal." I paused whilst the tower gave some instructions to a Lufthansa departure.

"Alternators?" I asked.

"On and warning lights out."

"Windshield demist?"

"On."

"Engine anti-ice and fuel heaters?"

"Tested and not required." The radio broke in again, this time to give us our airways clearance which Steve copied efficiently and read back We carried out the pre take-off check list and I ran the right engine up to full power, still concerned about the prop fault. Everything seemed normal but I harbour deep suspicions when a fault is either not traced or 'cured' by wiping off with a rag. I glared at the prop blade indicator light, daring it to flicker but it remained well behaved. Steve glanced at me, obviously wondering why I was displaying such paranoia. Ah well, I thought, he has a good deal to learn. The tower cleared us for line up and take off. I steered us onto the runway and lined up on the centreline markings.

"You have control," I said.

"I have control." Steve pushed the power levers up to full power and released the brakes.

"Oil pressures normal," I said. "And the pitch lock is in 'FLIGHT' position." This final check is vital on the Dart engine. Without going into too much technical stuff, the prop has a setting where the blades turn totally flat so that there is no resistance during start-up. At this setting, the blades produce virtually nothing in the way of thrust. This setting is known as 'ground fine' pitch. To prevent the prop assuming this completely unhelpful setting in the air, there is an electro-mechanical device known as the 'pitch lock' which is engaged as the power levers are advanced. Okay? Enough of the technicalities? Fine, then I'll get on with the story.

We charged down the runway and rose smoothly into the air. As soon as we were safely airborne and climbing, Steve called for gear up. A very short time later the flaps came up and we were established in the climbing turn required by the departure procedure. Probably because we were fairly light on both passengers and on fuel, the aircraft was climbing manfully. The various checkpoints came up on schedule and eventually we were able to bid farewell to Marseilles tower and settle down in the cruise across France. We skimmed easily over a thin cloud layer some fifty feet below us. It is fascinating to descend to the surface of such cloud layers and let the propeller tips set the vapour swirling in confusion. It is at such times when the impression of speed is truly apparent. A favourite pursuit amongst bored airline crews is 'drilling holes in clouds'. One charges full tilt at a seemingly solid white mountain and as the point of contact approaches there is inevitably a moment of nervousness. Plunging headlong into the unknown and into the darkness goes against the grain for the normally cautious members of the flying fraternity but in civilian flying, there is little else to invoke excitement. So absorbed in idle thoughts we crossed France and reached Paris airspace. The checkpoints came and passed. Refreshments were served to the passengers. The air was smooth with scarcely a ripple to disrupt our course. My co-pilot and I breathed a sigh of relief as the English Channel appeared on the horizon. Seemingly content that we were clearing their airspace, Paris cleared us to start our descent. Our preferred height for the Channel crossing was five thousand feet and the company preferred our descents to be gentle in order to spare passenger discomfort as the Herald pressurisation system was somewhat given to erratic behaviour.

We crossed the coast of France as we descended through six thousand feet. The sea below us sparkled in the afternoon sunshine. Steve nudged the aircraft down the last two hundred feet. I pulled the aircraft tech log from its stowage and started to fill in the various figures required by the authorities, the company, the engineers, her Majesty the Queen, the Archbishop of Canterbury and almost anyone else in the world who could find a reason for determining how this flight had progressed. Like most pilots, I resented paperwork. Even completing my own flying logbook was a chore. I settled to the task with a sigh of resignation and by the time I had completed the entries and snapped the book shut, we were almost over England. Dover slid beneath our wings and I could see the gentle rolling green of the Downs. Almost home, I thought. I picked up the PA microphone to make the obligatory speech, (thank you for flying with us today, we hope your trip has been a pleasant one, sorry about the delay, folks, but we're almost home now and so on.)

"Ladies and gentlemen, this is the captain," I started. There was a loud bang from the right hand side of the aircraft. We swung violently to the right. Steve gasped and pushed full left rudder. I looked at the engine RPM indicators. The right engine was heading briskly towards maximum and the associated torque meter showed a drop. The bloody prop had gone right into ground fine and the engine was revelling in the lack of effort and spinning the prop up to the danger speed, where the blades might simply fly off and slice through the cabin.

"Right engine overspeed!" I shouted. I checked the stop withdrawal lever, which is supposed to prevent such occurrences. The lever was definitely in the 'Flight' position. I pulled the power lever fully closed. The engine showed no inclination to slow down. "I have control. Get in the back and get the passengers clear of the plane of the prop. Get them as far back as you can." He climbed out of the seat and started to reach for his jacket. "Never mind your bloody jacket You sort out the people and I'll take care of the aircraft."

To add to our woes, the prop was showing a definite disinclination to feather. In conditions such as we were experiencing, the propeller is supposed to feather automatically, that is the blades turn edge on into the airstream so that they cause least possible resistance. Typically, they had not auto-feathered and the immense drag caused by the flat blades was presenting me with a situation where I was holding almost full opposite rudder just to keep us reasonably straight. I pulled the high-pressure fuel cock to the manual feathering position. The Flight Manual claims that this action will initiate the feathering sequence. Needless to say, on this occasion, the book appeared to require a little in the way of editing. I quickly wound on a huge amount of rudder trim to try and reduce the pedal force and initiated the manual feathering sequence again.

In the cabin, Steve and the cabin crew were hurrying anxious passengers towards the rear of the cabin. At last, the RPM started to decrease so the immediate danger of a prop failure was averted. Our problems were not quite over, however. For reasons best known to itself, the propeller was refusing to feather despite my persistent attempts. The electric motor, which provides oil pressure for feathering, had either failed or popped its circuit breaker.

I had to make the radio call.

"Manston radar, BAF461, abeam Biggin Hill, flight level five zero, we have an engine problem and will be asymmetric for the rest of this flight. We intend to continue to Southend for landing."

"BAF461, Manston, do you require further assistance at this time?"

"Negative on that, Manston. Not unless you can fix a buggered engine."

"Sorry 461 I'm not an engineer"

"Roger. We will continue to Southend then."

"BAF461 you are clear to change to Southend Approach at your discretion."

"Ahhh…we'll stick with you for a few minutes. Four Six One"

In situations such as this, the Flight manual dictates several courses of action. We must firstly slow the aircraft to minimum safe flying speed. By doing this, I would lose some of the rudder authority, which I badly needed just to keep the aircraft straight. I compromised by slowing down a little and by doing so, reduced the power being generously provided by the still perfect left engine. This also had the effect of causing us to start a descent. The book told me to descend to a safe altitude, but I did not feel that less than our present five thousand feet could be referred to as safe. Steve came back to his seat.

"They are all in the back," he said. "One guy said he saw flames coming from the engine."

"There's always someone who says that. There is no reason to suspect that we have an engine fire." A thought struck me. "Go back again and ask him if he actually saw flames, or was it just smoke." Steve left on his mission, leaving me to fight the recalcitrant aircraft. With the help of the rudder trim it was a fairly easy task, although the real test would come when we put the landing gear down and slowed for landing.

"He says, yes it was only smoke." Steve had come back and climbed into his seat. "Why does that make a difference?"

"Because if it was just smoke, it could be an oil line burst. Probably the prop control oil line. If that's the case, we won't be able to feather the prop at all and we will be stuck with this bloody drag all the way down." Steve looked concerned. I made a decision.

"I'm going in flapless. A higher speed will give us better control authority. I'll leave the landing gear until late and accept whatever problems a late selection give us. I would like to think that you agree but if you don't then speak now or forever hold your peace."

"Sounds okay to me, boss. Not that I would know! The training school didn't cover this!"

I decided to let Steve have the aircraft so that I would have a chance to think before the landing.

"You have control." He looked at me incredulously.

"You sure about this?" I nodded. "I have control." I gradually released the control pressure until I was able to take my hands off the yoke.

"Christ! It's flying like a sack of shit!" Always ready with words of comfort and encouragement, I warned him that it would get a whole lot worse when we slowed down. It was time to brief the passengers.

"Ladies and gentlemen, it's the captain again. As I was saying before the little interruption, we are now getting close to Southend. You are probably aware that we are having problems with one engine. It is likely that the landing will be a trifle on the firm side so I am asking you to make sure that your seat belts are really secure and that you follow any instructions given by the cabin crew exactly." I wondered if I should tell them about crash positions, then decided against that. "We will be landing in about ten minutes so if you need to have a quick smoke, do so now, but please be very careful. Thank you very much." It was time to talk to Southend. I thanked Manston for seeing us through their airspace and changed frequency to Southend.

"Southend Approach, BAF461, four thousand feet coming up to the Estuary. Be advised that we are asymmetric at this time and having some control difficulty."

"461, Southend, are you declaring an emergency?"

"We're asymmetric so I suppose that constitutes an emergency. I would like the rescue on standby but that's all."

"461, you are cleared to final approach, runway two four, QFE one zero one four. We will clear all the other aircraft from the circuit to make you number one to land."

"Southend, 461 we appreciate that. We're over the Estuary now descending to two thousand feet." Steve looked at me anxiously.

"Okay," I said. "I have control."

"You have control." I took the aircraft and settled myself firmly in the seat. Steve started the landing checklist.

"We'll do the final approach checks now please, Steve, except for the gear and flaps. I want to get the feel of the thing as early as possible." He worked out our flapless approach speed. I decided to add a few knots for safety. It was going to be hard enough countering the drag from the useless propeller without reducing the effectiveness of the flying controls by getting the airspeed too low. We turned right to give us a long approach. We flew out over the Blackwater River and turned gently to the left to line up on the distant runway. The effort of turning left took almost every scrap of control authority available. I cautiously reduced the power on the good engine. The aircraft slowed obediently. I was unable to see the useless engine from my seat, but the dials showing zero glared insolently with scant regard for my distaste. I coaxed the unresponsive aircraft onto our approach course and carefully started to reduce power. Steve was right about the flying characteristics. It certainly *was* flying like a sack of shit We droned on uncomfortably. The old mill long used by students as a position marker for final approach slid beneath our wings. Seven hundred feet. Steve had his finger on the landing gear selector, ready to drop the wheels as soon as I gave the word. One mile out.

"Tower, 461 is finals for two four."

"461 clear to land or overshoot at your discretion, no conflicting traffic, surface wind two seven zero at ten knots." I acknowledged the transmission and smiled wryly. With one engine shut down and a propeller generating as much drag as a barn door, we stood little chance of overshooting from a bad approach. At least the wind was favourable. The slight crosswind would help to keep us straight. A quick glance across the cockpit revealed that Steve appeared to be quite frightened, his face drawn and strained and his fists clenched tightly. Strangely, I felt quite calm, having a kind of naïve confidence that the gentle Herald would not try to kill us.

"Gear down!"

"Gear down!" Steve mashed the button hard and the landing gear started to extend. The additional drag as the spindly legs confronted the airflow slowed us down and I added a little power to stop us sinking too fast. Immediately, the aircraft started to swing back to the right. I put the left wing down to try to correct the swing. Looking up from the instruments, I saw to my horror that we were drifting off the centre line. Reduce the power again. We were now sinking too fast. Flaps. We needed flaps.

"Take off flap! Steve, give me take off flap!" As the flaps came down our descent stopped. I carefully reduced the power. We were still to the right of the centre line but at the right height and pretty close to the right speed. I dropped the left wing a little more and very slowly the aircraft turned back to the runway centre. Now we were in exactly the correct position. Slowly we allowed the airplane to sink. Three hundred feet. A little less power. Two hundred. Drifting right again. One fifty. Starting to seriously drift. We were going to land on the grass if I wasn't careful. I had to get the wing up. If I did, we would certainly start drifting too much. I took a huge chance, levelled off and chopped the power to the good engine. The Herald dropped out of the sky from thirty feet up like a falling grand piano. We hit the ground hard and bounced. Just the once. Steve slammed the pitch stop on the good engine. I started braking as carefully as possible, trying to keep us straight. Incredibly, we stayed on the runway although the grass got frighteningly close. The runway markers flashed past but I felt confident that most of our worries were behind us.

"461, Tower, the emergency vehicles are right behind you."

"Thanks tower. They might care to have a look at the left brake when we stop. Might be a bit on the warm side, otherwise I think we're okay."

"Roger 461. Are you able to clear the runway or do you need assistance?"

"Could you advise our Operations that we will be clearing the runway to the right and that we will require transport for twenty two passengers and two cabin crew."

We turned right at the end of the runway and shut down our remaining engine. Steve and I stood at the doorway to say goodbye to our departing passengers. One of the passengers was a tiny lady, perhaps eighty years old. She grasped my hand and her eyes twinkled as she smiled up at me.

"That was fun. Do you know, young man, I have flown almost all round the world. Australia, Canada, America and all over Europe. Up till now, I had never ever been in an aeroplane with a bad fault. That was really quite dangerous wasn't it?"

"I've had better days ma'am," I grinned at her.

"I just *bet* you have," she said. To my astonishment, she winked at me and skipped down the steps. A middle-aged man, just behind her said to us,

"My mother is just impossible! She was a ferry pilot during the war. Flown Liberators, Hurricanes and all sorts of stuff. Got thousands of flying hours. She still can't get enough of flying. That made her day. Thanks."

From the doorway, I watched the little old lady accepting assistance from the driver to board the bus. She stopped and looked back at the aircraft and waved at us, her broad smile clearly visible. I turned to Steve.

"Another satisfied customer! Isn't flying just *wonderful!*"

Epilogue

The flight deck of the Airbus 321 is darkened. The instrument displays are bright and very clear. The Distance Measuring equipment (DME) clicks down, showing the miles to the next waypoint. A line stretching up and down the display shows our proposed track. Apart from short radio transmissions, no one has spoken for some time. I am aware of the subdued hum of the two huge CFM56 engines that are propelling us through the rarefied atmosphere that exists at thirty-three thousand feet. Our speed is seventy-eight per cent of the speed of sound.

The Traffic Collision Avoidance System known as Tee-cass shows that there is another aircraft some fifteen miles ahead of us, cruising at the same level as we are. The thought of this separation gives us comfort because we can only see the flashing of his strobe lights in the far distance. We arrive at the waypoint and the aircraft imperceptibly alters course by a few degrees to take up a new heading. The majority of the passengers are unaware of this necessary change. They have been given a hot meal, cooked in the microwave ovens and served by attractive cabin crew. Some of the passengers are watching the in-flight movie. Some are sleeping in the rather cramped accommodation. Even after all these years, the charter airlines still cram as many souls on board as they possibly can.

The push of a button changes the display on the screen to show the condition of the engines and aircraft systems. All is well, both engines and the three hydraulic systems are functioning perfectly. The display returns to indicate our progress over the Bay of Biscay. From the navigational computers, we are able to accurately predict to fractions of a minute our arrival time at the subsequent waypoint, a hypothetical point in space designated by the Air Traffic authorities in order to maintain order in the crowded skies. Such estimates are, and always have been essential to allow the controllers to ensure adequate separation of aircraft. We are exactly on time.

There is a tremendous sense of peace and order here. To chatter without due cause would be to disturb the tranquillity of the moment. Even in the cabin, the only sounds come from fractious children and the low chat of passengers queuing to use the toilets. I consider that the peace that was very common on night flights on my introduction to charter flying is the same sensation that I am now experiencing many years later. The aircraft have changed beyond all recognition. A very efficient and very expensive Flight Management Computer flies this aircraft which is hurrying us through the night sky. Compared to the elderly aircraft that carried happy holidaymakers then, this airplane is faster, flies higher, uses less fuel and carries more passengers. It is also very much quieter, although the hysterical outbursts of anti aircraft protesters would appear to indicate otherwise.

The display shows that we have arrived at the final waypoint. Our track line on the screen shows a small arrow a few miles ahead. At this point, we will commence our descent. Even this small calculation is taken care of by the pre loaded flight plan. When we reach the arrow, a selection on the autopilot puts the aircraft into a gentle descent. As we pass between the islands the First Officer who is the handling pilot disengages the autopilot. He selects the Instrument Landing System display and watches as the bar moves across the instrument. Smoothly he turns the aircraft to the left and the bar centres vertically as we line up on the distant runway. I ask him if he intends to land the aircraft manually instead of using the autoland facility. He replies in the affirmative. The approach is perfect and the mainwheels kiss the runway.

When we have turned off the runway and we are taxiing towards the terminal building, he turns to me. He gives me the grin that I have known since he was just a little boy. I am immensely proud. I have now completed the full circle from being an eleven year old kid trying to persuade balsawood model aircraft to fly to this point where I am sitting in the jump seat of an Airbus watching my son at work. He has been kind enough to say that his interest in aviation came from me. That may or may not be a good thing because this industry has had more than a fair share of difficulties and in the light of the dreadful events of September 11 2001 the problems are obviously far from being over. I reiterate, however that I have an enormous sense of pride in seeing my son taking his place in a business that is unlike any other.

AM October 2001

0-595-24729-6

Printed in the United Kingdom
by Lightning Source UK Ltd.
93540